The Hidden CAMINO

A spiritual journey into the heart of the pilgrimage, where nothing is as it first seems

Louise Sommer

Yellow Bird Press

Published by Yellow Bird Press, Australia
First published in Australia by The Sommer Institute

Cataloguing-in-Publication details available from the National Library of
Australia

ISBN: 978-0-9942170-2-8 (ebk)
ISBN: 978-0-9942170-3-5 (pbk)
Project editor: Carol Campbell
Text design and layout: Yellow Bird Press
2nd edition cover design: Natalie Winter
1st edition text and cover design: Publicious
Map design: Natalie Winter
Yellow Bird Press logo design: Rick Sherman, RANGE studio

I received an invitation.
I really had no choice
but to accept. The call came from Her
and She made sure that I walked the road
the way it was meant
a long time ago.
This is my story.

Louise Sommer

FRANCE

St. Jean
Roncesvalles
Zubiri
Pamplona
Puente la Reina
Lorca
Estella
Viana
Navarette
Nájera
Santo Domingo de Calzada
St. Juan de Ortega
Burgos
Hontanas
Castrojeriz
Boadilla del Camino
Terradillos de Templarios
Sahagún
Leon
Astorga
Foncebadón
Molinaseca
Ponferrada
Villafranca del Bierzo
Vega de Valcarce
Hospital de la Condesa
Santiago de Compostela
Finisterre

Bilbao
Lugo

Zaragoza

Madrid

SPAIN

PORTUGAL

N

CONTENTS

AUTHOR'S NOTE

Except for the names of Richard, Susie and Ida, all other names, and most nationalities, have been changed to protect the identity and privacy of those mentioned. Some incidents have been altered to maintain the flow of the story, but in no way do these changes affect or change its authenticity or truth.

It is important to note: The Roman Catholic Church laid the foundations of Christianity as we know it. Numerous branches of Christianity throughout history have broken away from the Roman Catholic Church, and many hold wildly differing views. I am very much aware of this. So when I use the terms Christianity and pre-Christianity, I am only referring to the Roman Catholic Church.

INTRODUCTION

The Camino is said to follow beneath the Milky Way, and that the stars will guide the pilgrim along the pathway. The term 'Milky Way' comes from the Vikings who believed the Milky Way was a river of milk, from which the gods drank and received their divine powers.

Could it be that this River of Milk, that guides the pilgrim, is the Light of Divinity? And could it be that the human who walks this way becomes nourished and enlightened, too, just like the gods?

The Camino is a pilgrimage in the north of Spain, and it means The Way. Many people also call it The Way of Saint James, but only a few know that the Camino existed long before Christianity.

Back then the end destination was Finisterra, coming from the latin words *Finis Terrae*. The correct translation is the 'End of the Earth', not the 'End of the World', as some say. This is particularly important, because the End of the Earth is connected to the Celtic legend of Tir-na-Nóg; the physical world as we know it, the End of the Earth is where the divine world of Tir-na-Nóg begins. The Way, had also been a sacred path for the Celts.

For the Celts, Finisterra was considered the place where heaven and earth, spirit and matter met. It was here the druidesses and druids performed their most sacred rituals and initiations. It was indeed a sacred place. Tir-na-Nóg is the Land of Eternal Youth, a paradise located west of the known world. It is inhabited by enchanting female creatures whose beauty surpasses all. Here, only music, strength, life energy and pleasure exist.

There are only two ways to reach Tir-na-Nóg: you must have received either an invitation or you must have walked the hard and difficult way, looking deep into your own soul. You see, just as Oisin, when he travelled with the nymph Niamph on her magical horse, so must every human have a guide to Tir-na-Nóg. Only they know the way to the Land of Eternal Youth. Only they have horses with golden manes who can fly you across the big ocean to the island in the west.

At Finisterra, one can find the burial tomb of the Celtic goddess, Orcabella. She was the old crone goddess, the hag who, in the Middle Ages, was made into the evil witch we all know from fairytales. But in pre-Christian times, the crone goddess was the seer and the teacher. She was the one who knew about the forces that drove life. She was death and she was wisdom. She, just like Finisterra, was the sacred place where a human, after having walked the long hard road, entered the last stage of transformation before the rebirth.

The tradition says that, at sunset, you must stand and look out over the ocean at Finisterra. Here, the sun sets over to the west, the direction of Tir-na-Nóg. The night is your initiation. As the sun rise above the well known world, the earth, your transformation is complete. Collect the first shell you find on the beach. This is your gift, your proof of having walked the Way of Orcabella, the Way for Enlightenment.

For the Celts, the new day always began at sunset, that very time when the sun is at its most golden and glowing. And the sun was, indeed, worshipped at Finisterra for more than 4000 centuries, as was the goddess. *For those with eyes to see...*

THE START OF MY JOURNEY

It was January, 2010, when something changed in my life that would lead me to walk the Camino. To that point, there was nothing out of the ordinary happening. I was busy at work and studying for my Masters degree. It wasn't an especially happy or unhappy time; my life just seemed to be muddling along.

But then these goddesses from around the world walked into my dreams and turned everything upside down. In the beginning, I understood them to be archetypes of the Great Goddess. But then, who was the Great Goddess? It was a concept that was hard for me to understand. So I was short of terminology, and I was a little confused on how to label these visitors to my dreams. In fact, these dreams were confusing. Full stop.

The first time I brought the dreams up with my therapist, I found the process extremely difficult. What would my therapist think? Was my ego about to freak out or was I about to have a meltdown? I hardly knew what to do. I mean, what had I done to deserve such divine and love-filled dreams?

I have to admit that the whole situation was out of my comfort zone – especially during the first few months. Then it became more frustrating because the energies I experienced in my dreams were so powerful. It felt as if the planets had suddenly rotated in some odd way and a golden gate had opened just like that, without any further introduction.

Over a period of nearly two years, my dreams taught me to *see* and they taught me to *hear*. And before long, I found myself in a place where earth and sky met.

This book is the account of my journey on the Camino and my meeting with its hidden story; a journey that was so much larger than me. Where I thought I would end up in the east, I would end up in the west, and I never knew my next step before I had taken it. But the journey began a long time before I even thought about the Camino.

THE DREAMS

The very first dream that came to me was about the Church of Mary Magdalene.

It is late evening and I come walking towards a big wooden gate next to a moat. I pass through the gate and continue walking towards a mighty church made from red bricks.

As I enter the church I can see that there is no ceiling, only the night sky above me where the stars sparkle in the distance. The floor appears to be made of stone pathways, from which enormous white pillars rise and disappear out into the sky. There is no floor between the pathways, so the church floats on a invisible base of dark blue.

The white pillars are decorated with beautiful animals, whales, dolphins, symbols of torches with large flames, stars, scallop shells, Egyptian symbols and many others. I recognise the symbols from across many cultures and ages, and know they were used to describe the connection with our innate spirituality.

This place is indeed sacred. It is filled with a presence of an unbelieveble stillness, mystery and knowledge.

Impressed and humbled, I walk around and look in amazement. Never in my entire life did I think a place of such beauty could exist.

Reaching the eastern side of the church, I walk up onto a plateau where I have a good view over the building. From here, I can see that the pathways are formed in the shape of a eight-pointed star. In the dream, I remember that the number eight, in some traditions, refers to Venus. Someone tells me that this is the very Church of Mary Magdalene.

As I walk towards what I think is the altar and centre of the church, I see a heavily pregnant Mary Magdalene, wearing a long green gown. She is walking along the stone pathways, crying. She looks devastated and walks around restlessly. Her unhappiness fills my heart, so I ask her why she is so unhappy. She tells me it is because she has lost her husband. She has been searching for him for almost two thousand years without success.

Her long search has etched her footprints into the stones of the pathways.

I had tears in my eyes when I woke the next morning. My heart was still broken as I felt her grief in telling me her sad story. But I also felt deeply touched by the extremely moving design of the church and the fact that it was actually her church. The dream had been so alive that it felt like I had actually been there.

I knew it was normal to be affected by dreams for a short while, but as the day progressed the intensity of this dream continued. It was impossible to shake it off and, as the hours passed, the more emotional I felt. That day, no matter where I went or what I did, Mary Magdalene seemed to appear. It was extremely eerie and a little unreal. But if I thought that this was just a single night's dream, I was mistaken. This dream was only the first of many that continued for almost the next two years – especially the first year and a half, where they came almost nightly; strong, insisting and incredibly beautiful.

Mary Magdalene was the first of the many goddesses I was to dream about. However, she was quickly accompanied by dreams about the Grail. In the first dream, the Grail was a necklace. After that, the Grail would have different shapes: the map of a country or the sun. But no matter what shape it had, it would always be a shining golden light. Shortly after the Grail, the Norse goddess, Freya, appeared. Just like the Grail, she too, was connected to spring – the Rebirth of Life. Mary Magdalene on the other hand, is closely related to the Summer Solstice as her feast day is July 22. The day of Summer Solstice is June 22.

Like so many other things related to my dreams and the following journey, very little made sense before the end. However, noticing that the times of spring and Summer Solstice were central in my dreams, I felt this would be a process of maturation. The day of Summer Solstice was actually a part of a longer celebration that went over several weeks. In ancient Scandinavian shamanistic traditions, the time of Summer Solstice was when the connection with the Divine invisible worlds and Earth, was the closest and strongest. It was considered a time when humans could access the most powerful energy of manifestation.

It wasn't that I disliked the dreams; it was more the intensity of them that was so hard to handle. It was as if they were stirring up a pot of emotions I didn't feel like stirring up at all. I suppose it also made me a little nervous dreaming about Mary Magdalene and the Grail in this way because they were religious figures, and I was not a religious person.

I was, however, quite pleased to dream about Freya as she was a part of my native Nordic mythology. But as I thought about it, so was Mary Magdalene! She was a part of the Christian religion which had shaped the history of my country for centuries. Realising this, I started to feel much more comfortable with it. It did puzzle me, though; why did I dream about *her church*?

A few days later, I found myself hurrying along one of the main streets in Copenhagen, trying to get to the Metro before rush hour. I became caught up with hundreds of people, all trying to find their way around and through the endless, annoying inner-city construction works. Would they ever end?

In an effort to escape the chaos, I decided to take a detour. But just as I was about to cross a busy square, I suddenly felt very clear in my head and was overcome by an urge to turn left, deeper into the crowds of people. That was odd? I was trying to get away from them, not closer.

Out of curiosity, I decided to follow my instinct to see where it would lead me. Maybe a little surprised, I ended up in a bookshop. Inside, I walked directly up to a book about Mary Magdalene as if someone was showing me the way. I looked at the book for a moment before picking it up and letting the pages run through my fingers, wondering why.

On the first page where I stopped to read, the text read that in 1969, the Roman Catholic Church had officially altered its long term position in describing Mary Magdalene as a prostitute. What!? I had never heard about this, and due to my recent dreams about Mary Magdalene, I couldn't help but feel there was something significant about this coincidence.

As I walked away from the bookshop, I wondered why I had never come across this information before. I had studied parts of church history for many years and still not seen any reference to this change. Maybe I had been looking in the wrong places. But still, this was a major deal, the references should have been there somewhere. So I went home and began searching for information about the church's rather secretive admission. And what I found shocked me.

In my research, I discovered that Pope John Paul II in 1988, had written an Apostolic letter titled *Mulieris Dignitatem*; 'On the dignity and vocation of women'. In this letter, the Pope had referred to Mary Magdalene as *Apostola Apostolorum*, that is, 'the Apostle to the Apostles.' Indicating, that Mary Magdalene was a teacher to the other Apostles although it didn't specifically describe how. The title *Apostola Apostolorum* was given to Mary Magdalene as she was the first to witness the resurrected Jesus, to receive the instructions from Him and as such, was the bearer of this news to the other Apostles. But who, or what, I wondered, had created Magdalene as a repentant sinner to begin with? After much research, I discovered that it was Pope Gregory the Great who, in 591AD, had declared Mary Magdalene a prostitute. From what I could understand, Pope Gregory the Great had been in the need of a 'perfect sinner', and therefore had interpreted the relevant sections of Luke's gospel to suit his own ends. But he also made two other 'changes' that would support his claim of Magdalene as a prostitute; he (deliberately?) confused the different Marys mentioned in the gospel and he decided that the 'seven deadly sins' meant being possessed by evil. This was an interpretation that was built on a manipulated lie created to make Magdalene 'the perfect sinner'. But never the less, my research proved that Mary Magdalene had never been a prostitute to begin with! So the questions were; who had Mary Magdalene been *before* her narrative had been changed into a sinful woman? And why was the Roman Catholic church, even to this day, still preaching (almost thirty years after Pope John Paul's II Apostolic letter) that Mary Magdalene was a prostitute and of no importance? The shocking answers to these questions wouldn't become clear to me before the end of the Camino.

I felt sick to my stomach when learning of this. How could something so important go so unnoticed? But the fact that it had, made me realise more that ever, that Mary Magdalene mirrored what the church had done towards women – done towards me. Mary Magdalene had become an archetype of the supressed and depowered woman, but there was a time when she had been so much more. Sorry, I am getting ahead of my story here. Let me just say that there was indeed a very good reason as to why she was the first goddess to appear in my dreams and why she was associated with the Summer Solstice.

THE INVITATION

Shortly after I had dreamt about Freya the first time, I had a dream about another goddess. I didn't know her name or who she was, and didn't find out before a friend showed me a picture of an ancient Brazilian goddess. The picture she showed me sent chills up and down my spine. The woman, and the scene in the picture, was exactly the same as I had experienced in my dream. What really made a difference in seeing this, was the fact that someone else had 'met' her, too. She wasn't just a figment of my imagination. Her name was Lemanja, and my therapist later told me she was considered the goddess of the ocean and the stars.

I stand on a beach and see a clear blue sky filled with small shining stars. The ocean rolls onto the shore with lazy calm waves and I am all alone. When I turn my head to the left I see an indescribably beautiful woman come walking towards me along the water's edge. Her long dark hair tumbles over her shoulders and down her back and dances in the breeze like the light blue robe she is wearing. It is as if something around her shines like a full moon. I wonder how someone like her can be so real.

Her deep brown eyes look into mine, and I feel embraced by her unconditional love and kindness. She smiles gently, but says nothing. I keep staring at her, mesmerised. How can anybody love me this much? How can anybody see so much beauty in me? I don't understand it, but her love is so strong that it overcomes my negative emotions. As she comes close to me, she reaches out her hand and says, 'Come'.

I had been given an invitation. When I awoke the following morning, I was suffused with all the love I had experienced. Her presence wavered back and forth within my body. In the reflection of her love for me, I realised how little I actually loved myself, my body and my femininity. It stood unquestionably clear to me, that I had become my own worst friend. But not only that, I had also let the world around me convince me that this was true.

The incredible thing was, that the strength of Lemanja's love was so powerful that it won over the negative feelings I had about myself. It was just so hard to understand that in me, something so beautiful, so wise and divine, could exist. It was as if all these women rebelled against my lack of self-esteem and insisted on showing me a different reality. It was time to free myself from these illusions, to open my eyes and actually see.

To my relief, my therapist told me, that my dreams were normal archetypical dreams. There was nothing partcularly unusual about that. I thought: 'Okay, I know about Jungian psychology; I can deal with that.' But once back home, I began studying his theory about archetypes more closely – a study that soon led me even deeper into my interest of alchemy.

I left my session that day thinking I had seen the last of these dreams. Everything could go back to normal. But no, they continued at full speed. My dreams about Mary Magdalene, the Grail, Freya and Lemanja remained, especially those involving Mary Magdalene and her church. But other goddessees also joined in. And as with Lemanja, women with identities I hadn't known of previously, entered my dreams.

I found this rather interesting as there wasn't any obvious or logical connection between them and myself. How could they appear in my dreams when I had never heard of them before? And so, ever so slowly, I started to understand that they were not only archetypes for something in me; they were also universal archetypes connected to what Jung called, the 'collective conscious'. I called it 'that greater something' because my experiences made me feel that I was a part of something much bigger. Over the years, I learnt that my dreams contained many levels of information at the same time, embracing me in a vast context of history, culture, society and spirituality.

The intensity of the dreams started to create a snowball effect of thoughts, which placed women, and particularly women in history, in the centre. And one day, whilst moving from one meeting to another, thinking about some of my recent dreams and a book I was reading, I found myself wondering why I had heard only about so few women in history. Taking into consideration that half the world's population were women, they obviously must have been there. So why were they only mentioned as a sideline or in a negative context, if at all? And so, my study in Christianity changed to focus on women. I even expanded my search field and started to look deeper into the pre-Christian times of ancient Europe. (These times are often described as times of 'matriarchal cultures', which is somewhat incorrect. I like to refer to them as times of the 'goddess cultures' as that is my main focus in this book.)

It was a new and exciting road that made so many things clear to me, but it also created many more questions. One of them was related to the origin of the Virgin Mary. To be honest, I didn't even know that she had 'an origin'. She was Jesus' mother; that was it! But I was to learn, that when it came to women in history and religion, very little was as it seemed.

As time went by, my therapist started to question why I kept having these dreams, so intense and over such a long period of time. What she didn't tell me, until after the Camino, was that archetypical dreams as strong as mine indicated that a huge change would occur in my life. Not just a nice little change, but a change that moved mountains, and only the future knew how these changes would be manifested.

For almost 2000 years, we in Europe have learnt not to see Her and not to hear Her. Maybe this was one of the reasons I was so lost when my dreams began. For what do we do when we no longer can ignore Her and that part of ourselves anymore? With spirituality locked up in either (patriarchial) religions or an airy-fairy New Age movement, it is difficult to know where to turn. We can end up with depression and a narcissistic ego thinking we are something 'chosen' or we live in fear of our 'different' self. Where do we as women turn when the history and culture we grow up in constantly portray us as invisible or wrong, banishing our spirituality into legends such as the Mists of Avalon and fairytales like Cinderella?

Due to the awakening and subsequent questioning resulting from the dreams I became increasingly frustrated and restless. Although I did find my studies interesting and inspiring, I also felt an inner pressure building up. I started to feel that I needed to do something, change something. But what? How?

It took me a long time before I was able to admit why I had such difficulty listening to my dreams. Where I had felt good about the intellectual approach to them, it was much harder to embrace the emotions the dreams awakened as they triggered a confusion and pain I felt about my own womanhood. So what did I do? I fought like a Viking. I fought the healing from the dreams so hard when all I should have done was to surrender. But I wouldn't. And so, frustrations, restlessness and irritation built up along with self-doubt.

It was about this time, that I dreamt about a woman I called my grandmother. She wasn't my maternal grandmother, but we had met in my early twenties and had immediately developed a deep connection. As time passed, I had become her and her husband's 'adopted' granddaughter.

My grandmother sits on a sofa together with her beloved husband. She looks at me with her ever so warm and caring eyes.

'My dearest grandchild,' she says, 'it's all about the dance of life ... You must learn to listen to the music in your heart and you must learn to follow the path that is yours. First you learn each single step, then you learn the wholeness, and then you learn the flow of movement within the body; the dance itself.'

I felt very reassured and much more at peace when I woke up. Here was a figure that I knew. My grandmother had been a very special person to me, and had taught me innumerable valuable lessons about life. Later the same day, I climbed the stairs to my attic and found all the papers, books and folders my grandmother had left me before her death. Looking though some of the papers, I noticed a lot of the material was about the Grail. I couldn't help smiling. I had never paid any attention to it before. But I suppose that's the way it is. We see when we are ready.

In some of my grandmother's notes, I saw references that went far back into history. Like many others, I had thought the Grail was a Christian legend. However, according to my grandmother, the Grail had a much older history. Apparently, the Grail could be traced back to the cult of the Norse goddess Inanna as well as the religions of ancient Egypt and of the Middle East. To my surprise, I also discovered that the Grail, in the shape of a chalice, had appeared first in the Middle Ages. Before then, the Grail had been a stone (for example, the Philosophers Stone, the stone in the legend of King Arthur), a magic cauldron, an urn and the Horn of Abundance. Today, many consider the actual Grail to be the children of Mary Magdalene and Jesus. However my grandmother's notes also mentioned that the Grail had strong links to the Celtic goddess Eriu, who in ancient Ireland had been the Grail maiden personifying Mother Nature and her Power of Creation. The ritual of Eriu was celebrated in the spring.

Feeling overwhelmed about all this new information, I recovered a book my grandmother and her husband had given me. It was about the Grail, too. Why had I never thought about this before, I wondered. I flicked through some pages before deciding to read it. I thought back on all the talks my grandmother and I had together over the years and I always looked forward to the next visit. I could talk about everything with my grandmother. With her I shared all my dreams, my deepest thoughts and my life experiences without ever fearing judgement or misunderstanding; I knew that she would always understand.

It took a long time to heal the hole she left behind. For a whole week following her death I had dreams about her. In these dreams, I saw her dance, spinning around, having so much fun.

'Look,' she said and laughed, 'Look! I'm feeling good. I can dance. Be happy for me.'

But it was hard to be happy for her as my loss was too great. I knew she had suffered enormously with back pain for more than three decades, and it was something that had limited her daily physical activities to a routine of regularly changing between standing, sitting and lying down. And yet, she would always be filled with an inner peace, an inner knowing, always driven towards helping other people through life. I often wondered how anyone could become such a good human being.

Some time after her death, her husband found a note in her diary, where she had predicted her time of passing. But that's the way it was with my grandmother. All of her life she had experienced dreams and visions. Today I wondered if her dreams and visions had helped her rise above her pain and physical limitations and become the wise and compassionate woman that I loved. For this reason, dreams about my grandmother always meant a lot to me. I knew they appeared to tell me that everything was okay and give me advice on how to deal with whatever situation I was facing.

My grandmother was a sort of a crone figure to me. She had been the living example that it was how we acted, and who we were as a person, that really mattered. I leant back and lay down on my wooden floor and closed my eyes. I was happy that she could dance and have fun again. If anyone deserved it, she did.

And just like that, for the first time ever, I allowed myself to open up to all the love and wisdom that the women in my dreams showed me. The ceiling didn't fall down on my head and my toaster didn't explode. Nothing happened, except that I started to feel a whole lot better about myself. I finally accepted the invitation..

THE CAMINO DECIDES ITSELF

During my Christmas break, and after having had the dreams for a year, I finally understood that I was in the midst of a deep transformation and it was huge. It was an end, and it heralded a new beginning. The time after New Year was as busy as usual. Many reports had to be done before the summer holidays started and a new computer system took a toll on my energy as well. One week into January, our young intern returned from her holidays and the first thing she told me, as she stepped into the office, was that she had bought a book about the Camino.

Dream one

I stand on a small earthen path looking out over huge golden fields as far as my eyes can see. When I look down onto the path where I stand, I can see that it is golden, too. Some of the fields have been harvested and the crops collected into beautiful golden sheaves.

The sky is clear blue and the sun embraces everything with its warm rays of light. Birds fly around and sing. In the distance there are two other paths: one comes from the east and one from the west. I know that these paths will eventually merge with mine, somewhere further ahead. I often see another pilgrim on the path from the east, and sometimes one from the west too. I feel in total harmony and balance within this enchanting landscape.

Dream two

I stand next to the Camino and see infinite amounts of milk running along the pathway. As I look up, I see that the Camino is filled with cows as far as the eye can see. From their udders, milk runs in abundance and transforms the pathway into a river of milk. Amongst the cows I see a woman walking towards me. She is very beautiful and has an unusually strong presence. She wears a crown with two large horns. When close, she tells me that she is the mother of the cows. She is Hathor.

I had no idea who Hathor was and had to Google her the first thing in the morning. I was quite surprised to learn that not only was she was an Egyptian goddess, she also stood for rebirth/resurrection and fertility, and was considered to house the sun within her.

Egyptian, Norse, Brazilian, Christian, Celtic ... they came from everywhere in my dreams, and most of them had to do with spring. But I still had difficulty understanding what all of this was about. After my dream about Hathor, my understanding of the meaning of the Milky Way changed and the Camino became The Way, where the divine nourishment from the Great Goddess ran in plenty. There it was again: the Great Goddess. I didn't even particularly like the term, and yet I found myself using it. But I did understand that milk ran in abundance because She was the Abundance of Life. Hathor told me that I would drink of this divine milk as I walked the Camino. In fact, I was already drinking it and anyone who walked the Camino would be able to do so.

The milk that comes from a mother's udder is life's important nourishment for the small infant. I was now drinking the same nourishment from my divine mother. No wonder the dreams had been so powerful and transforming! For the first time I felt a true and deep inner change take place. I came to understand that no matter what I had heard or not heard about the Camino, I had no doubt that my pilgrimage was connected to the Way of the Goddess. I had absolutely no idea what this meant but I had a strong feeling that I was about to find out. For well over a year, I had been guided towards this journey. I was ready.

For those with eyes to see, and ears to hear.

ST JEAN-PIED-DE-PORT

On 19 June, 2011, I caught the last plane from Copenhagen to Paris. From Charles de Gaulle airport, I continued on by train and arrived at about midnight at Gare du Nord, close to where I was staying the night. The streets leading away from the station were dirty and dark, and my hotel room was the size of a matchbox. Even the hotel's credit card machine was broken, so I had to pay with cash. However, seeing what the place looked like, I figured it was probably a better idea anyway.

Once up in my tiny room, I took a shower and prepared for the next day. I even arranged my clothes in the order I would put them on the following morning and fell asleep the moment my head hit the pillow. It had been a long day, but less than five hours later, my alarm clock went off. I wasn't sure how long it would take me to get to Montparnasse station so I figured I'd better leave enough time in case I became lost.

A colleague of mine, who often travelled to Paris, had been kind enough to give me two tickets and the timetable for the Metro. The next morning when trying to find my way through Gare du Nord, I thought of him fondly, for the knowledge was a big help in a somewhat stressful situation. I didn't know the Metro system, I didn't speak French and I was afraid I would get lost and miss my train; however, I did make it on time to Montparnasse.

Montparnasse was a huge station. The platform, from where my TGV train was leaving, was filled with nice little eateries and places to sit. The aroma of fresh bakeries and coffee permeated the air while people in transit dashed between the stalls and trains. I had plenty of time to buy a warm quiche lorraine and a freshly squeezed orange juice for breakfast. I took my food, surprised at how friendly the waiter had been (he even said some words in English!), and sat on a bench. From there, I had a good view to where my train was waiting. I had also bought two warm and very tasty looking croissants – I am a sucker for French croissants. They should have been for later in the journey, but the mouthwatering smell convinced me that I should eat them. So I did! Loving every bit of it.

Even though I usually preferred sleeping in until about 9am, I felt quite awake and energetic that morning. People who passed me looked puzzled at my happy smile. I bet they thought that only a nutcase would be this fresh so early. But I couldn't help it, the smiles just kept popping up. Sometimes, happy feelings can be like champagne. They just kept bubbling inside, making their way to the surface whether you want them to or not. I suppose I felt a little bit like champagne that morning.

I headed towards my train a bit before departure time to make sure it didn't leave without me. Finding my seat and leaving my blue backpack up on the shelf, I felt well prepared for the long train ride that lay ahead of me. I would first take the TGV train from Montparnasse to Bordeaux, which was about a four-hour trip. From there, I would continue with local trains to Dax, and then from Dax to Bayonne and from Bayonne to St Jean, where I would arrive somewhere about 6pm.

As the train hit top speed and I found myself sliding through the lovely countryside of northern France, I couldn't help feeling uplifted and surrounded by joy. I didn't have many thoughts at this time; I just felt so happy that I was finally on my way. Now I could lean back, relax and enjoy the ride. I felt so guided, so safe, and so connected to something wonderful I couldn't explain.

I hadn't been sure about starting in St Jean to begin with. For quite some time I had leant more towards starting in Monserrat and then hitting the main road from there. St Jean had seemed too touristy. I preferred starting in a place with more historical interest. But then I would miss crossing the Pyrenees, so I finally decided on St Jean. Sitting in the TGV train, I was pleased with my decision and found the long train ride a good way to start my journey. Never having walked a pilgrimage before, I really had no idea what I was getting myself into. The feeling of freedom and being in nature all day made my head dizzy with ecstasy. Living in a big city, I missed nature and space. This was, by the way, also my official reason for walking the

Camino. Nobody else, except for my therapist, knew about my dreams.

I saw my first pilgrim of the day at Dax station. My reaction was a little weird. It was as if someone had trespassed on my territory in such a way that I almost felt angry. This made me laugh. I suppose I had been thinking that I was the only pilgrim, although I had to admit that it was nice to see that I wasn't. Later on, in Bayonne, when I reached the platform for my train to St Jean, I felt as if I had walked into a different world. It was overwhelming to see so many pilgrims. Everywhere I looked, I saw people dressed in shorts (those where you unzip the lower legs), T-shirts and hats and carrying backpacks.

Nobody, except pilgrims dressed like this, so we really stood out. Some people spoke with loud voices; others were quieter and then there were those who said nothing. Some pilgrims sat and looked around or read a book. Others would fiddle nervously with their hats. A few Catholics would grasp their rosaries firmly while they attempted to smile at everybody around them. The atmosphere was buzzing, a mixture of excitement, nervousness, vulnerability, magic, adventure, hope and fear of loneliness. Everybody had their own mission; their own hopes, dreams and reasons for walking the Camino. What we all shared in common, at that very moment, was the train that would take us to our destination, the promised land of the unknown. The train was already there with its doors open, but only a few people had entered.

I wondered if any of these pilgrims had been guided here by their dreams, just like me. I took a deep breath and looked up into the sky. Who could tell? It was now late afternoon and the sun was starting to set. The heat of the day was still hanging heavily in the air and birds flew around, filling the air with their songs. The platform, where the train was waiting to take us to St Jean, was a little away from the main station. It was surrounded by numerous trees, bushes and flowers. As I gazed down the tracks in the direction of where the train would go, the terrain looked more rugged. I even saw a pretty stream that ran alongside.

Standing there, taking it all in, I realised just how special and beautiful my journey so far had been. It had opened my eyes and taken me in directions I could never have foreseen. However, standing amongst all these pilgrims, something odd happened to me. I suddenly started to lose my feeling of identity and direction as I became part of a 'uniform' crowd of pilgrims. As I felt the energy that had sustained my journey drain away, I realised I had to make a choice. I could either give into the feeling of becoming 'just one in a crowd', or I could choose to stay in the light of my own journey. I chose the latter. Having made this choice, all my energy returned. My connection to the pilgrims as a group also changed. Instead of losing the harmony I was feeling, I became one with a path so many had walked before me for thousands of years. I was about to walk in the light of their footsteps, their histories and their lives. Alone, and yet never alone; in this light, we were all connected.

I approached the train slowly, thinking it might be a good time to board before the rush, although I couldn't see anywhere that said when the train was actually going to leave. For some reason, I didn't think about taking out my train ticket and looking at it. The idea of time had already disappeared from my life – or maybe, I just didn't care. I looked down at my brown walking boots. They would be my best friends for the next six weeks and I hoped that my training and preparations had been good enough. I then lifted my head and stood there for a few moments, looking up at the sun, thinking. I couldn't help wondering if any of these pilgrims would become my friends along the way. Again, who knew? So I turned around and walked into the train.

Inside I spotted a good seat with the perfect view where I could watch people as they entered. A smile spread across my face as I walked towards it. I had finally come to the last train ride of the day. It did surprise me, however, that the train was so small. It was only two carriages long and looked a little bit like the metro trains in Copenhagen. Five to 10 minutes later, a bell rang and a train conductor started to shout something in French. All the pilgrims immediately started to move. As they entered the train I couldn't help notice the look of insecurity that emanated from most of them. I smiled at a woman as she took a seat close to me. She looked at me with serious eyes for a few seconds, before returning a hesitant smile. Many others didn't smile at all. They didn't even look at each other.

As the two carriages filled up, I was shocked to see how huge the backpacks were that many people were carrying. With backpacks this large, you would have room for tents, twenty outfits and bulky towels. I couldn't imagine why people would bring all these things. Suddenly my own small backpack, weighing only 5½ kilograms, seemed petite and very light.

I think there were over a hundred people piled in together in the two carriages when the train finally left Bayonne station. Backpacks were stacked onto shelves, heaped in piles next to the doors, under the seats and on their owners' laps. There were backpacks everywhere! More than half the pilgrims had also brought old-fashioned wooden hiking poles. Together with the backpacks, these also took up a lot of space. Only the brave would dare to move around in this train. It was a wonderful sight and an adventurous sight. I wish I had taken a picture.

As I sat and watched the people on the train, I couldn't help but notice how the pilgrims were both seeking and yet rejecting contact at the same time. The flickering of the eyes and the restless body movements. It was as if we didn't know how to behave being outside our usual defined world. Our vulnerabilty became so obvious to us. It was a vulnerabilty that really was about our sensitivity and ability to react to the world; something that was looked on as a weakness by many. Maybe we just had become too alienated towards ourselves and our feelings, and called that 'weakness'. I felt like giving some of them a big hug, saying that everything would be fine, but I didn't, of course. I just sat quietly in my seat.

Looking out of the window as the train started, a small stream danced along our way, sometimes big and wide, other times thin and soft, always changing shape. As the train slowly climbed, the stream disappeared into the distance below us. Stillness spread through the train and all the commotion there had been at the station transformed into a quiet presence. We were waiting. Waiting for the train to arrive in St Jean. Waiting to start our pilgrimage. Waiting for the adventure to begin. Waiting for all the things we hoped for. Waiting for the last minutes of our rail journey to arrive so we could reach the beginning. We were, after all, the pilgrims of tomorrow.

The train was on time and arrived in St Jean about 6pm. The pilgrims left the train in a noisy chaos of backpacks and hiking poles. I heard two people behind me who spoke in Danish so I sped up. I didn't feel like talking to them and relate to being a Dane on a pilgrimage. I was in a state of mind where I was without nationality, without limitations and without name tags. I was simply, just me, and I wasn't ready to connect with my fellow pilgrims yet.

Once outside the small train station, the pilgrims disappeared in a huge wave down the road. I presumed that everybody else but me knew where we were heading. Half-confused, I let myself get caught up in the wave whilst looking for a sign that could enlighten me on the right direction into town, but found none. I had looked at a map of St Jean at home and the walk between the train station and my *albergue*, that special place where only pilgrims can stay, had looked quite easy. In fact, it had looked so easy that I thought I wouldn't need a map. Well, I did! The obliging tourist signs I had expected remained absent, and all I could do was to follow along and hope I would end up at the right place.

As I was carried along towards town, I felt like one small fish in a large school. This was when the young Danish couple approached me. They wanted to know if I knew where their albergue was. Revealing myself, I answered them in Danish. Not only did I not know where their albergue was, I had absolutely no idea where my own was. And so began a friendship that would last until our roads separated many hundreds of kilometres later. That was typical of the Camino.

The young Danish couple, Søren and Ditte, talked non-stop while the 'school of pilgrims' moved through the streets of St Jean in seemingly random fashion. We walked up some stairs, crossed roads and took a lot of turns that I didn't remember from the map. But I didn't seem to remember much about the map anyway. Then suddenly, out of the blue, I saw the sign for L'Esprit de Chemin. Surprised, I stopped and exclaimed loud and clear: 'That's my albergue!'

I couldn't believe my luck! Søren, who almost bumped into me because I had stopped in the middle of the crowded road, looked at it dismissively. 'That's not the right place to stay,' he said, as he and Ditte pushed on past me at full speed.

I looked after them for a moment, thinking, that I had never heard anything about a 'right' place to stay. I shrugged my shoulders and headed towards L'Esprit's colourful front door. As I approached my albergue, a noisy commotion was occuring a little further up the alley. I turned to see what was going on, thinking that it couldn't possibly be from the pilgrims. But it was! The commotion was right in front of the pilgrims office – the most famous office in St Jean. It was the place where a pilgrim received their first official Camino stamp, become registered, and was given a map of the route over the Pyrenees into Roncesvalles. This was also the place where one could buy a pilgrim's pass if they had not done so beforehand.

It was an odd experience to see how the formerly semi-organised wave of pilgrims had turned into a noisy chaotic mass of backpacks, boots, walking sticks, loud voices and bodies. Everybody was trying to fit into the small office, but it was just not physically possible (not that it seemed to have dawned on anyone, though). Pushing and squeezing like crazy, the noise from their boots and big wooden hiking poles sounded like the stamping of impatient horses. The din that ensued drowned out the individual voices of the excited and impatient pilgrims. I stared at them, not knowing what to think. But the fact was this: once you got the stamp, you had – officially – begun your Camino. And we had been waiting a long time for this moment. Not wanting to join the chaos, I decided to check into my albergue first, and return later to register as I had two full hours before it closed.

Standing next to the entrance door into L'Esprit, was a beautiful old lantern with a lit candle inside. An old wooden hiking pole of Saint James rested peacefully beside it. It was as if he had left it there for only a short moment. With the dried flowers on the door it all had a very middle-aged romantic look, and, most importantly, it gave me a feeling of being welcome.

As I opened the door, a small old-fashioned bell rang. It took a couple of seconds before I got used to the darkness in what seemed to be a very narrow hallway. I slowly walked further inside, trying not to disturb any of the pictures on the walls. Not that I was successful as I managed knocking a small picture frame down onto the floor with my backpack. Bending over to pick it up, I could hear some voices from behind a doorway further down the hallway. It sounded like they were coming from a kitchen. Carefully I put my backpack down on the floor, still working hard on not to upset anything (although it was a bit difficult). As I poked my head through the open doorway I let out a quiet 'Hello'.

Two women, who were busy cooking, turned around and replied with two big smiling 'Hellos' in return. The entire kitchen table was stacked with heaps of fresh vegetables and herbs the ladies were preparing to cook.

'Come in, come in! Sit down,' said the elder of the two, as she walked towards me, pointing to some tables and chairs.

A little awkwardly I sat down. I could see that they were busy and I didn't want to disturb them. But the ladies laughed. They immediately included me in their conversation without me having to do anything. The younger, called Antoinette, quickly took a cup from one of the shelves and poured me some tea.

'You must be tired?' she asked, while she sat down on the chair next to me. She looked at me kindly, as if she had all the time in the world. I nodded in agreement and took a sip of the hot tea.

'Where do you come from?' Antoinette asked, whilst pouring herself a cup of tea.

'I have travelled by train from Paris since early this morning, but I come from Denmark – do you know where that is?'

She did and went on to tell me a funny story about some Danish pilgrims she had met. We laughed. Antoinette herself came from Canada. The older woman was from France. Emanuelle, I think her name was. They both worked as *hospitalarios*. This is a term for former pilgrims who worked in albergues, because they wished to return the love and care that had been given to them on their pilgrimage. Emanuelle had walked the Camino before together with her husband. She had also wished to return some of the help and hospitality she had received on her walk. Antoinette, on the other hand, was doing it in the opposite way. She hadn't walked the Camino yet, but dreamt about it. This was her way of starting.

It was difficult not to cast longing looks toward the delicious food they were preparing. The many different fresh vegetables, herbs, marinated meats, grilled chicken and bean salads made my mouth water. While I sat and hoped dinner was going to be soon, Emanuelle turned around from her pot of stew and asked: 'Are you the one who is allergic to wine and garlic?'

'Yes!' I replied, with a smile and a sigh of relief, 'I am.' It is always a little difficult with my food allergies, and I never know how people will react. Some will, however, still put garlic in food, even though they said they didn't. It made me very happy that it wasn't the case here. It turned out that Emanuelle had set a portion aside for me, before adding the garlic and the wine. And with regards to the wine that was always served with the pilgrims dinner, I said she could drink mine. Emanuelle looked at me with a big grin on her face.

'I think I get enough,' she laughed, as she raised her glass of red wine. Standing on the bench beside her was a half empty bottle of wine!

I didn't know which albergue Søren and Ditte were staying at, but I was so happy to be here. It was my friend, Ida, who had advised me to stay at L'Esprit.

After having finished my tea, Antoinette showed me to the room where I would sleep. We walked out from the kitchen and upstairs. On the door into my room, a beautiful orange-yellow labyrinth was painted. The arms and the legs of the human in the middle made up the pathways of the labyrinth. As it was very pretty, I couldn't help but comment on it. Antoinette looked surprised and asked if I knew anything about labyrinths. 'A little,' I replied.

She nodded, opened the door quietly and we walked into the room. 'That's yours,' she said, and pointed to a bed in the corner. Then she turned and walked downstairs back into the kitchen. There was a bunk bed, which a French couple occupied, and a single bed for me in the corner. On my bed, a white sheet had been folded nicely, and placed on top of a blue blanket. Leaning against it was a small square-shaped piece of paper, with a pretty blue flower drawn on it wishing me welcome in several languages. As a final touch, a caramel sweet, had been placed in front of the paper. I took it and unwrapped the caramel slowly. I couldn't help being impressed with all the little details that had been arranged to make me feel welcome. Me, a single pilgrim out of thousands.

My French roommates had left their backpacks on their mattresses together with some clothes. They had obviously gone out. After having looked around the place, I decided to get some rest before dinner. So many thoughts ran through my head: the excitement of finally being there, knowing that I would spend the next six weeks in nature, completely free from calendars and work. All I had to do was to follow the scallop shell, eat when I was hungry and take breaks when I was tired. Freedom. I longed so deeply to feel free, to enjoy life and just surrender to the magic of it. But, in my life, there had never been room or time for it. Days were locked into work, demands and necessary activities.

As I lay on the bed trying to relax, I felt how difficult it had been to breathe in the life that I had lived, and how I had to struggle more and more not to lose the meaning of it all. For a time my thoughts moved to my work, and how a recent change of management had created an exhausting and aggressive work environment. It had made bullying and the resulting stress a normal part of the day. However, to admit to being stressed was considered a weakness, and was not looked upon kindly – even my studies weren't looked upon kindly. It was frustrating to see how people's behaviour had changed towards the negative. At one point, my new leader had told me that one could say a lot about another person by looking at how long they stayed at their workplaces. I thought to myself that you also could say a lot about the leader and the management by looking at how much stress, bullying and fear there was amongst the employees. The whole situation made me sad. Sad for him and sad for those who thought so badly about other people. How we treated other people said a lot about how we felt about ourselves, and taking our issues out on others was downright draining.

The bell on the door rang downstairs. I could hear a group of pilgrims walk in. The noise of their backpacks and boots being thrown down in the hallway and Antoinette's voice welcoming them reached me in the little room. I smiled and stretched like a lazy cat before getting out of bed. It was time to register at the pilgrims office and have a look around St Jean.

Except for three older male employees, the pilgrims office was now empty. They gave me a friendly smile as I entered, although they seemed a little puzzled that my first stamp had been from my albergue and not from them, which was the accepted custom. I filled out my registration papers, received a photocopied map of the way to Roncesvalles, and had my credential stamped. One of the men looked at me as he gave me the map and said: 'Don't take the forest way just before you get to Roncesvalles.'

A temp from work had advised the same thing, but I hadn't understood what he meant, so I just thanked the kind men and left. 'Buen Camino!' they said. 'Have a blessed journey.'

'Thank you!' I replied. Then I turned around and walked out through the small door. Once outside, I discovered that most of the albergues in St Jean were located on this very street. It was a part of the Camino route and was paved with pretty cobblestones. Beautiful and well-kept old houses were lined up on each side of the street. Turning left from the pilgrims office, I walked up a hill and passed some fascinating ruins. I didn't have the energy to explore them, though. Instead, I walked up a little further and enjoyed the view over the spectacular and lush mountain landscape. It was such a thrill knowing that I would be walking in those mountains the following day.

Walking back down the hill, past the pilgrims office and my albergue, I came across various shops selling professional pilgrim gear and other outdoor accessories. At the very bottom of the hill, I found the most romantic gothic church dating from the 14th century, which I immediately went in to inspect. It was a thing of mine; after having started my studies in the Catholic part of Christianity, women etc., I always, whenever travelling in Europe, visit every Catholic church I pass. I used to do it because I enjoyed looking at all the art work they displayed, but now I did it for other reasons as well. I had, in fact, tested a few friends' patience with these visits. They never asked why I did it, though, so I kept the reasons to myself.

The gothic church was located next to a small arched bridge which crossed the river. It was really a picture-postcard perfect scene. Along the river, old romantic houses in traditional colours were lined up with flowers outside their windows. What a place to live, I thought. The next morning I would have to walk this way, passing the church and crossing the bridge when walking out of St Jean and up into the mountains – onto *The Road of The Scallop Shell*. I stood there for a while and looked back down the road.

For the last half hour before dinner I sat in the backyard of L'Esprit and enjoyed the sunset. I finally started to unwind and forget about work and all the other things that had previously occupied my mind. The dinner was healthy and nutritious, and was served in the cosy backyard behind the kitchen. About 25 people showed up for dinner. The two hospitalarios had prepared a brown-bean salad, a green salad filled with herbs, a chicken and meat stew with beans, freshly baked bread, steamed vegetables and a green lentil soup. All of this was served with a half bottle of red wine per person. For dessert, Emanuelle had cut up fresh fruit, topped with sweet whipped cream. The food was delicious and all the pilgrims were a lot happier and more talkative after dinner, although I suspected that the wine had played a role in this.

Feeling satisfied, I enjoyed the company of my fellow pilgrims. It was rather surprising that most of them were at least 10 years older than me. I had thought that most of the pilgrims would have been much younger. During our conversations, I learnt that one woman had to go home because her father was ill, another had walked from France to Leon in Spain, and then all the way back to St Jean, and a third had walked a completely different way. I was close to being the only one in the entire company, who was going to walk directly from St Jean to Santiago de Compostela.

I had a good time during dinner and loved the way the two hospitalaros knew how to create a positive and relaxed atmosphere. It was easy to see that those who had walked the Camino before were the talkative ones. The rest of us would mostly just sit, a little bit shy, and listen carefully to what they said, occasionally asking questions. Around nine o'clock most of us said goodnight and went to bed. That night, I had this dream:

I come walking along a pretty earth track. It is evening, but still very light. I arrive at some very old and beautiful stone ruins, made from rose-coloured adobe sandstones.

Somewhere in the wall, I see a loose stone, so I walk over and remove it. I place my face close to the hole and peer through with one eye. To my surprise, I see out into the universe; infinite, enchanting, stunning and welcoming. In the distance, a radiant female figure comes toward me. Her beauty is of divine dimensions.

As she draws closer, I am totally amazed and just stare at her. Her radiance makes me feel completly safe and calm. She comes so close, that I can look deeply into her eyes. In them, I see the entire universe, galaxies and the most amazing colours. She keeps looking at me, kind, loving, but also very direct. She continues to approach me until she is so close, that I only can see one of her eyes, looking at me through the hole in the wall. When she speaks, her voice comes from the beauty of the endless universe. She says: 'In you, I see faithfulness.'

I woke up immediately after these words. Today was the day of the summer solstice, my first walking day on the Camino. I could still feel and see the woman of my dream clearly. What was the meaning of that dream? Faithfulness? As I turned over onto my back and looked out into the darkness, I felt an immense feeling of happiness well up within me. The word 'faithfulness' kept spinning through my head.

During my upbringing I had experienced so much falseness and betrayal that it had made me sick. To live with authenticity, freedom and integrity had been my golden principle and dream since I was young. These values had been my goals since I turned 18 and left home, but to actually live this way had been an uphill struggle most of the time. Sometimes I could have made life easier for myself and not acted with integrity; but I just couldn't. I had seen too many people live ignoble lives, and I just knew that it wasn't the way for me. Yet, I still felt I had let myself down too many times, but this dream told me something else. Not only had I managed to be faithful towards myself, I had also been faithful to the spiritual and divine in myself. Could anyone had given me a bigger compliment? I didn't think so.

If the French couple had woken up, they would have seen some teeth shining in the darkness. That was me, smiling like crazy. Probably, for the first time in my life, I felt a sense of pride about myself. I had actually had the courage and will to follow my heart and intuition, and fight for my convictions, even though the price sometimes had been the loss of other people's recognition and inclusion in female groups. But I knew now, that I was exactly where I wanted to be. No matter where I stood in other people's eyes, I liked where I stood in mine. At that moment, my alarm clock rang. It was 6am and still dark outside. A new day was about to begin.

THE DAY OF SUMMER SOLSTICE

I had hidden my phone under my pillow and turned the volume down as far as I could. I tried, as quietly as possible, to collect my things and tiptoe out to the toilet. It was almost impossible and I could hear how much noise I made. Searching for my blouse, I dropped my comb on the floor. Getting back up, I hit the small lamp on my bedside table that nearly tipped over. When I tried to get my towel from inside the backpack, five other things came out, making more noise. I looked up and saw the French couple were now awake. I realised I hadn't arranged my things properly before going to sleep. Apologetically, I took all my things under one arm and walked out, still in my nightwear.

Out in the hallway, other pilgrims were trying to get dressed in the dark as quietly as possible, since there were many pilgrims still sleeping in their rooms. I couldn't help but smile at every person with whom I made eye contact. My dream that night had meant so much to me. The fact that my dream had appeared the night before starting on my pilgrimage was even more incredible. Whilst I dressed next to the staircase, several pilgrims stood in line for a shower. Not wanting to waste my time, as I had showered the evening before, I packed my backpack and went downstairs. I could smell the coffee and breakfast being cooked. Knowing what dinner had been like, I was sure I had something to look forward to.

Down in the kitchen, I was met by Emanuelle and Antoinette's heartwarming smiles followed by a welcoming 'Good morning'. The breakfast table was filled with different kinds of muesli, bread, milk, yogurt, cheese, butter, jam, juice, tea and coffee. Emanuelle was already standing by

29

the stove cooking delicious omelettes, and Antoinette was cutting up herbs and vegetables. I was utterly amazed by their energy and dedication, especially at this time of the morning. Their eyes did look a little tired, so I asked what it was like to be a hospitalario. While serving myself breakfast from the many items on the table, Emanuelle told me that they got up between 4 and 5am; prepared breakfast and made delicious omelette sandwiches for those of us who had been lucky enough to have ordered one. After the pilgrims left, they would then clean the albergue and make ready for the next pilgrims. Then they would have one or two hours of rest, before starting on dinner. I looked at them in admiration.

'You truly prove that it is the love of one's work that makes the wheel turn around,' I said. 'You look so happy all the time. And not just a pretend smile so-I-look-like-I-am-happy. I can really feel how much you love doing this.'

Emanuelle's face lit up with a bright smile as she lifted the pan containing the omelette. 'You know,' she said, 'it feels so good and wonderful to be able to give the pilgrims a good start. I know how much it meant from my own walk.'

She told me how she had put the menu together so the food had a high content of protein. 'You will need it,' she said, 'there won't be much protein in your diet once you get to Spain.'

With great skill, she deftly flipped the omelette over and put it into the sandwich roll. It was burning hot. She wrapped it in silver foil and placed it next to my plate. The fresh aroma of garden herbs was so enticing that I felt like eating it then and there. I shrugged my shoulders with joy, looking forward to my lunch, while I took another spoonful of muesli. I felt very lucky indeed, staying at this wonderful place.

My Camino started with me missing the obvious marked road, where I should have turned right. Instead I continued walking in the wrong direction. I did wonder where all the other pilgrims had disappeared to, but continued on for a further 10 minutes. Still no signpost as I had been told at the pilgrims office, so I stopped and looked around. 'I must have missed a turn or something,' I mumbled to myself whilst unfolding my map.

The early morning mist was hanging low and covered the landscape in a mysterious white-blue haze, with only the sounds coming from cow bells in the distance. There was no sign of a disappearing backpack anywhere to be seen. Not even a farmer in view. I was completely alone, which was a both great and unusual feeling at the same time. A few minutes later, the noise from a car came through the mist. The noise was followed by a very small, and very old, car, barely keeping it all together. The road was still wet from the night before, so the car left small patterned tyre marks as it slowly passed me by. An old man sat behind the steering wheel, and looked at me, a little confused. I raised my hand to greet him. He stared at me for a few seconds, still confused, before slowly nodding his head. Then he continued on this way.

'Okay!' I said out loud, 'that confirms it! If he gets confused seeing me here, I am definitely going the wrong way!' I turned around and walked back into St Jean. As the water from the fine mist dripped from my nose, I couldn't help laughing. 'What a grand way to start the Camino,' I chuckled to myself, 'going wrong like that.' Oh well, at least I came to see that part of St Jean, too.

As I backtracked to the T-junction and to the sign I had missed before, pilgrims re-appeared. This time, I turned the same way as they did. I walked on at a fast pace and soon left the other pilgrims behind me. Having no idea how much energy I would use crossing the Pyrenees into Roncesvalles, I walked on without a care in the world, but the road started to ascend quickly. 'It will be over in a minute,' I thought, and kept up my fast pace.

I passed a few small farms and many large green fields. The mist was still hanging low. A few sheep eating their breakfast looked up at me through the haze. However, the ascent hadn't come anywhere near an end. I believed, for some reason, that crossing the Pyrenees would be a fairly easy walk. So whilst I was breathing in the clean, fresh mountain air that smelled of trees, grass, flowers and earth, I ignored the fact that the road was getting steeper and steeper – thinking, mistakenly, that it would level out just around the next corner.

The absence of modern-day traffic was soothing to my ears. It was unbelievably relaxing not to have the constant noise of cars or people around me all the time. Only on rare occasions would a small tractor pass me on the road, usually driven by a tired looking farmer. As the mist started to clear, I saw a falcon sitting close by on a small haystack. Since it didn't seem to be bothered by me, I slowly moved closer to the fence and took a picture. 'What a majestic bird!' I thought. I stood for a while and appreciated its beauty before I moved on, upwards, into the Pyrenees.

The climb was now getting seriously harder, but the stunning nature distracted me from thinking about it: the grandeur, the lush green colours and the continuously changing scenery. Fuelled by a surplus of energy, I could feel the strength in my legs and body pushing me forward. After having walked for about two hours I decided it was time for a break, even though I didn't feel tired. During my preparations, I had promised myself that I would take frequent rest breaks, so that I could enjoy my walk as much as possible. Now was a good time to start keeping that promise.

After having passed through a forest, the view cleared and I saw a perfect spot for my first stop. It was situated further up the road under a big oak tree, with lots of soft grass covering the ground beneath it. A couple of fat cows were walking around behind a little stonewall next to the tree. Upon reaching my chosen spot, I found an American girl had arrived ahead of me. 'Is it okay if I sit here, too?' I asked her.

'Of course,' she said and smiled whilst making room for me. Her Camino had also started from St Jean. She was busy looking at a blister on one of her heels. Seeing the size of it I felt sorry for her. Little did I know her blister was nothing compared to what I would witness later on. Looking up from her foot I caught a glimpse of her backpack. It was absolutely huge. Spilling out of it were several books, lots of clothes and huge towels.

'Oh, my gosh!' I said, pointing at all the things she had brought with her. I couldn't help but comment. The girl laughed and shrugged her shoulders. She hadn't been able to decide on what to leave behind, so she had brought it all.

A short time later a Scottish vet, named Scott, decided to join us. 'Is it okay if I sit with you?' he asked.

'Of course!' we said and made room for him.

Even though we had never met before, we all sat under the large Oak and talked as if we had been friends for a very long time. I experienced very quickly on the Camino that it didn't matter what type of work you did, how much money you earned, or what education you had. What mattered was who you were as a person, and how you treated your fellow pilgrims. People actually listened to each other here. For that reason, we rarely talked about trivial things. Instead we talked about more personal things like why we walked the Camino, our inner journeys and, of course, our feet.

As I continued my walk, leaving the American girl and Scott behind, I couldn't help but feel how the amazing landscape moved something within me. The green fields looked endless. With the absence of the masses of people, and the noise that usually accompanied them, I began to question if a big city really was the right place for me to live.

After the oak tree, the road became even steeper. It became so steep that, instead of walking, I felt as if I was scrambling on all fours up along the road. Sweat trickled down my face and I constantly had to dry it with my small chamois. I had somehow forgotten that I was actually climbing the Pyrenees, one of the highest mountain ranges in Europe. I didn't realise my struggles wouldn't be over until I reached Roncesvalles, *many* exhausting hours later.

One minute I would find myself walking above the clouds, the next, below the clouds. The scenery above the clouds was a white and dreamy expanse with mountain tops poking through. The scenery below the clouds was filled with the beautiful greenness of the Pyrenees. It was really fantastic and somewhat breathtaking. I realised I hadn't experienced so much vastness and lush vegetation for eons. Well, for a very long time anyway. Having become so accustomed to the polluted air in the city, the fresh air here in the Pyrenees felt like breathing in pure prana. Never had I experienced such an intense happiness. It ran as a force through my body and gave me energy to continue the climb.

After walking for a few hours, the mist from the morning had evaporated, and the sun was shining in a crystal-clear blue sky. Small white wispy clouds quickly came and went, casting fleeting shadows on the ground. When reaching a place where I had a clear view over the mountains, I stopped to have a rest and admire the scenery. The mountains continued as far as my gaze could see; some even wore snow on their peaks. I took off my boots and socks, placing them on a nearby stone in the sunshine so they could dry. Ida, my friend who had walked the Camino before, had given me this advice. She had said that by doing this, I would reduce the chances of blisters, help my feet cool down and reduce swelling. Either way, it just felt wonderful to get my feet out of the boots.

I sat in absolute stillness, releasing my tensions and remembering how I, as a little girl, would sit for hours and look at books with pictures in them from all over the world. I wasn't even old enough to read them, but it didn't matter. The pictures spoke for themselves, and I dreamt of exploring all these fascinating places when I grew up. Maybe that was when my destiny had been sealed. I remembered promising myself that when I grew up, I would travel out into the big, fascinating world and discover its many secrets. But life had a way of its own. My journeys out in the world had also become my journeys into myself. So during my 20s and into my 30s, I grew up to become an adult who saw herself more as a citizen of the world rather than just of one country.

During my many journeys and despite cultural differences, I came to feel that we humans after all, weren't that different deep inside. Who doesn't wish to be loved and respected for who they are? Who doesn't wish to be healthy, have good friends, enough food on the table every day and a meaningful life? Many of these early experiences became the reason for my choice of a career in psychology and social education. And sitting here, on my way across the Pyrenees, I saw how far I had travelled in life, inside and out. And, somehow, the Camino seemed to be linked to the end of all of these travels.

Still deep in thought, I caught sight of a pilgrim further back along the road as she struggled up the mountainside. Her big backpack danced from side to side, buffeted like a ship in a storm. Her boots were unlaced, and she looked really miserable. A little while later, two young men followed. They looked even worse. As they passed me by, I could hear one of them complaining incessantly about his blisters while trying to catch his breath. I looked down at my own feet and examined them carefully. They seemed fine.

Shortly after, my socks were almost dry. I felt rejuvenated as I donned my dry socks and boots. Back on the road, I enjoyed the small talks I had with other pilgrims I met. I still walked too fast, but since I had a lot of energy, I didn't worry about the consequences of using it up so quickly. I was in good shape, felt very strong and well prepared. Nobody had warned me about how hard the walk would be, except for the forest path just before Roncesvalles. So I remained in this more or less naive frame of mind, thinking that I could easily cross the Pyrenees.

It did confuse me a little, however, that my map didn't seem to fit with the landmarks that I passed, but as long as all the other pilgrims went in the same direction as me, I thought I was fine. Really, all I had to do was to follow the yellow arrows, together with the red and white stripes; the French sign for the Camino. The arrow told me which direction to go, and once in Spain, the stripes would be replaced with the famous scallop shell. The problem was, it transpired, that I had stopped looking for the yellow arrows. I had just followed the pilgrims who walked in front of me.

Somewhere close to what I guessed was the top of the mountain, I teamed up with a Canadian. His name was Pierre, and he had walked all the way from Switzerland. This was his second Camino. Pierre was about 70 years old, extremely fit and looked remarkably like Santa Claus. He had a huge knowledge about the Knights Templar and the Freemasons. He seemed, however, unusually secretive when we discussed those subjects. Sometimes he would give me a feeling that he had said too much. So I started to suspect him of belonging to some sort of secret society. When I asked him if he belonged to one of these groups, he flatly denied it. This always made me laugh, whilst Pierre looked at me with a secretive smile. We found out that we had a lot in common, so we walked for a long time together. Pierre turned out to be a warm and considerate person, who always showed a genuine care for his fellow pilgrims. Wherever he was, his presence alone would ensure that nobody felt unsafe or alone.

Together with Pierre, I reached the actual top of the mountain. When the pilgrims who had been walking in front of us, turned off the paved road onto a muddy track we followed. Why look for arrows when you're in the middle of an interesting conversation and the pilgrims in front of you seemed to know where they were going? Pierre and I walked together for a long time along the muddy track. The track would meander through the undulationg countryside like water in a creek. The area was often covered in a mist, making it impossible to see ahead. Often it seemed as if a sheep or a fence had popped out from the mist. Then, out of nowhere, a paved road appeared. We stopped, looking at it curiously. Where did that come from? We stood there for a while, trying to get our bearings.

Seeing other pilgrims walking past us along the road, which headed north, we followed and continued together until Pierre stopped to talk to other pilgrims he seemed to know. By the time I reached a small but famous statue of the Virgin Mary, I was almost out of water as I hadn't passed any of the water fountains I had expected to. But, not only that, I also finally found my location on the map. Looking at it for a while I realised I had taken a huge detour. As it turned out, I had taken a totally different road from St Jean than orginally planned. Prior to leaving St Jean, I had decided to take the easy road across the Pyreness because it had several water fountains along its way. But I had somehow managed to take a third unmarked route. This explained why I hadn't passed any fountains and, subsequently, ran short of water. The detour I had taken with Pierre was my second 'navigational' mistake. No wonder my map hadn't worked at all!

Shortly after, when I met up with Pierre again, we had a really good laugh over this. 'I hadn't even thought about it,' he said, still laughing, 'I just followed the people in front of us, thinking they knew the way.'

'Me too,' I said, a little surprised, 'I used to be pretty good at finding my way around using a map.'

But Pierre and I weren't the only people who had taken the huge detour. The people in front of us had followed those in front of them, and those behind Pierre and I had followed us – each of us thinking that we knew where we were going. Humans are such great herd animals. In spite of the mistake, our detour had led us into one of the most untouched and mystical places in the Pyrenees. Who said a detour had to be a bad thing?

Walking across the mountain top I felt great pleasure as I watched the sheep, horses and cows roaming freely. There were no fences on the flattened top of the mountain, so the animals could wander around as they pleased. Later that night, at dinner, I would describe them as 'happy cows and happy horses' to the Scottish vet. Scott, of course, burst out in laughter. This was about the funniest description of animals he had ever heard.

Somewhere after the Virgin Mary statue, I started to feel thirsty. Really thirsty. I must have sweated so much fluid during the hours I had been walking. Looking around, I tried to find a solution. At first, there appeared to be none. But then I noticed the many small springs that ran down through the fields. The water looked very clean, so I drank from one of them. A German woman, who had seen me drink the water, called to me that I shouldn't drink it. 'Why not?' I asked.

'Animal urine and the chemical sprays used on the fields may have contaminated the water. And if they have, the water will make you sick.' Since I didn't want to get sick, I had to drink what I had left in my water bottle, which wasn't much.

I walked for over an hour before coming to the next, and last, water fountain prior to reaching Roncesvalles. By the time I finally reached the fountain, I felt utterly exhausted and totally dehydrated. I immediately drank half a litre of fresh cold water, and then filled my water bottles to the brim. Feeling better I found a little spot to lie down and rest. It turned out that the toughness of the hike from St Jean to Roncesvalles had surprised many. It wasn't only me. Laying in the grass, looking up into the sky, I wondered if I'd ever make it to Roncesvalles before dark. It felt as if I would never make my body move again.

After my snooze, I still felt quite spent. My feet and legs hurt and my energy supply was down to zero. I had no more food or snacks that I could eat, but at least I had water. There was only one thing I could do, and that was to force myself to continue. So, as I started to walk again, I began to feel an unexpected irritation and anger towards the Camino. Angry at myself for getting into this situation and irritated for being so stupid. In fact, for the rest of my descent into Roncesvalles, the Camino turned into the most stupid idea in the whole world. Even with my four and a half months of preparation for the Camino, a walk this hard, and on the first day, was too much.

It didn't help, that a new-age woman, had decided to walk with me, talking non-stop in 'bumper sticker' clichés. All she could say was the usual passive phrase of 'everything had a purpose' and that everything and everyone was about *you* with only one aim: to teach you something about yourself. Well, maybe the purpose was to grow up and start using your own voice instead of limiting yourself to a 'bumper sticker' language. However, the real reason I disliked these kind of attitudes, was the person's arrogance and total lack of humility. Most people who thought this way were only able to see themselves – thinking that the world was totally there for their benefit. They were indifferent to what happened in the world and to the people living in it, with no empathy or awareness of others and their realities. Our planet is a very small planet. It resides in a galaxy that is one out of an unknown number in a universe that is infinite. How can we claim to know *the truth*? That was the arrogance I perceived. A healthy person would always learn and grow throughout life, not having a need for the world to revolve purely around them.

Not feeling comfortable in her company, I decided to walk on ahead by myself, so I quickly sped up. Eight hours after having left St Jean, I finally reached the pathway that passed through the forest down to Roncesvalles. A Swedish couple, that I had come to know during the day, stood and looked at a signpost as I arrived. One sign pointed towards the forest, giving an approximate time for the walk down to Roncesvalles. The other sign pointed in the other direction, indicating the alternative route to Roncesvalles. The time for this route being almost twice as long as for the forest walk. After a short discussion, the Swedish couple decided to take the long way. I decided on the shorter forest way. The walk went pretty much like this:

I thought I was a lot smarter than the Swedish couple. What could be wrong with a beautiful walk down through a forest? Looking from where I was standing, it didn't look as bad as I had been told and the forest was so shaded that it made the air nice and cool. So I started to think that people had exaggerated. Well, I was right about the last part, the coolness that is, for as I started to walk, the forest road quickly turned into the steepest pathway one could imagine, almost like a roller coaster. The loose gravel and polished stones offered no secure footing so I had to zig-zag very carefully every inch of the way. By the time I realised my mistake, it was too late to turn around. I just didn't have the energy to walk back up.

As I scrambled very carefully down the pathway, the sudden sound of skidding feet made me turn around and look. Back up the pathway I saw two young men. One was clinging desperately to a tree, whilst watching his friend frantically struggling to avoid falling on the loose surface. As the friend slipped, the other one let go of the tree. The moment he stepped on the pathway, his feet slipped from under him and he joined his friend in rapid descent. Being afraid that the men would fall again and take me with them this time, I yelled a warning up to them. Not only did I have to worry about myself now, I also had to worry about suddenly being 'run over'. Making sure that my own feet were steady on the ground (well, as steady as they could be), I started to give the two men instructions on how to zig-zag correctly from side to side. They thanked me, with much gratitude, whilst working hard to follow the instructions I had given them. Feeling a little relieved, I continued to walk on. Hearing their laughter a few minutes later, I turned around to see what they were up to.

This time, I found them clinging to each other, their legs shaking, looking like two old ladies crossing the street. Even though I knew I shouldn't, I started to laugh out loud. But the moment I did, my feet started to slide on the stones and I only just managed to keep my balance, by putting one hand on the ground to steady myself. 'Okay, stop laughing!' I said to myself, but it was hard not to. The situation was so comical.

The descent was difficult and inescapable. I tried to walk off the pathway, a bit into the forest where I almost stepped on a snake, but it was just as difficult. A little disappointed and frustrated, I walked back out to the pathway. I soon lost sight of the two men behind me, although I could still hear them. After I became accustomed to the terrain, well, sort of, I managed to maintain a pretty okay speed, that was only a little faster than 'turtle speed'. But it only lasted until the next time my foot slipped on some stones. This time I skidded hard and landed on my bum in one big cloud of dust. Surprised, I sat there for a moment before realising, that it was actually quite comfortable in that position.

The steepness of the road behind me, pushed my backpack up so high, that it worked like the back of a chair. I could hear the men in the distance falling again so I tipped my head back and began to laugh. I laughed so hard that tears ran down my cheeks. This was the most insane situation ever. I didn't know how I was going to make it to the bottom or even how to get up from where I was sitting. The muscles in my legs were shaking so hard, that I didn't feel they would support me anymore. The pain was burning and I was beyond exhaustion. It was just crazy!

To add insult to injury, further down the pathway, I managed to twist my ankle. That was one of the worst things that could happen. Limping into a grassy clearing, I lay down and rested my foot on some wood to keep it elevated, not knowing what to do. I didn't even have energy to find out how bad it was. Thankfully, a pilgrim passed by shortly after. His name was Rodney. He was Irish, a Catholic and a chiropractor with many facial freckles. His eyes were deep green and his hair short and red.

Upon seeing me, he stopped and asked what was wrong. I told him what had happened and he took off his backpack before having a look at my ankle. 'You should get up and continue to walk right away,' he said, after explaining a sprain to me (as if I didn't already know).

Not sure that I would be able to get up, I replied that I would rest for a few more minutes first. Rodney looked at me thoughtfully, while putting on his backpack, nodded and then walked on. Shortly after that, Pierre came walking by, with what I would come to know as his entourage. They all stopped and asked what had happened and I explained once again. They stayed with me for a while, just chatting and filling me with a lot of love and healing energy. I was surprisingly feeling better in their company. A few minutes after they had walked on, I heard Pierre's voice calling out to me.

'We are less than three minutes from where you are,' he called, 'and there is a sign here that says we have reached the monastery at Roncesvalles. It is only a short walk from where you are.'

'Thanks!' I yelled back, supressing tears of exhaustion and gratitude.

Thankfully, when I stood up, my ankle seemed okay. Although sore, I was able to put weight on it without any problem. Thinking they were further away, I prepared myself for a longer walk. But it turned out that Pierre, his group and Rodney were all standing just around the corner from where I had been resting, waiting for me. They looked at me compassionately, and made sure that I reached the monastery with no further problems. I felt extremely touched by the love and care they showed me, and grateful for reaching my destination at last.

Upon arrival, I found the Swedish couple sitting outside the front door relaxing. It looked as if they had checked in a long time ago. I forced myself to give them a smile, but it sure didn't come from the heart. While Pierre and his group disappeared somewhere inside, Rodney and I checked in.

The monastery in Roncesvalles was beautiful and very well kept, both on the inside and the outside. Upon entering the large front gate, three men stood greeting us as we came inside. Well, greeting might be an exaggeration, but they were polite. I was a little confused about whether or not these men were monks, because I thought only nuns lived here. The odd thing was that the men became seriously cranky when I asked where the nuns lived. It apparently didn't help the situation, either, when I asked why there weren't any.

I think I would have been able to freeze a chicken from the cold angry stares they gave me. Even Rodney, being a devoted Catholic, was puzzled by their reaction. 'Nuns or monks … they are both Catholics,' he said. 'Why would they get so upset about that?'

'I don't know,' I said and gave him a blank look, 'but for some reason, they are.'

We walked upstairs into a huge dormitory that was divided into small cubicles, with four beds in each. The beds were arranged as bunk beds. As I walked into the dormitory, it was like seeing old friends again. Meeting the pilgrims I had come to know during the struggles of the day felt really good. We would smile and greet each other warmly, asking how the day had been. To my great surprise, it so happened that Ditte, Søren, Rodney and I would share a small, walled-off cubicle. It felt as if I were home again, safe and sound with my new pilgrim family with everybody having survived the day.

I quickly had a shower, washed my clothes, made my bed and prepared my things for the next morning. Constantly in the back on my mind, I kept wondering why there weren't any nuns present in this monastery. I felt as if there was something seriously wrong with what I was seeing. Ever since I heard the name, Roncesvalles, I had been convinced that it would be inhabited by nuns or simply just a place that somehow was related to women. But whatever it was, the males here surely didn't like to talk about that topic!

Later I went for a stroll to explore the place. Every time I passed the men (or monks) downstairs, they stared coldly at me until I was out of their sight. They even refused to tell me where I could do my laundry. Rodney noticed this and shook his head. I just smiled, thinking their behaviour was downright ridiculous and consequently found the laundry person myself – a woman, of course. The only woman, and only kind person I met, who worked in the monastery of Roncesvalles.

Whilst waiting for my washing to be done, I went to visit a church, which was part of the monastery. Here, I found many conspicuous symbols that referred to the feminine. In a rose window, I saw a woman within each single rose petal. Seeing so many women, and symbols like the rose within this church, made me question the assumption that this place had been for monks only. And again, I kept having this feeling that something wasn't quite right. It felt as if the women and the feminine symbols within this church were like a pink elephant in the room, or like the scapegoat of the family. It was either consciously ignored or a hotly debated topic. According to the way the men behaved, it seemed to be consciously ignored.

My stroll ended as I reached the open lawn that lay behind the buildings, the same place where I had arrived earlier from the Pyrenees. It was very quiet now. The main gates of the monastery were closed and it seemed as if all the pilgrims had arrived. I enjoyed standing on the lawn being the only pilgrim there. Everybody else was sleeping or resting. Behind me, I could hear the church organ starting to play. I turned around and looked up at the rose window again. It looked even prettier with the music coming from behind it.

I looked back towards the mountains, where I had come from earlier. They were covered by an emerald-green forest. I couldn't help but notice how exuberant and mighty the trees seemed. Dark clouds were moving in and warning that rain would be coming soon. I walked to the more sheltered side of the thick walls, underneath the big rose window, and lay down. The music stopped as the service began. In the silence, I could now hear the thunder in the distance and felt a warm wind caress my face. I felt so peaceful and loved. Was this place the reason for feeling like that, I wondered.

It occured to me, that this monastery was surrounded by an atmosphere of peace, presence and tranquility. There was something very special about the trees here. It was as if they knew something, as if the place was 'alive'. Maybe it was the way the trees danced in the wind. I didn't know. But it was exactly the way I had thought a place devoted to the goddess would feel. I knew I was wrong thinking this way because the men had told me that there had never ever been any nuns or women here. I gave up trying to understand the contradictions between the facts I had been given, and my own inner feelings. Eventually I closed my eyes and fell asleep.

I am at the very same place where I had fallen asleep in front of the church. Close to me, out on the big lawn, I see a white marble statue of a woman. She is the Sleeping Lady from Malta, lying on her side, sleeping. I stand for a while and look at her, wondering why she is asleep. I decide to ask her and walk towards her.

'Why do you sleep?' I ask.

The moment I ask the question, the statue comes alive and she opens her eyes and looks at me. Her eyes are crystal blue and as deep as the ocean.

'I am not asleep', she says, 'I am travelling in the underworld. My eyes are closed because I look inside. I look into the inner worlds, the worlds within me and the worlds that are invisible to the physical eye.'

She smiles and looks at me for a while. Then the picture changes. Now I see her standing closer to the surrounding trees. She is totally naked, with long golden hair. She looks like a true Venus. As she stands there, her golden hair dances in the wind. She is the wind, She is the trees and She is the mountains. She is everything that Roncesvalles encompasses. She says to me: 'Eyes look both inside and out, and so must you, Louise, look both ways.'

It was the loud peals of thunder and soft raindrops falling on my face that woke me, but I kept my eyes closed. My body felt deeply relaxed, resting safely on the earth beneath me. I didn't feel like moving at all. When I finally opened my eyes, everything looked and felt just like it had in my dream. I wondered for a second if I had been dreaming at all. And even though I couldn't see Her anymore, I felt Her presence very clearly. I still didn't feel like getting up, even as the raindrops started to fall more rapidly.

Instead, I spread my arms out to both sides, breathing in the wonderful smell of rain that bore the sweetness of the forest and the fresh air from the Pyrenees. I really loved this place and felt that it touched the very centre of my heart. Even the rain felt kind and caring.

Unfortunately, as the wind and rain became stronger, it was time to go. I gazed one last time upon the rose window, and looked at all the women within the petals, before running inside. I wondered who they were and why they were there?

Little did I know at the time, that a child in the middle ages had experienced a vison of Our Lady right here. And what I was to learn much later, was that Roncesvalles, in pre-Christian times, actually had been a special place for goddess worship.

CATHARSIS

The light was turned on at 5am sharp, waking all the pilgrims. It was wrong to say that I felt fully rested. My night had been terrible. After having such a beautiful experience the day before, followed by a nice dinner with fellow pilgrims, my night had turned into something of a nightmare. Every single part of my body hurt. My feet burnt as if they were being barbecued over an open fire. My body ached and burnt like I had a fever. It had been impossible to find any position where I could find any kind of rest. It had been quite annoying watching Søren and Ditte sleeping peacefully while Rodney's satisfied snoring echoed from the bunk beneath me. I couldn't understand why they weren't suffering like me, even just a little bit.

It was about 1am when I had the brilliant idea to take some painkillers. Unfortunately, I also realised, that I was in too much pain to move, let alone climb down the ladder. So I just had to endure it. Thankfully, the burning wore off after a while, allowing me a few hours of sleep before we were all awakened. Shortly after the light was turned on, I walked out to have a cold shower. To my surprise, my body felt a lot better than expected, and much of the pain had disappeared. Returning to the dormitory, most of the pilgrims were up and about. They seemed to be walking around aimlessly, not having developed a morning routine as yet. Rodney had gone; he must have left when it was still very dark. Ditte and Søren were, as usual, talking non-stop with their seemingly endless energy.

As I packed I discovered that my biggest problem, at that very moment, was breakfast. Eating breakfast was the first thing I did every morning. But right now, I had no idea where I could get any, so I sat on Rodney's empty bed eating almonds and fruit, thinking about what to do. After a few minutes, I decided to start walking. There had to be something along the way. So I left Ditte and Søren, who had gone to the bathroom, and walked downstairs to find my boots. As I walked out into the fresh morning air, I had the feeling that the 'cold-eyed' men were more than happy to see me leave, hoping never to see me again.

When I left the monastery, the darkness of the night was slowly lifting, letting in the first light of day. The place was surrounded by a heavy mist with raindrops dripping from the trees. Only a few other pilgrims were out, slowly moving around. The path I was to follow from Roncesvalles seemed mysterious and Avalonish, because of the thick, silvery-green coloured mist. In the stillness, as I walked along a small path under the trees, I heard someone come running. I stopped and looked back, concerned that something serious had happened. But no. It was simply a man who seemed to be running the Camino. I stood and stared at him as he passed and disappeared into the mist. Running the Camino? Who would *run* the Camino?

I passed several small places called *bars*, they were really more like cafés, on the way. They all had signs advertising breakfast, but they looked closed. So I kept walking. It took me a day or two before understanding that bars on the Camino were actually often open, even though they looked closed.

The mist continued to create an Avalonish feel to the scenery as I walked through fields of thick green grass and flowers. It was strange walking alone in the stillness, with the feeling that possibly only the pilgrims were awake at this time of day. Sheep would stand and stare after me, while absently chewing on the grass. Barbed wire fences with their spider webs would appear from time to time, decorated with beautiful drops of mist shining like small diamonds, lined up like pearls on a necklace. And with the mist hovering above them, small lavender coloured flowers stood out like lilac stars in the night. I never thought nature could be that enchanting. Even the silence was special. With time, I would come to know this special kind of stillness, that was so typical for the early mornings on the Camino. It was that special kind of silence, when there were no cars, no airplanes and no noise from humans. It was incredible.

Later in the morning, after having walked for about three hours, I reached a little village called Espinal. Time seemed to pass quickly when walking or I just seemed to disappear into a 'no time' zone. But in Espinal, I finally saw a sign for a bar where I could get some breakfast – and it was even open! 'Hurray!' I thought.

Pilgrims were sitting outside, drinking coffee and eating breakfast. In the middle of them all, I saw Rodney sitting holding his cup of coffee, looking at me with a huge self-satisfied grin on his face. On the table in front of him, stood an empty plate. He must have been sitting there for hours. I smiled and walked up to him. As I sat down, I realised, just how wonderful it was to get off my feet. I looked around at what people were eating, hoping to see some appetising, nourishing food. But no. As if reading my mind, Rodney advised me to buy a sandwich. 'It's the best they have,' he muttered.

I looked at him rather dissatisfied. The best they have? That didn't sound promising. I wanted a proper breakfast, not a sandwich. Inside the bar a real Spanish senora, dressed all in white, stood behind the counter. Apart from coffee and tea, I could choose between tortilla (a thick omelette with potatoes) and a sandwich made from a white breadstick filled with a tasty cheese and chorizo sausage. What I really would have liked was eggs, bacon and some fresh fruit – food with lots of energy in it. Having no choice, I ended up ordering two sandwiches, saving one for later, and a cup of tea. When I returned to the table outside, I found Rodney was getting ready to leave. 'See you!' he smiled, and walked off.

I was about to take the first bite of my sandwich when Scott, the Scottish vet, appeared in the company of another man. He waved as they walked over to me. I learnt later, that Scott was a real charmer, and one who many young women on the Camino chased after. I even met some who had stood and waited for him at remote intersections along the way. But whereas he did enjoy the attention, he was a man who had escaped from a stressful work situation and a recent painful divorce. As he threw his backback down on one of the chairs, he introduced his companion. 'This is Richard. He's from Australia.' As he introduced his friend, he turned his head towards the bar, commenting: 'I hope they have some good coffee in here.'

Richard and I shook hands. He was the stereotype of a 'typical' Australian – tanned and fit. Richard took his backpack off and placed it carefully down on the ground and left his blue walking pole against the chair that Scott had put his backpack on. He looked at me with a kind expression and asked: 'Do they have good coffee here?'

'I don't know. I don't drink coffee,' I said, shrugging my shoulders.

'Don't drink coffee?! How can anyone not drink coffee?' Richard laughed and showed a pair of sparkling brown eyes.

Richard and Scott came back from the bar with two *cortados* – each! A cortado is a strong black Spanish coffee, served in a very small cup. Scott had apparently been pretty liberal with the wine during dinner the night before, later followed by a bottle of grappa. When I asked Scott why he had been drinking so much, he told me he needed it in order to get a good night's sleep. Richard, on the other hand was a doctor, and his breakfast was, by definition, strong coffee. Neither of them ate anything. Instead, they entertained me, telling all about the previous evening. It sounded like they had been having a good time together. Apparently, they shared a mutual interest in horses.

Finishing breakfast, we walked out of Espinal together. On the way, in front of a kiosk, three American college girls caught our attention. They all wore flip-flops, tiny shorts and carried absolutely huge backpacks filled to the brim. All the backpacks hung haphazardly on their backs, looking as if a twister had just spat them out. They constantly laughed and giggled. When one of the straps suddenly broke on one of the girls' backpacks, it left it dangling at a precarious angle. Richard went over to help her. Another girl dropped her waterbottle and managed to spray water all over people's feet and boots, and breaking her flip-flops whilst trying to avoid getting wet herself. We shook our heads, hoping that somebody would watch over these girls. They sure would need it.

Leaving the girls behind, Scott disappeared deep into his own thoughts, maintaining his own walking pace. Richard and I, walking easily at the same pace, began talking. He quickly gave me the impression of being an interesting person, and I couldn't help but notice his ability to actually listen, something that made our conversations so much more relaxed and natural. Engrossed in our discussion, it took a while before we noticed that Scott had moved on ahead of us. We called after him, teasing him about abandoning us. Scott stopped and laughed. He explained that he really wasn't a walker and, if he didn't push himself, he was afraid he wouldn't achieve anything. Scott only had two weeks to walk as far as possible and that was the way it was with the Camino. You could only do it one way, and that was your way.

Around lunchtime, I arrived in Zubiri with Richard and Scott. Physically tired, Scott had slowed his pace and joined back up with us, already complaining about pain in his back. After eating together, Scott decided to carry on. My feet were hurting so badly I decided to stay in Zubiri. Richard, who also felt tired, decided to stay as well and checked into a small hotel. I, on the other hand, checked into the first albergue I came across after crossing a small bridge. Richard and I went off to our respective accommodations to rest, agreeing to meet for dinner some hours later.

When I entered my albergue, a South African man was sitting on a bench next to a large wooden dinner table. He seemed to be the only person in the albergue besides myself. He sat completely absorbed, attending to his feet. All the bottles of different kinds of ointments, needles and roles of bandages that were on the table next to him made me wonder if there had been an accident. It certainly looked as if he had been seriously injured. I stood watching him a time while I patiently waited for a person to come and check me in. Five minutes later, a door opened. 'Hellooo.'

I turned around and saw a woman with long dark hair walk into the room. 'Would you like a bed?' she asked, greeting me warmly.

'Yes, please,' I replied, as I reached for my pilgrim's pass and some money. A pilgrim was always carefully registered at every place she or he stayed. It was a security procedure in case a pilgrim disappeared.

'Here you go,' she smiled, and handed me my pass back. I looked at the stamp I had received. I just loved them. Each stamp was different with various symbols, names and colours. They were usually rather pretty and artistic, each having their own story to tell. Since I was only the second pilgrim to arrive, I could choose whatever bed I wanted in the two rooms. Each room contained four bunk beds, and we shared one small bathroom.

Exhausted, I sat down on the first bed I came to. I wanted to go to sleep right away. But knowing that I needed to wash my clothes and allow time for them to dry, I stood up and went out to launder the gear I had worn all day. I hung them to dry outside the window of my room on some washing lines. The window gave a panoramic view into people's backyards, which were filled with broken-down stone walls, grass, trees, endless clothes lines filled with laundry and large white sheets. It was like a scene out of a movie. The different corners of the yards were home to old, rusted-out cars and retired tractors. Cats were lying in the sun licking their fur, bees were busy visiting the different flowers, dogs were barking and, in the distance, an old lady plucked flowers that grew in front of her house. I leant my head against the window frame and smiled. I felt so grateful and so humble for experiencing this. I felt that what I saw in this backyard was more real than the life I lived in Copenhagen. Thousands of years of history emanated from the earth here, embracing everything around it. Our world was truly created by the steps we took and left behind us.

As I stood in the window, taking it all in, my heart opened up and I became a part of the world I saw around me and feeling as if I were the luckiest person alive. I would not have chosen to be born in any other place than in Europe and, at that moment in time, I would not have been anywhere else than at that window, looking out into those backyards.

I took a long hot shower, hoping that it would help ease my pains. After that, it was time for my siesta. Just as I was about to fall asleep, a Brazilian girl walked in still wearing her boots. Usually they would be left outside to prevent bringing bugs and too much dirt in the rooms. Letting the door slam behind her, the girl walked directly to the bed opposite me. She threw herself on the bed, leaving her backpack and boots in a pile in the middle of the floor. It was time to reach for my earplugs.

Upon waking an hour or so later, I discovered five more pilgrims had arrived. Most of them were lying on their beds sleeping. The Brazilian girl was in the exact same position as when I last saw her. So were her pile of belongings. I looked out through the open window for a while, enjoying the breeze that came in. Here on the Camino, I came to life in a way that I had never known before. It literally felt as if the Camino was saturated with life energy.

During the afternoon, I started to become more aware of a wonderful closeness and kindness that existed between the pilgrims. Most showed respect and sensitivity to their fellow pilgrims. This meant that we would show consideration towards each other's hardships, both emotional and physical, at the moment of our meeting. Everybody was included in the community and ready to help each other, no matter if one felt like talking or not. The thing was, that on a pilgrimage, everybody needed their own space and on their own terms. As a result, people who followed these unwritten guidelines seemed to experience a greater kind of harmony.

The next morning, Richard and I left Zubiri together. As much as I enjoyed his company and our talks, they also started to stress me. The constant talking prevented me from feeling the earth under my feet and the sky above my head. I needed to *feel* the nature that was around me, the places I passed and the space where I could wonder and marvel. I knew that all of this was essential for me, and I could feel that it was important that I respected it. But I didn't. Instead, I walked with Richard for the following two days, talking non-stop. We talked about everything, from philosophy, religion, politics and history to health.

He was very interesting to talk to and not afraid of a woman who had read widely, seen and done many things and who had thought a lot about life. I felt our conversations were equal in a unique way that enriched us both, and because our discussions were so exciting and interesting, I stayed with him.

When we reached Puente La Reina two days later, I felt as if my chest was about to explode. The inner pressure was unbearable and, since I was talking all the time, I couldn't hear or feel what the pressure was about. I did try to suppress it during that evening because we had such a good time with Søren, Ditte, Scott and all the other pilgrims. But early the next morning, while it was still dark, the signals became very clear. It was time to head off alone. After a sad goodbye, Richard and I went our separate ways. He went off to eat breakfast with the other pilgrims whilst I put on my backpack and left the albergue. The tears were waiting for me the moment I set foot on the sidewalk. It was so early that I still could see the stars on the night sky ahead of me while, at the same time, the sun was preparing to rise behind me in the east.

Apart from the young Brazilian girl who was walking ahead of me, I was by myself, alone. I tried hard to fight back the tears, feeling embarassed by them, so I just wanted to get out of the village, as fast as I could. Upon taking a left turn, I reached a charming square. It was then, in the middle of it, that I looked up into the sky. At that moment, I remembered last night's dream. For some unknown reason, the memory hit me really hard. In my dream, I had been standing on that exact same spot, as I did now. This morning, however, I only saw the sky where night and day met, but in my dream ... I had seen *Her*.

I come walking, all by myself, carrying my blue backpack. I feel really good, happy and content. As I reach the middle of the square, a movement in the sky catches my eye, so I look up. There, amidst the millions of stars and galaxies in the dark blue night sky, I see the outline of the exact same women that I had seen in my dream on the day I started my Camino. This time, there is no wall between us. She looks down at me with her endless presence, her love and compassion. It strikes me that she looks much larger and even more beautiful than in my other dream. Her eyes are as deep as the universe, and they sparkle like a million stars. Infinite amounts of milk-coloured liquid, with sparkles of gold, run out from the stars that shape her breasts.

From where I stand, I can see that the liquid runs down into the earth, and through the earth up into my body. It brings life to my cells and life to the earth that I stand on. It also brings life to the stars in the sky and the planets that move in our universe.

I stand in amazement and look at what I see. It makes me realise how small and insignificant I am, compared with all of the beauty I see around me. Yet, all the love I feel surrounding me says that I am indeed a part of it. I look back up to see if the Goddess is still there. She is. She smiles the most loving smile as our eyes meet and a stony hardness in my heart melts. The separation I had felt between myself, my spirituality and all the life that I was a part of, evaporated. Instead, a softness of comfort and oneness filled me and I felt a weight was lifted off my chest.

'See me,' she says. 'Hear me!'

I tilt my head to one side. 'I will,' I say.

In Her, I saw the purity of life's energy unpolluted and all-consuming.

Remembering the dream, tears started to run like a million raindrops, and there was no way I could stop them. I rushed across the square and down the cobbled street as fast as I could. I cried so hard that I could hardly breathe and I felt as if my entire world had opened and collapsed at one and the same time. Feeling touched inside by something truly divine, I also felt terrified. The wisdom that She radiated, Her love and Her all-surrounding presence – it was as if, for a timeless moment, Her love had been my love.

She had opened my inner ocean of feelings and freed something deep within me. She had made me come truly alive and it was impossible not to surrender to the ocean of tears. It was time to let go, to let it all out and *listen*. I remembered Ida and what she had told me: 'There will be days on the Camino when you will feel like crying, but that is what the Camino does to you. Just let go and cry.'

I thought she had exaggerated back then. Now, sobbing my way out of town, I realised that she was right. I continued to cry non-stop for the next four hours or so. Every time I thought I had no more tears left, a new wave of emotions would hit me, and I started to cry again. I cried for all the spirituality I had repressed in myself, and for the times in my life that had been so hard. I cried because my body needed to, and I cried for all the times I should have cried, but never did. I cried over the man I had just left behind, and the many times I had let people put me down, when I shouldn't have let them. I cried because all of my life I had longed for the kind of community I experienced here on the Camino. It was a community that was filled with mutual respect, space and a closeness filled with a freedom to be who I truly was. I cried because, for the first time in so many years, I had stopped and breathed in so deeply that I could actually feel it in my stomach. I cried because the smile that I smiled when breathing out was so free and honest. It was like the first smile of my life. It was the smile of a newborn child. And I cried because it was all I could do.

As the tears and crying subsided, I felt an inner stillness and physical lightness. My breathing became easy and untroubled, and my feet almost flew above the path that I was walking on. My heart was once again filled with an endless gratitude for being on this amazing earth, the beauty and diversity of which was beyond description. I walked away from the track onto a grassy verge and took off my backpack. Here I found a shady spot under a tree, hidden away from the other pilgrims. I lay down and closed my eyes, letting the morning sun create pretty patterns of yellow light and shadows through my eyelids, and, as my body rested on the soft grass, birds sang and insects hummed in their own joyful way. An ant crossed my left wrist, as if in a hurry and a bee found something interesting on the tip of my dirty boots. I had indeed returned to nature. I thought of Descartes who had said: 'I think, therefore I am.' But for me, it was rather: 'I feel the life in me, therefore I am.'

I rested in the shade for a while, surrendering to my feelings of tranquility and freedom. It was as if I had cried out everything I had held inside, emptied what I had needed to empty. The separation that once had filled me, was now beginning to heal and a new sense of oneness was starting to sprout.

I opened my eyes and stared up into the sky through the many branches of the tree. Its leaves were large and green, constantly changing form and colour depending on how the sunlight reflected off them. My heart and chest felt lighter! I remembered how, many years ago, I had learnt that there had been times when the sun had been regarded as a goddess and the moon as a god. It had turned out that these sun goddesses and moon gods had existed in many ancient cultures from all around the world. They even had co-existing sun god/goddesses and moon god/goddesses.

Of sun goddesses there had been: Sól or Sunna, as some had called her, from Scandinavia; Amaterasu from Japan; Hepa and Arinna from the Hittites; Shemesh from Ugarit; Aditi from India; Aine from Ireland; Belwe from Lapland; Sekhmet from Egypt; and Bila from the Aborigines in Australia. Of moon gods there had been: Arma from the Hittites; Khons, Thoth, Osiris, Min and Duau from Egypt; Mên from Western Asia Minor; Sin/Nanna from Sumeria; Tsuki-Yomi from Japan; and Yarikh from Ugarit. Yarikh was also the consort of the sun goddess Nikkal. Another famous couple were Shiva and Parvati from India, who have been illustrated in pictures where Shiva represented the moon and Parvati represented the sun. I had one of those pictures myself at home. It had been a gift from a friend.

The beautiful thing was, that the moon gods had represented the values, such as healing and fertility. Values that we today usually define as soft and feminine. The sun goddesses had, on the other hand, represented the values that we today define as masculine, such as power and strength. The masculine and feminine aspects of both the sun and the moon had, in other words, existed side by side, together a long time ago. When I had looked at these cultures I realised something important; there once had been a time when masculinity and femininity were defined very differently from the way they are today. This also meant that men and women and the way they regarded each other also had been understood in a complex, much deeper and more diverse way.

It had been a bit of a shock for me to realise that the definitions and truths that I had been brought up with, about femininity and masculinity, were not universal truths at all. Far from it. Beside our physical differences, the terms 'masculinity' and 'femininity' were man-made concepts. Looking at ancient history, the form and shape of these terminologies had been changed and redefined much to the detriment of the feminine aspect and women, especially throughout the Christian era. The approach to wholeness in the ancient cultures seemed to have created an attitude that focused on a deeply spiritual and phenomenological equality. They were not dichotomies as we view masculinity and femininity today.

It seemed clear to me that when we had removed the feminine aspect from men, and the masculine aspect from women, we had castrated ourselves. In doing so, we created a separation, not only inside our psyches, but also between men and women. This separation was unfortunately re-enforced by the church and, thus, eliminated the feeling and knowledge about wholeness and our innate spirituality.

As I lay there, looking up at the morning sun, I thought that maybe these cultures had been able to grasp just how deep and diverse we human beings are. Now, all these years later and somewhat wiser, I wondered if Carl Jung had studied these ancient cultures when he developed his theory about the anima and the animus, because his theory didn't seem that new to me. It certainly had a lot in common with ancient cultures and alchemy, which I knew Jung had studied for many years.

Leaving those numerous thoughts behind me, I started to drift into a state of deep relaxation of half-sleep. My breathing moved into a slow rhythm and a feeling of inner stillness descended upon me. I let the warmth of the sun penetrate my body while I listened to the peaceful sounds of the insects. At one point, I became aware of a sensation that I could only describe as a pulse. Small and quiet, but still a pulse. It was like a heartbeat, coming from deep inside the earth. As I started to pay attention, the heartbeat gave me a feeling of balance within, a balance that connected me to the earth below and the sky above. First, the pulse would expand, then contract, and then it paused. One movement led to the other and, after a while, it became one collective movement. I called it the heartbeat of the earth. Slowly, as I fell asleep, the heartbeat and I seemed to fall into a kind of harmomy.

Awakening sometime later, I felt rested and grounded. It was time to continue my walk. I got back to my feet, put on my backpack, tightened the straps and walked back towards the path. A pilgrim who passed me by as I reached the pathway gave me a quiet nod. He walked at a pace that seemed comfortable for him, and in a way that seemed so full of harmony. My eyes followed him as he disappeared around a corner. Once out of sight, I started to walk and felt remarkably well. My emotions, my body and my head felt as clear as spring water, so I straightened my back and fell happily into a comfortable pace. I was new, and I was on my way. I had no idea to where, but that was a part of the adventure.

I stopped in Lorca for lunch. Lorca is a small and extremely charming village. It was well kept and cozy. Pierre, of course, was sitting at the entrance to a bar when I arrived. He smiled warmly and waved to me. As I walked towards him, he pulled out a chair for me at his table. As I sat down, I gave him what felt like the most honest, and yet fragile, smile I ever had smiled. I wondered if he could see I had been crying, afraid he might ask me why. But he looked at me thoughtfully with those warm caring eyes. So I relaxed, having nothing to worry about.

'How are you?' he asked gently.

'Good,' I replied, 'and yourself?'

'I'm fine,' Pierre said, 'I'm just having a short break.' There was silence for a few seconds. Other pilgrims were sitting on benches outside along cobblestone walls, resting and drinking coffee.

'You need something to eat and drink,' Pierre stated with a knowing look. Without waiting for my reply, he called the waitress over. After they had exchanged a few words in Spanish, he looked over at me and asked: 'Will an omelette with salad and a soft drink suffice?'

'Yes, please! That will be fine. Thank you very much,' I replied, feeling grateful and somewhat surprised. How did he come up with that?

At the same time, a man wearing a blue T-shirt showed up. Pierre gave him a discreet nod and quickly finished his coffee. He then paid for my lunch and turned his attention to me. I couldn't help but notice that the man in the blue T-shirt stood patiently, waiting at a respectful distance.

'I have to go now,' Pierre said suddenly, reaching for his backback. 'Enjoy your lunch and take care.'

'You, too. And thank you so much for the food. It was really nice of you.'

'No problem.' He had a quiet laugh and started to walk off with his friend.

I looked after him wistfully. Due to the emotional turmoils of my day, his sensitive gesture touched me even more. All the pain and emotions I had released during the morning had made me feel vulnerable and unprotected. Pierre had been there, at the right time and in the right place, with empathy and caring. The biggest protection in the world. It made me feel humble and grateful, and it proved to me once again, how deeply we affect each other with our behaviour and actions.

As I sat, watching Pierre and his friend disappear down the road, it occurred to me that something strange seemed to happen everytime Pierre was around. Wherever he was, someone would come up and wait at a respectful distance, never uttering a world. Pierre would then give them a discreet nod. The group, or a single person, would then just look at Pierre and wait patiently for him. Pierre, on the other hand, would finish his coffee and prepare to move on. This pattern of behaviour happened every single time.

My lunch was tasty, and I enjoyed every bit of it. From time to time a fellow pilgrim I knew passed by. Most stopped for a chat and updated me on the latest happenings and their experiences, especially as the first blisters had made their arrival and caused problems for many of them. However, what I had experienced earlier that day remained untold. How did one explain those experiences anyway? I didn't even bother trying.

Sitting and relaxing after my lunch, I thought about whether I should stay in Lorca, or if I should continue on to Estella. A casual employee from work, who had walked the Camino the year previously, had said that Estella wasn't worth visiting. Intuitively, I had felt otherwise. I had a feeling that Estella was indeed worth visiting. Moving my feet I paid close attention to how my body was feeling. It was fine. I was still full of energy, so I decided to walk on.

The day was hot now, but a light breeze made it a comfortable walk. There was so much that I loved about walking along the ever-changing scenery of the Camino. Everything was so incredibly beautiful. When walking I had time to notice the small things: a particularly beautiful flower hiding in the grass, the colours, the funny shape of a cloud and the beautiful old lady who sat outside her house. I loved the feeling of the sun on my skin, the breeze that once in a while would come and cool me down and the sound of my boots striking the pathway. I passed houses that must have been more than 500 years old that seemed to emanate the essences of those who had once lived there. I loved the pilgrims who rested in their own space, having no need for other people to act in a specific way, or to involve others in their private emotional projects of needs and control. We were just ourselves on a pilgrimage. So simple, so real and these simple days brought me so much joy. They allowed me to feel 'champagne bubbles' deep inside without any particular reason.

Shortly after leaving Lorca I met a small blond woman carrying one of those huge backpacks. She trudged up the hill towards me, and it wasn't until she got closer that I recognised her. Her name was Alice. Her backpack weighed about 25 kilograms, and it was way to big for her petite frame. When Alice carried her backpack, she leant forwards like an old lady carrying heavy loads back from the fields. She always walked fast while keeping up her non-stop talking. Whenever she stopped for a break, she would still be busy making hundreds of phone calls and posting things on

Facebook.

Alice was the only person I saw use a phone or an iPad on the Camino. I had to say I enjoyed the relative absence of these distracting devices. At the albergues, a few pilgrims would check their emails from time to time, but most seemed glad to get away from such time-demanding technology. I was, that's for sure. There wasn't one minute that I missed it. I really liked Alice. I didn't mind all her incessant chatter too much. So when she called out, I stopped and waited for her as she huffed and puffed her way up the hill. As she came nearer, I called with a grin: 'How are you doing?' and pointed towards her backpack.

'Hi!' she laughed. 'Fine, fine. I'm doing fine.' She stopped to catch her breath. She dried the sweat of her face with one hand while resting the other on her left thigh. Her blond hair was neatly tied up into a ponytail underneath her hat.

'That's good,' I said, looking at her for a short while. She gave me the feeling that she was doing well, but I was still curious about her backpack. So when she finally made it to where I stood, I asked, 'What's it like with your backpack? Still shipping your things ahead to Santiago?'

'Arggg … you know. It's really heavy, but I'm getting used to it,' she said, taking another pause to catch her breath before continuing. 'It's been good today, so I don't know,' she grimaced, giving me the impression that she was a bit uncertain about the situation.

I nodded and tilted my head to one side, giving her a thoughtful smile. 'Okay,' I answered and paused for a moment. 'That's brilliant, and if you don't have any pain, it's even better.'

'Yeah …' Alice grimaced again, sighing. 'Well, we'll see. I might ship some off next time I come to a post office.'

We started to walk slowly along the small earth track that went through green fields that were filled with tall grass and wild flowers. Trees would occasionally line the pathway and provide much-appreciated shade. We had been talking for a short time when Alice said she had heard that Richard had stopped in Lorca with some of the other pilgrims. We continued on in silence until we came upon a lonely looking donkey. As we stopped to feed it with grass and wild flowers from the other side of the fence, I thought about Winnie the Pooh, which had been one of my favourite books as a child. And even though the tiger was my favourite character, I always had a special love for the donkey. Now, as an adult, whenever I saw a donkey, I still think about the stories of Winnie the Pooh. Great stories always seemed to bring me happy memories at unexpected times. They were like magic: ageless and timeless.

Alice and I climbed the fence and stayed with the donkey for a while. It was a sweet animal that even let us give him a hug. I think the donkey was the most, if not the only, social animal I met on the entire Camino. I quickly discovered that dogs and cats here weren't treated as they were in Denmark. Here I found the country dogs especially aggressive, but as long as I left them alone, they would leave me alone. If I tried to make contact, they could turn into rather aggressive animals. As Alice and I walked on, I enjoyed the pretty pathway and all the small fields we passed. The fields were filled with golden corn, and along the edge of the ditches were wild flowers in various colours, filling the air with an ever-present fragrance of sweetness and sunshine.

Insects joyfully flew between the flowers, and the cutest birds would sing from their branches in the trees. A charming old ramshackled stable, full of hay, added a decorative touch standing in the field behind a line of green bushes alongside the small road where we walked. There were no cars anywhere and the only sounds I heard came from nature, our boots and when we spoke. It was impossible not to feel content and happy.

Most of the pains in my body, from crossing the Pyrenees, had by now disappeared. The only thing that was still present, although to various degrees, was the pain in my feet. I did notice, however, that my feet had started to move more confidently on the different types of surfaces. I smiled, spread my arms out wide and took a deep breath. This was something the Camino was beginning to teach me – taking deep breaths and breathing out slowly.

Close to Estella, I started to experience a tingling sensation in my body, as if I expected something really good or exciting to happen. Since I never knew what was around the next corner, there was no logic to the feeling. But turning a corner shortly afterwards, a majestic 14th century gothic church, Iglesia del Santo Sepulchro and the shining Convento Santo Domino greeted us. We had reached Estella. These impressive old buildings stood tall and enchanting on top of a cliff, right next to each other, welcoming us to this special town. The moment I saw the church, I felt a shiver down my spine, followed by an intense flush of happiness. In a clear moment of deja vú, I saw myself in this very church, many hundreds of years ago. In my experience, I was standing in front of the altar, as a young woman, preaching the way of the goddess. This church had once been Her church. Dedicated to *Her* knowledge and *Her* wisdom.

I was stunned by the experience and somewhat taken aback. Where the idea of past lives was old news to me, I found the flashback intriguing as women were not allowed to preach in churches in those days, and she certainly would not be preaching in the name of the goddess. But, then again, who knows the real truth of history? The churches in Europe had been used for many different purposes throughout the ages. Some were secret; some were not. I didn't get much time to think about my flashback or history, as Alice started talking again. We crossed an empty parking lot and sat down in the shade of some trees, where we had a clear view of the church. There was something very special about it. A newer church had been built right next to Iglesia del Santo Sepulchro and Santo Domingo for some odd reason. It was as if they had been thrown together in a random and clumsy way, and looked terrible. I decided to pay them all a visit later.

As Alice and I sat and talked about where to find an albergue, I started to notice a beautiful soft rosy light radiating from the top of Santa Sepulchro, a bit like an an aura surrounding the building. At first I thought it was something I had in my eye, so I kept looking back to double-check. But the rosy light kept shining in its own gentle way, filling the air with a soothing kind of love. It somehow reminded me of the energy I had experienced in Roncesvalles, although this time it felt more angelic. It truly felt as if this place had once been a most beloved home of mine. And the rosy light was connected to this time.

Alice handed her guidebook over and pointed to some albergues. 'What do you think?' she asked. 'Which one should we take?'

I looked at the page she pointed to but had difficulty concentrating. I didn't really feel like going to any of them. I much rather wanted to sit in this soothing loving energy and look at the soft colours that surrounded Santo Sepulchro. Alice seemed to be distracted, too. She forgot all about the book as well and leant back relaxing on her backpack, gazing at the sights around us. Just behind where we were sitting, a river flowed into the city. We turned around and sat facing it.

'I would love to stay in a place next to this river,' I said, almost to myself.

'Yeah, me too,' Alice said, equally absent minded. 'It's really nice here.'

Again we sat in silence, just looking around, neither of us showing any interest in moving. About ten minutes or so later, I noticed a small sign close to us. The sign had the shape of a yellow arrow that said albergue. Looking at the sign, I nudged Alice with my elbow. 'Look!'

'Look at what?' Alice replied lazily, half-asleep, looking in the other direction.

'There's a sign that says albergue.'

Alice woke up from her dream world and turned her head slowly. 'There!' I said, and pointed towards the sign.

'Oh, so it is,' Alice replied with a surprised and lazy voice, 'so it is …'

THE CITY OF STARS

The albergue turned out to be only two minutes from the parking lot. When we entered Hospital de Peregrinos, we saw Don and Rodney sitting behind a couple of computers. They both looked up at the same time and smiled, their faces looking quite sunburnt. I ran into Rodney from time to time. He always seemed surprised to see me, for some odd reason. I met Scott almost every day, usually in the company of a younger and prettier girl. These companions of his usually acted with jealousy towards any other woman who dared seek his company.

Alice and I had a short chat with the two men before going upstairs. Thank God, it was only up to the first floor. At the end of the day, climbing steps was too painful and exhausting. Our dormitory was rather large and filled with bunk beds, which stood in pairs, two and two, and almost worked as double beds. Large old windows stood open and faced out towards the street, letting in fresh air and the cosy sounds of people passing beneath them. Some kind and polite Koreans had taken up most of the beds in our room. They tried to start up a conversation with me, but I constantly ruined it by asking where in Japan they were from. After a while, they stopped talking to me altogether.

Having completed my usual post walking routine, which was having a shower, changing my clothes, making my bed ready and finding a washing machine, I went outside to have a rest in the garden with Alice. I wondered what it was that the temp from work hadn't liked about this albergue or Estella, apart from the man at the front desk who was quite rude, irritable and totally incapable of providing any service at all. Alice and I had to ask him several times to obtain a coin for the washing mashine, and then for soap and then for directions on how to start it. Not that we got any help from him, but with a little bit of luck and support from Scott and some of the other pilgrims, we finally succeeded. There was nothing like great team work to make an old tired laundromat work!

Half-asleep out on the soft grass, I noticed Alice was busy with her iPad – as usual. This time, I think she was calling someone in France. Yesterday it had been Canada and then Spain. Today her call was about a special car she wanted to rent for herself and her family when she finished the Camino. I drifted off to sleep whilst Alice called different car rental companies. She woke me an hour later to tell me that the washing machine had finished, and that the next pilgrims stood anxiously waiting for it. I found I had some washing powder left over so I gave it to the people who were next in line for the troublesome laundromat. The couple looked at me in surprise.

'Thank you!' they said with a huge smile. 'Don't you want any money for it?'

'Ah, no!' I said, smiling. Of course I didn't want any money for it. But small things like that made such a huge difference to pilgrims.

There was laundry hanging everywhere on the lines in the garden. The chairs, and even the small crevices in the walls, worked as places for the pilgrims to hang their clean laundry to dry. Thanks to the hot weather, the clothes dried quickly and most pilgrims were considerate enough to remove them as soon as they were dry. This created a continuous flow of available drying space. Well, sort of! One pilgrim had placed his newly washed clothes on his head, arms and legs while sitting in the sun relaxing. Others would hang their clothes on the edges of the bunk beds, adding to the mess, but nobody really cared. It was important that our clothes were clean and dry for the next day. Many pilgrims, like myself, only carried two sets of clothes, one set for walking and one set for after. More than this would be an unnecessary weight in our backpacks. It was all about the bare essentials.

After hanging her clothes out to dry, Alice went back to her little screen. Rodney was still working on his computer, surfing Facebook, and Scott had gone upstairs to have a snooze. I packed my journal in my little green multi-purpose bag, together with a bottle of water, and went out to explore Estella. I went directly towards Iglesia del Santo Sepulchro, but ended up in the newer church that stood just in front of it. I tried another way. Again, I ended up in front of the newer church. That was odd, I thought. I stood scanning my surroundings for a while and looked for a road or pathway that would take me to my desired destination. But there was nothing to be found. A little frustrated, I walked back to the newer church, which I discovered was actually a museum. The staff here were incredibly friendly and helpful, but Iglesia del Santo Sepulchro and Convento Santo Domingo remained locked, closed and *no disponible* (not available).

'We're so sorry, but they are!' they kept saying.

I looked at them for a minute, disappointed, not able to understand why it was *no disponible*. I knew there was no point persisting with my request, so I thanked them politely before walking away. Maybe it was because of my flashback earlier on that I felt this way. But still, I needed to see it and I needed to feel it. So I was not at all pleased about the rejection. I walked out of the church-museum, paying little attention to the exhibition. Standing outside in the tiny square, I turned and looked back towards the church, wondering if I should climb the fence, the wall maybe, or the cliffs? Which would be easiest? How far should I go to get in? After some reflection, I came to the conclusion that it wasn't good behaviour, especially for a pilgrim, to break in like that. And bad behaviour from one pilgrim gave the other pilgrims a bad name. I left the place feeling disenchanted, let alone annoyed, and started to walk around Estella.

An hour or so later, I found myself on a romantic terrace belonging to the church of San Pedro. The terrace was located at the very top of some steps, hidden in a quiet corner behind a gate. A wall of stones protected the visitor from a deadly fall and the noise from all the cars on the busy road beneath. Outside the wall, old treetops hid the terrace from the rest of the town. From here, I had a beautiful view across old roof tops to none other than the gothic church and the convent.

San Pedro was my fourth church visit in Estella. As I stood on the terrace looking out, I really appreciated the beautiful atmosphere surrounding this charming town. The little streets and plazas were filled with bars, shops, restaurants, pilgrims and locals. Cars seemed miraculously able to squeeze themselves in and out of the small parking spots. Estella even managed to have room for a noisy and busy road passing in front of the church of San Pedro. Everything just seemed to meld in its own wonderous way.

Luckily, the heat of the day had mellowed into a comfortable and soft warmth. A few birds seemed to appreciate the dust found between the stones on the terrace. I felt I was in a safe corner that protected me from the rest of the world, allowing me to surrender to the softness of my inner being.

I turned away from the wall and looked towards the steps that led up to a closed wooden door – one of the many that led into San Pedro. 'That's a good spot,' I thought to myself and walked over and brushed some sand from one of the steps and sat down. It was time to write about my day. Delving into my green bag, I took out my journal and a pen, and began to write.

I began with my dream about the universal goddess. Then I wrote about my hours of crying, the pulse, meeting Pierre in Lorca, walking with Alice into Estella, my tingling sensations, the Koreans and the (closed) Gothic church and Convento. I wrote to get it all out of my system. I wanted to document my journey so I could go back and remember it in the times to come. I even wrote how the Virgin Mary, on the altarpiece in the old church of St Jean, had been placed equal to Jesus. In Roncesvalles, the mosaic windows had been filled with women, and, in Zubiri, I had seen a powerful Mary Magdalene with the Grail. Actually, Mary Magdalene and several other women had been extremely present and visible in several places on the Camino up until now, even though women were basically absent throughout the written history of these places and in the stories of the Camino. Why was that? And why had the men in Roncesvalles reacted the way they had when I mentioned women? I thought back to Mary Magdalene and the whole prostitution manipulation and how so many other women in history had been made invisible. Was there a pattern here?

Writing my dreams, thoughts and experiences down was such a great way to process the day, as it gave me time to reflect and absorb everything. Sitting there, in my little secure corner of the world, I let it all out. Sometimes, I would take a break from writing and rest my head thoughtfully in my hands. I watched the birds in the trees and looked at an insect passing by. I let my fingertips run through the soft dry, brown sand and felt peaceful as I looked up into the bright blue sky. The soothing energy of the Camino wrapped itself around me, lovingly embracing me, making me feel grounded in my experiences.

In the stillness of the afternoon, I understood that it was through walking the paths of the Camino that I had come into contact with the pulse of the earth. Inspired, I got up and walked out to the middle of the terrace. I closed my eyes and began to listen. Ever so slowly, my body began to move in a dance that was choreographed by this stream of life. As I danced, my body opened up and became the cauldron of the energy I had seen run through everything. To be in contact with this pulse was the same as being in contact with my very own inner being.

Somewhere in my dance, I couldn't help but wonder if my grandmother, in my dream, had been indicating that I should learn to live my life in coordination with this pulse? And was this what Indigenous people and ancient civilisations from around the world have experienced for centuries? That special connection to everything that was. I felt it was. As I listened, I understood that what I was experiencing was a part of my innate spirituality. A connection; a force of golden energy, *me*.

In this light I also understood, that when we suppress and abuse others, we block the connection to our own innate spirituality and everything around us. When we lose this connection, we turn to steal it from others to survive. In this way, we think we regain our lost energy, and so, the game of power and control begins. Unfortunately, it is a game that only leads us further away from our inner source of life and strength.

I felt myself letting go of times where I had allowed other people to steal my energy and took back what was mine. In doing so, I saw just how weak and unhappy those people really were, and I saw that only by taking responsibilty, could they, and I, change this game that causes so much emotional poverty in our world. As I surrendered to these sensations and understandings, my inner world and the outer world started to merge together. I became one with the pulse of the dance that slowly permeated my whole being, as deep negative feelings of anger and negativity washed out of me. The dance was like a cleansing ritual, and finally I truly understood what my grandmother had meant.

It is all about learning the dance of life.

She had meant, that I had to learn to live in harmony with the pulse of life within myself. Again, I remembered all the dreams after her death where she had danced – always so happy and joyful. 'Be happy for me,' she had said in those dreams. It had been so hard, but today I danced for her and I danced with her. I danced for the stars and the earth, and I danced for myself. I didn't need any music, for the music was in the stillness. And in the stillness, I found myself.

THE FLEUR-DE-LIS

I had packed my gear and was walking down the stairs from the San Pedro church when I thought about my grandmother and remembered, with a smile, a dream she once told me about. She had been about the age of thirty back then. In the dream, she had been shown a big box. The box had been divided into several empty rooms, equally sized. A man had pointed towards the box and told her that each room represented one of the world's religions. She had then been urged to notice just how small and limited each room in the box was, and how infinite and beautiful the world around it was.

When my grandmother told me about this vision for the first time, I had been quite struck by the wisdom of it. It had also challenged me because it approached religion in a totally different way than I had ever been taught. The dream had been my first lesson about the fact that spirituality and religion didn't have much to do with each other. Religion was like a limited box, a set of rules that dictated how to perceive the world, how to act and how to think. Spirituality, on the other hand, was an inner state of being that existed outside the box. It was subjective and individual for it could only be experienced.

During the travels in my 20s, I had learnt that we each had to seek and try to understand the mysteries we wished to know. The road would always be our own individual journey and the responsibility would also entirely be our own, as nobody else could do the work for us.

Once down on the street again, I found a small shop where I bought lasagna and some vegetables. Good fresh vegetables, except for onions, were virtually non-existent along the Camino. And those you could find tasted terrible. So when I saw the broccoli and carrots I bought them on the spot. I didn't feel like going out to eat anyway. Instead, I ended up sharing my food with a Russian pilgrim back at the albergue. After we had finished our dinner, we gave our leftovers to another pilgrim who was about to eat only a piece of dry toast. He looked grateful as he began to dig into the lasagna and vegetables.

After dinner I headed out through reception to have another look at Estella. A Mexican dentist I had met on my way across the Pyrenees asked if he could join me.

'Of course,' I said. Like a true host, he showed me around Estella like it was his own home town. He was good company, and I always enjoyed having a chat with the fellow pilgrims I met along the way. By now, I could spot a pilgrim in a flash. The pain in our bodies, the tiredness on our happy faces and the way we dressed usually made us stand out.

Just as it was getting dark, we passed a group of locals from Navarra, who were standing in a circle around a large candle-lit lantern. They stood on one of the beautiful walking streets close to my albergue and sang the most beautiful traditional songs from Navarra. I forgot all about my companion and stopped to listen. There was an enchanted feeling to these songs. Never having heard songs like this before made it even more fascinating. I wanted to take a photograph but felt it would be wrong because of the special energy that surrounded the group. Instead, the Mexican and I just stood with a little crowd of onlookers and listened intently. When the group finished their singing, about ten minutes later, my friend wanted to explore more, but I decided to return home. I had a feeling that Richard would call, and I was right! When I picked up my phone back at the albergue, I saw Richard had indeed tried to call me, twice.

From the messages he had left on my voicemail, I understood that he was staying back in Lorca together with some Dutch nurses. I immediately tried to ring back on the number shown, but it didn't work. Rodney, who had been sitting in the kitchen watching me unsuccesfully make the call, also tried to ring with the same result. The number just didn't work. And so it happened that I took out my diary and opened it up to write down Richard's number, and Rodney, like a grashopper on speed, suddenly jumped up and stared crazily at my book. I looked up at him quite bemused. He acted like a person who had just seen a ghost. His eyes were wide open, his freckled face had turned red and his index finger, violently shaking, pointed towards the book. I could even see small drops of sweat appearing on his face.

'That symbol!' His voice was shaking, full of disbelief. I stared at him open-mouthed, completely bewildered, as my eyes followed the direction of his shaking finger that pointed to a symbol on a page in my open dairy.

'Yes?' I said slowly, somewhat confused as I looked back up at him, 'That is a fleur-de-lis and ...?'

Rodney stared at me for a moment before frantically starting to walk around in circles in the kitchen. He walked in a stressful way, rubbing his hands over his head and through his sparse red hair. He even started to laugh nervously. After pacing around in circles for what felt like a couple of minutes, he came back and sat on the bench next to me. For a moment he seemed almost normal again.

'Give me the phone,' he muttered and reached for it. Once again he tried to ring Richard. While he was doing this for a couple of minutes, I couldn't help but stare at him. From freaking out about a symbol in my notebook, he now, after having no luck getting through on the number, asked some Spaniards to help me out. Confusion from my side was an understatement. The moment the Spanish couple took over the mission of trying to contact Richard, Rodney turned his attention back to me. He was obviously still upset. I could see it in his eyes.

Even his body seemed tense and on guard, ready to jump, and sweat was threatening to break out on his face again. He looked at me quite thoughtfully for a while, and then, with a calm hand, slowly pulled my dairy towards him, still looking into my eyes watchfully. Slowly he opened to the page with the fleur-de-lis, still looking at me with an intense and testing look. Once opened on the page, he purposely pointed at the symbol with his finger. 'That is a bad symbol!' he stated firmly.

I felt as if I were an actress in a movie but didn't know the script. His behaviour was so out of place. In fact, the whole scene was so absurd that it was hard not to laugh. 'Why is that a bad symbol?' I queried, trying to hide a smile.

'Why do you have that symbol?!' he said in a demanding manner. His tone now had become serious and direct.

'I don't know ... it's just there in a book that I bought by chance ... it's a mass produced book. Anyway, why is that a bad symbol?'

'Why do you have that symbol?' he demanded again. This time he sounded angry, although I did not find him threatening.

I had no idea whether this man had been taking drugs, but his behaviour was totally weird. This symbol clearly had a special meaning to him and caused him distress. And somewhere in all of this, it seemed as if he believed I knew the significance of the fleur-de-lis – and that the picture in my book had a much deeper meaning. I, on the other hand, just wanted to know what he was on about and what significance the symbol had for him, so I could help him. But no, Rodney made it very hard to make any sense of it all. Instead, he impatiently made the situation even more confusing.

'Why?' he asked again, in a demanding, but now much calmer way. 'Why do you have that symbol in your book?'

I gave him a questioning look. 'Well, it's a, um, mass-produced notebook, as I said before … and, um, I don't know why someone has put the flower in it. I mean, it's a very common symbol for God's sake!' I couldn't supress my irritation any longer.

Rodney, not satisfied with my answer, got up quickly, took a few steps and then stopped. He then started again to walk in his customary circles. As he was walking, he looked back at me, stressed, almost heartbroken. Then he stopped, just to look at the book once more before looking away again. After having walked around in numerous circles scratching his head and obviously deep in thought, he turned around and came back and sat next to me. I almost got a headache watching him.

Meanwhile, the Spanish couple had progressed to looking at the local phonebooks and even calling the neighbours, trying to locate where Richard was staying. They sat opposite Rodney and me at a big wooden table in the kitchen, seemingly totally unaware of the scene that was going on in front of them.

I looked back at Rodney. He seemed highly stressed again and I felt lost in a translation that apparently never had occured. Was there something I had missed? So I said rather impatiently: 'Rodney, this conversation is ridiculous. It's going in circles just like you! You could at least make the effort and explain to me what all of this is about!'

Rodney didn't say anything but his eyes looked as if they were about to pop out of his head. I started to think that maybe his reaction was because some people believed the fleur-de-lis symbolised the offsprings of Mary Magdalene and Jesus. Apparently, this theory had upset some Catholics, but

I decided to let it be. He seemed to be stressed enough already.

A few minutes later, Rodney calmed down and looked at me again with compassionate, almost forgiving eyes, as if he had decided that I wasn't one of these bad people who belonged to the symbol. Where I had tried to understand him and his connection to the flower, it seemed as if he had been torn between trusting me as his friend or having to see me as an enemy. It now seemed as if he had made his decision on where I belonged in this matter. He sat down on the bench next to me in a matter-of-fact way.

'I'm sorry,' he said in a friendly manner, as he looked apologetically at me, 'but I can't tell you. I'm a devoted Catholic, and for us that is a bad symbol.'

'Okay,' I sighed, and replied in a ruder way than I had meant to, 'but don't the Catholics in general have problems with a lot of things? And in this context, it is rather difficult for me to understand why a small flower can create such an absurd scene from you, Rodney!'

He gave a relieved laugh and seemed to relax. His eyes were once again back to being normal. He nodded his head and looked down towards his hands, which were resting in his lap. He smiled to himself.

'Yeah,' he said with a charming laugh, looking back up at me, 'You're right about that for sure. But I am truly sorry ... I cannot say any more, even if I wanted to.' He got up from the bench, gave my right shoulder a friendly squeeze with his right hand and, as he was leaving, said: 'Good luck with Richard. I hope you manage to get through to him.'

I never saw Rodney again, and his secrets remain a mystery to this day. The Spanish couple handed me my phone, shook their heads and apologised. None of the phone numbers worked in Lorca, which they said was not unusual in small rural villages in Spain. I thanked them for their help. The couple just shugged their shoulders and continued their conversation, as if they hadn't just spent a half an hour helping me find a number. That was the way of the Camino. It was just natural to help whenever one could. No wonder the community between the pilgrims affected everybody so deeply.

Later that same evening, as the moon was rising into the sky and merging with the descending darkness of the night, the same group of locals appeared beneath the windows of my albergue. Once again, the group gathered in a perfect circle around the lantern with its white burning candle.

Sometimes, we need the darkness to show us how beautiful the light is. At other times, we need the light to illuminate the beauty of the dark night. And then again, a small flame in a lantern, lit by someone else, is all we need to find our way.

As I listened to the songs, I felt touched by something utterly deep and spiritual as my heart and spirit soared with their ancient melodies. Standing in the window I stared up into the starry sky, reflecting about my life. I was beginning to realise that I was living a life that I couldn't identify with anymore. It was time to let in the changes for real, so I opened up and stopped fighting them. When I did this, I discovered a place in my heart that was full of sunshine. I knew then that I was ready to move ahead on new and unknown roads that lay ahead of me. I merged with the spirit of the Navarettes, appreciating the power and life that ran through their tunes. They taught me, that by sharing the connection to their roots, they helped me connect to mine. They knew who they were and where they came from, celebrating it through their songs. Had I ever really known who I was?

I looked at the people around me and thought of my travels, education, studies about women, work and all the other things I had done and learnt. It occurred to me that I actually had grown to have a pretty clear understanding of who I was and why. But the whole journey with my dreams, the related studies and now, the Camino, were bringing this insight to a whole new level.

Very early the next morning, while the other pilgrims were still asleep, the same group of Navarettes were gathering silently. They lit the white candle in the lantern and placed it carefully in the middle of their perfect circle. Once again, the magical songs of Navarra danced through the air, calling the pilgrims back from their dreamworld, preparing them for a new day on the Camino.

The locals of Navarra were known as being a difficult, proud, stubborn and even hot-blooded people. But that morning, I understood them. I understood that all they were doing was celebrating an inheritance of knowledge, magic and belonging. Something so many of us had forgotten and lost. On this morning, the circle shared their magic and tradition with the pilgrims, not knowing that a Danish woman was listening and remembering with them. That morning, something very beautiful, that had remained hidden inside of me appeared. I thanked the group quietly as they doused the flame of the candle, and walked away.

Immediately after the songs ended, the pilgrims in my room got up and started to move around. I stayed in my bed. My body was tired and I needed more rest. By the time I finally stood outside the albergue, ready to depart, the sun had made its entrance and coloured the sky in beautiful rose and purple hues. Looking at the colours, I felt an urge to return to the gothic church. The hospilario, who stood outside the albergue guiding the pilgrims on their way, looked at me with confusion as I turned right instead of left.

'No, no,' he said, and signalled for me to go the other way.

Assuming he didn't speak any English, I held up my camera indicating that I wanted to take some photos and pointed in the direction of Iglesia del Santo Sepulchro. Judged by the confused look on his face, I either didn't convince him, or he just didn't understand. He stared after me as I walked 'the wrong way'. When I returned five minutes later, he was gone. On my way out through Estella, I passed a number of pilgrims who were sitting around, scattered randomly on numerous roadside benches. One of these was Scott. He was lying down, grey-faced, and told me, in a voice full of suffering, that it had been his birthday the night before. And for Scott, that meant having a lot to drink.

'Do you need anything?' I asked, whilst laughing quietly to myself.

'No,' he grunted, 'but thanks anyway.' Scott tried not to laugh at his own predicament, as he knew this would make him feel even worse.

'Okay then ... have a nice day.' I smiled and walked on, giving the other hung-over pilgrims an energetic 'Buen Camino!' as I passed them by. I thought, in truth, there were many ways to walk this pilgrimage and enjoy the experiences it held.

As I left this pretty town, I felt it had been a huge emotional cleansing for me. I walked out feeling so much clearer about who I was and what I had left behind. However, I quickly came back to earth as the exhaustion in my body started to kick in. It needed more protein than the customary Spanish cuisine could provide, and it was starting to become an issue that made me think fondly about Emanuelle from L'Esprit in St Jean (although I hadn't been too keen on all those beans). So that morning, I found myself walking at a much slower pace. Apart from the physical tiredness, I also needed to slow down to process the other effects the Camino were starting to have on me.

'Estella' means star, and refers to the Star of the Alchemists and the eight-pointed star of Venus. It also refers to a shower of stars, followed by a vision of The Virgin Mary seen by shepherds in 1085. Thus, Estella became the City of Stars; stars that shone their light of enlightenment and transformation as people from all walks of life passed though. Some would feel it. Some might even see Her and hear whispers of secrets from forgotten times. And then again, some would just pass through, thinking it was just another town on the road to Santiago. But many hundreds of years ago, a young woman had been standing in this very City of Stars, teaching the way of the Goddess. She too, was long forgotten.

THE SCALLOP SHELL

Every morning on the Camino was a new day of freedom, joy and adventure. As much as I loved every place I had stayed so far, the happiness that hit me when I was back on the road in the morning never ceased to go unnoticed.

Leaving Estella behind, I passed the famous winery, Bodegas Irache with its *Fuente del Vino*, which had installed two taps where pilgrims could have a free sip of wine on their journey. It was an old custom and very generous of the wine growers. As I would discover this morning, times had changed. Pilgrims would not just have a sip of red wine from their scallop shells any more. Instead, they would fill up their entire water bottle with the wine. And not just one, sometimes even two. Therefore, there was only wine enough for the very few and a big disappointment for the many who passed the empty wine taps. It didn't bother me, because I didn't drink wine; however, I heard a lot of comments from many who missed out, as well as from those who filled not only one bottle, but two, with wine.

Having left the outskirts of a town, I started along a dusty road that took me through huge fields of wheat, barley and corn. I walked peacefully, at a slow pace, and took time to appreciate the beautiful blue colour of the sky. I marvelled at all the small stones that were spread across my path and the sounds my boots made as I walked along. The corn stood tall and shone like gold in the sunlight. The earth that I walked upon was dry and was of dusty brown colour.

As I walked slowly through the fields, noticing the landscape surrounding me, it dawned on me that it looked exactly as it had in my dreams from before the Camino. I stopped and shook my head. It had to be my imagination. But no, it really was the scenery from my dreams about the Camino. It was as if a curtain lifted and my actual walk on the Camino merged together with my dreams and became a living reality. I had dreamt about this pathway; I had dreamt about the corn and the colours; I had dreamt about all of it; and whatever doubts I might have felt about my experience, I now saw clearer than ever the path that I was now walking.

'Good morning,' a voice said from behind me.

I turned around and saw the dentist from Mexico. He looked healthier and happier each time I saw him. When I had met him in the Pyrenees the first time, he had not only been dehydrated and exhausted, and walking in a zig-zag kind of way. He had also seemed somewhat lost.

'Good morning,' I replied, lifting my hand to greet him. 'Feeling good today?'

'Yep, all good,' he said as he smiled. 'And you?'

'Yeah, all good!'

After our morning greeting, we walked on together in silence. A common custom amongst the pilgrims, as we walked at our own pace. My thoughts went back to the Camino, and I felt a gratitude and humility towards the new insights I was being shown. This was yet another teaching from the Camino:

If you expect a miracle, expect to meet your real self.

I could choose between fighting the changes, or surrendering to the Camino's power of transformation. It wasn't like the famous 'crossroad' situation you hear about in Oprah's shows. The dreams had come to me, seeking my attention and guiding me on my journey. I never felt I had been in the situation of having to choose left or right. It had been more about feeling that I was doing the right thing.

At this point a scallop shell caught my eyes. It was the most important sign on the Camino. The scallop shell guaranteed that you were on the correct path, and was usually engraved on stones or posts. As I looked at the shell, like I done so many times before, two questions suddenly came to mind. *Why* was the scallop shell the symbol of the Camino? And *how* had it become a symbol for this deeply cherished pilgrimage? For some reason, even though I had thought about this before, these questions really struck me this time. So I stopped. I had this odd idea that the answers would 'fall from the sky', and decided to sit down in the grass to think about it.

I made myself comfortable and waited, but I didn't have to wait for long for, shortly after, the Swedish couple came walking along the track.

'Hi there!' they said, looking fresh and fit as always.

'Hi …'

'Are you okay?' the man asked and started to walk towards me, looking concerned.

'Yeah, thank you,' I replied. 'I'm fine. I'm just reflecting about the meaning of the scallop shell. Do you know why it became the symbol of the Camino?'

The couple looked at each other, and shook their heads. 'No idea,' said the man, looking questioningly at his wife.

'Oh! I think I know!' the wife suddenly said. 'We just talked to a French woman, and she mentioned something about it.'

Her husband's blue eyes lit up. 'That's right. She was quite interesting … ehh … I can't remember how she knew all these things, though. I don't remember her name either.'

The wife looked at me and said: ' Yeah, maybe you should wait for her. She will be coming along soon. Just look for a woman wearing a green hat.'

The Swedish couple looked at each other, satisfied with the help they had provided. 'Buen Camino!' they chorused in unison as they walked off.

I looked after them as they walked away. Since I hadn't planned to move anyway, I decided to stay and wait for the woman. Whilst waiting, I tried to summon up the few things I did know about the scallop shell.

I knew that many today considered that the scallop shell symbolised the many roads to Santiago and the rays of the sun. The scallop shell was almost synonymous with the pilgrimage now and the pilgrims themselves. I also knew that it was the symbol for the Roman goddess, Venus. I tried, but failed, to think of more that I knew about the scallop shell. So I closed my eyes and relaxed.

I awoke from my doze to the sounds of someone walking on the path close to me. Small stones were being kicked or squeezed out from under the boots in time with the slow rhythmic pace of the walker. Someone was quietly humming a tune. It sounded like a woman's voice, so I turned around and saw a woman wearing a green hat.

'Good morning,' she said, when she noticed me lying in the grass.

I sat up and put my hat back on to protect my head from the heat and my eyes from the sun. 'Good morning.'

'Are you okay?' she asked, slowing down as she approached me.

'Yes, I'm fine. Thank you for asking, but I was actually waiting for you.'

'Me? Why me?' she asked, puzzled, and stopped a few feet from my backpack.

'Yes, you,' I said and laughed, knowing it sounded like a cliché. 'A Swedish couple passed me a little while ago, and they said that I should ask the French women with a green hat about the scallop shell. They said that you would pass by here soon.'

The woman laughed and took off her hat to reveal her short-cropped dark hair. 'Oui, I have a green hat,' she said, smiling, 'and oui, I know the Swedish couple. So, what do you want to know about the scallop shell?'

She spoke with that typically cute French accent. I told her what I knew about the scallop shell, but that I still didn't understand how the shell had become the symbol of the pilgrimage to Santiago de Compostela.

'Ah!' she said and nodded. 'The million dollar question. 1 better sit. The answer might take a while.'

She took off her backpack and sat down on it. 'I'm Camille, by the way. What's your name?'

'I'm Louise – from Denmark.'

'Ah, oui.'

We both took out our bottles and drank some water. Camille found an apple in her bag, and took a couple of bites whilst thinking to herself. 'Let me make this very clear to begin with; nobody really knows why or how Christianity chose the scallop shell as the symbol for the Camino, but this is what we do know.'

Camille then began a long story that went all the way back to the time of the Celts and even further back to the cultures that built the megalithic monuments in this part of Spain. The scallop shell had been a sign related to fertility and goddess worship within Celtic cultures. The Romans took over this belief when arriving here, and inserted their own goddess, Venus, and the symbol for Venus, ever since early Roman times, was the scallop shell.

I nodded, listening carefully, while taking notes, as she went on. 'And what's important,' Camille noted, 'is to understand that the original Venus came from the Middle East. Her name has changed many times throughout history, but her original name meant 'risen from the foam', so this goddess figure has always been from the ocean. The scallop shell has, in that sense, been connected to the worship of goddesses for thousands of years before Christianity. And here on the Camino you have the sun and the goddess symbol as one and the same.'

Camilla took at break from talking, and finished her apple before throwing the core into the field behind me.

'So, to answer your question, the scallop shell has, in Europe, always been connected to the goddess and fertility in one way or the other, and these cultures had, as I said before, existed for thousands of years before Christianity. So the obvious answer is that the Church simply 'adopted' the scallop shell and replaced the goddess with Saint James – just like they have replaced so many pagan sites with their churches, and legends with male saints. The church either created the legend of Saint James to erase all traces of ancient cultures and female worship, or …' Camille said, while getting up and putting her backpack on, 'Saint James had been initiated into the pagan goddess cultures and their belief systems. And to cover it all up, the church kept Saint James as a Christian together with the scallop shell and did a hell of a good marketing job. Done and dusted.'

One could just about hear the sound of my jaw hitting the ground. I looked at her for a few seconds, shocked by her last comment. That couldn't be, I thought. That was too far out. But … could it? My mind was racing, trying to find anything that could argue against what Camille had just told me. Then, an answer slowly dawned on me. I looked at her, not knowing if I was brave enough to say it out loud, but doing so anyway.

'The church could do it,' I said slowly in a low voice, whilst still thinking,'… they could do it because the church has controlled knowledge and the documentation of history for more than a thousand years. In fact, it would be the easiest thing in the world for them.'

Camille seemed to be just as perplexed about the issue as I was. Still looking at her, I collected my thoughts and continued: 'For more than a thousand years, it was the church that had the means of writing and printing books, and thus they have been the ones creating the official version of "the truth".'

Camille nodded thoughtfully before she tightened the straps of her backpack and adjusted her hat. She looked up to the sky before answering. 'All I know for sure is this; if you follow the scallop shell, you will always walk in the light of the goddess. Think about that.' She smiled and walked off without uttering another word.

I sighed heavily. The Camino sure had its way. No wonder I had been dreaming about all these goddesses. I knew from Marija Gimbutas that these ancient matriarchial cultures had believed in partnership instead of man versus woman. They had valued creativity and inner enlightenment, instead of suppression and wars. And just like many indigenous cultures around the world, they had believed it was essential to live in balance with the earth and the spiritual world.

Thinking about what Camille had just told me, gave the scallop shell a quite different, and much deeper, meaning. For many pre-Christian religions, the sun had represented the source of life, even the soul. The scallop shell was also associated with fertility. Camille had told me that anthopologists had discovered that Celtic women wore scallop shells to enhance their fertility. But knowing these ancient cultures often used symbols as an analogy to illustrate a deeper meaning, I agreed with Camille, that 'fertility' was actually about the act of being 'impregnated by the divine powers of life', as in becoming enlightened rather than being pregnant as such. The pregnancy idea was, in my opinion, yet another example of the limited ways (especially) male scholars interpreted anything that had to do with women.

Suddenly, I remembered with extreme clarity, my dreams about Hathor and the milk that ran in abundance along the Camino. I also remembered the dream I had in Puenta La Reina about the starry goddess.

...Infinite amounts of milk coloured liquid, with sparkles of gold, run out from the stars that shape her breasts. From where I stand, I can see that the liquid runs down into the earth, and through the earth into my body. It brings life to my cells and life to the earth that I stand on. It also brings life to the stars in the sky and the planets that move in our universe.

The last resistance in me shattered and I was left awestruck. Tears ran down my cheeks and I surrendered. My dreams all along had been telling me about the origins of the Camino, and what was about to happen to me. The connection between my dreams, my experiences and the history of the Camino had stepped out from their hiding places and were beginning to reveal to me their secrets.

The scallop shell was indeed a powerful symbol. It was the very essence of this special walk towards transformation.

For those with eyes to see, and ears to hear.

THE ROADS MEET AGAIN

Shortly before reaching Villamayor de Monjardin, I stopped to look at a mysterious water house of some description. It was located on the right side of the dirt road where I was walking, and looked like an old water pool from India. It consisted of three walls, a roof and several steps inside, leading down into a pool filled with water. There was something about the building that reminded me of old Khmer architecture. However, as I stood looking at it, someone suddenly grabbed hold of my backpack and gave me a shove. Startled, I turned around feeling rather annoyed. It was Richard, standing there with a huge grin on his face.

'G'day!' he said in his Australian fashion. 'How are you going?'

My temporary moment of irritation vanished and, after a chat, we walked on together until we reached Villamayor de Monjardin where we stopped for lunch. Richard had his usual meal consisting of a piece of pastry and a cortado. It was beyond belief how this man managed to stay so slim and energetic with his diet. I asked how he, as a doctor and sportsman, could get away with eating like that. Richard smiled in his own charming way and shrugged his shoulders.

'But seriously, how do you have enough energy to walk the Camino? I can barely make it with the lack of protein I'm eating each day.'

I found I was hungry most of the time, and the Spanish 'white-sugar-air-bread', that I impolitely called it, made it worse. I often dreamt of a big steak with lots of fresh tasty vegetables. My breakfast would usually be something like toasted white bread with jam and butter. Lunch would be tortilla or a *bocadillo* (a white bread roll filled with cheese and chorizo).

Dinner was the only meal where I felt really satisfied, because they always served protein, like fish or meat, with a small amount of vegetables. Basically there wasn't much else to choose from, unless I went into the more expensive restaurants that I couldn't afford. So I had to make do with what I could get.

Later that same afternoon at Villamajor de Monjardin, I shared my protein worries with Richard and the two nurses from Holland. In the middle of it all John, a now good friend from South Africa, arrived. He looked like someone in great pain, and was obviously suffering. We all stared at him as he hobbled towards our table. Something was terribly wrong.

He was wearing thin flip-flops made of plastic, and his walking boots were tied to the back of his backpack. Richard looked at him, and his feet, with a serious look. I think we all did. John was a man in his forties. His short red hair went in all directions. He had green eyes and freckles covered his face. When he smiled, huge dimples would appear on his tanned face. He was somewhat overweight, and had hoped the Camino would help him get rid of some kilos, though sometimes I got the feeling that it was the work related stress he was really trying to get rid of.

John threw his large exhausted body down onto one of the plastic chairs and threw his backpack haphazardly onto the ground. He was profusely sweating, and kicked off his plastic thongs. My heart almost stopped!

'Oh my God, John!'

I couldn't believe what I was seeing. They looked like feet from a horror movie. My own feet hurt just looking at them.

John shrugged his shoulders, as if to say 'oh well'. Neither Richard, the Dutch nurses, nor I, had ever seen blisters this huge, or this bad. One blister took up the entire space of the sole of his right foot. On his left foot, three blisters shared the sole. They were all red, puffy and infected. It looked so painful I started to nervously chew on one of my fingernails.

Nobody said anything, not even John. We all just sat there, staring at his feet. Even the two Dutch nurses were speechless.

John looked at us, shrugged his shoulders again, threw up his arms and gave a resigned laugh.

'At least I have performed my part in supporting the pharmacists along the Camino,' he said with an ironic laugh, 'and trust me, I know, there are lots of them! I have spent many hundreds of euros on ointments, adhesive plasters and heaps of other kinds of bandages and creams in an effort to treat these blisters.'

I had first met John at the albergue in Zubiri. He had been the pilgrim I had seen sitting at the table with all his creams and bandages. That was six days ago, so he must have been suffering for quite some time. John's new boots, which he had been wearing since the start of his Camino, were now replaced by his flip-flops. And even though the flip-flops hadn't irritated his existing blisters and created pain, like the boots had, they had instead created new blisters on different areas of his feet.

While the nurses were busy commenting on his predicament and the state of his feet, Richard ran his hand across his brow, looking as if he was thinking 'holy shit'. I just stared at John, speechless. Never ever in my life had I seen blisters like those. It was a mystery how he was able to walk without screaming from the pain.

In the outside world, the talk about feet doesn't usually belong to dinner-table conversation. Here on the Camino, feet were the most common topic to be discussed, and at any time. Each day, when I had a break and took off my boots and socks, I would examine every single inch of my feet, looking out for the tell-tale signs of skin irritation and redness. So far, my only concern had been the nail on my right big toe. It had turned yellow. No soreness though, but I was watching it. Ditte and Søren, who in the beginning had managed to walk more than thirty kilometres daily, were also suffering from painful foot blisters. They had begun the Camino walking in their new boots. Søren had bought his boots the day before he had started. Ditte's were at least a few month older and had been worn a couple of times. Maybe this was the reason Ditte's blisters weren't quite as bad as Søren's.

Richard had been really helpful in treating other pilgrims' blisters, but there wasn't much he could do for John's. His feet were beyond repair. It was obvious, and nobody wanted to say it, but John would have to go home. No one could continue with feet like that. It simply wasn't possible. Noticing that John was comfortable with his feet elevated on a chair, I asked if he wanted anything from the bar.

'Yeah, a coke with ice would be nice,' he gratefully replied.

I walked into the bar and asked for a coke and a separate glass full of ice. I also brought him a glass of water, because it was so hot outside. When I arrived back at the table, John and Richard were deep in a heated discussion about soccer while the Dutch nurses had walked over to the albergue and were going through some things in their backpacks. I sat down on my chair and looked at the two men. Soccer? I thought, maybe somebody should be talking to John about going home. But we didn't. Only a pilgrim could understand why.

Villamayor de Monjardin was a nice little village – quiet and very peaceful. It was a good place to just sit and do nothing. It was also time for me to decide on whether I would walk further that day. I tipped my chair back and glanced towards the albergue to see if it was open yet. It wasn't. A sign on the door said it didn't open before 4pm. As I was thinking about whether I should wait or not, the tiredness of my body made the decision for me. I didn't feel like walking more that day. The temperature was soaring and there was not a single cloud in the sky. All I felt like doing was chilling out and meditating. It was my sixth straight day walking, so a long afternoon rest was well deserved.

When preparing for the Camino, I had expected the roads to be pretty flat, because the photos I had seen of the Camino had shown relatively flat terrain. I quickly learnt that this was not the case. The pathways were constantly going up and down hills, and even mountains. My feet reacted strongly to the different types of pathways I walked on, and in time I was able to predict how much foot pain I would have at the end of the day. Stones, concrete and bitumen were the worst; grass and earth the best.

Still tipped back, resting in my chair, my eyes caught sight of Susie. She came walking along the road, past the church, in her customary bright-coloured T-shirt. This day, it was green. Richard and John were still engaged in what seemed an interesting conversation about sport. I waved to Susie, by way of a greeting, hoping she would come over and join us.

Susie was a 50-year-old American divorcee with the most incredibly vibrant personality. Beside being a passionate teacher of Spanish, she was in truth a free-spirited women who 'ran with the wolves'. Independent, spiritual, compassionate and possessing a distinctive laugh.

Susie called back with her familiar 'cu-cu-ru-cuuu' greeting and came up to us with a huge smile. Richard, who immediatly recognised the greeting, turned around and called out, 'Hi Susie!'

'Come and join us,' we said.

She came over and slumped down in the chair next to us. 'Phew, it's so hot today! My feet are killing me,' she said whilst loosening her boots.

Despite sitting in the shade, we all felt as if we were melting. Our table was full of empty water glasses, soft drink containers, coffee cups and newly filled water bottles. All you could do in this heat was to drink lots of liquids.

After Susie had finished eating a cake, John began to mumble something about moving on. Richard, Susie and I stopped whatever we were doing, and looked at him.

'That doesn't sound like a good idea,' Susie said, being honest.

Richard agreed and said: 'Why don't you stop here for today? You can't walk any more on those feet.'

'Because,' John said, looking quite determined, 'I have walked so little, considering the total amount of time I have available to walk the Camino. So I have to move on today, otherwise I'll never make it.'

'Okay,' said Susie,' then why don't you just take a taxi to the town you had planned to reach today?'

The shock that went through the group was almost audible. A taxi!? But wasn't that a cardinal sin? Even cheating?

'Yes!' Susie said, as she looked seriously at us. 'I know it is frowned upon by pilgrims, but I have a certain distance I need to make every day together with sore feet due my new boots. So I take a taxi. In this way, I will make it to the end and see more of the sights along the way.'

Richard was the first to respond with a thoughtful nod. I sat and bit my lip, as I often do when reflecting on a conundrum. John sat thoughtfully and looked at her. I suppose we all could understand the point of her argument. After having recovered from our initial shock, Richard said he thought that would be a good idea in John's case.

John looked at me, as if seeking approval. 'Maybe you should consider it,' I said, pointing towards his swollen, red feet. 'Look at them. You can't even wear your flip-flops any more. Give your feet a rest and see how they feel tomorrow.'

John looked down at his feet. It wasn't easy for anyone to leave the Camino prematurely, or even to admit that one's feet were so bad they couldn't continue. We all understood that.

'Yeah,' he said quietly, with an expression of resignation, 'I suppose it's an acceptable solution under the circumstances.' Susie then walked into the bar and asked them to call John a cab.

It was a much relieved John who limped into the taxi fifteen minutes later. As the taxi drove off, he looked back at us through the window with a mixture of sadness and disappointment. We all sat and watched in silence as he was driven away.

It was still early afternoon and the albergue didn't open for another two hours. Susie looked at her watch and asked if Richard and I were going on.

'No, I'm staying,' I said, having accepted the fact that I also needed to listen to the limitations of my body. 'My body is tired, so I need to rest.'

Richard sat and thought for while before saying he also needed a break.

'Alrighty then,' Susie said, ' I suppose I had better go and have that lady call me another taxi, so I can make it to the next town.'

I didn't know why, but Susie's statement made us all laugh, and suddenly it seemed more acceptable for a pilgrim to take a taxi. For us, anyway.

As Susie walked into the bar, Richard and I picked up our backpacks and walked over to the albergue. We sat down on the steps in the shade and waited for it to open. I took off my boots and socks, and placed them in the sun to dry. It was always such a great sensation of freedom for my feet to feel the cool air, after having been locked up in what had become tight-fitting boots.

Just before the albergue opened, a group of Italian teenagers and their minder, a Catholic priest, arrived. Even though the teenagers were tired, the group was still full of youthful laughter and energy. One girl told us that they had been walking the Camino for a week and only had two days remaining before they were to return home.

Usually, teenagers travelling in groups are extremely loud and noisy, but this group was very different. Rarely had I seen a group of young people filled with so much harmony. I was impressed to see that nobody had taken on the role of a leader and used it to exclude anyone else. Instead, they all seemed to show a genuine care for each other, not having the need to create power games. It was also fun to watch how the boys and girls regularly teased each other. The priest, who didn't look particularly old, just smiled peacefully, letting the teenagers have fun and be themselves. A loving, warm aura surrounded him and it wasn't hard to see why the teenagers respected him so much. Around the same time, the two Dutch nurses showed up again. They never stopped talking and teasing Richard.

As I listened closely, I realised the nurses were two very interesting women. Behind their loud voices and laughter, there was a depth of compassion I found attractive. It was also great fun listening to how they stirred Richard to bring forth a charming smile from an otherwise serious-looking face. When the door to the albergue finally opened, pilgrims rushed in. They hurriedly took off their walking boots, leaving them on a wooden rack just inside the front door, and then raced up the stairs to get the best bunk beds. Richard and I ended up sharing a room with the large group of Italian teenagers.

Their priest had moved into another room with Renate, our German friend, and the Dutch nurses. I had to admit that I was impressed by the teenagers' self-discipline. First they made their beds, then they washed their clothes and, finally, they had a shower. I chose to wait to do my own laundry and delayed having my shower until they had all finished. They seemed to work so well together that I didn't want to disturb them. In the small passageway upstairs, next to where some of the girls stood and washed their clothes, a boy from their group sat by himself. He was busy trying to repair his hiking stick with the aid of a small, but rather sharp, pocket knife. A short time later, I heard him scream and rushed out to see what had happened.

Predictably, the boy had cut himself, and it didn't look good. Blood was running from his thumb, over his hand and onto his shirt. The poor boy sat helpless and ashen faced and looked as if he was about to faint. Because the cut looked so bad, I didn't know how to help him. So I rushed down the stairs and across the square to the bar where Richard and the two nurses sat talking.

'It looks really bad,' I said, explaining the situation. 'Can anyone help him?'

Before Richard had a chance to answer, the nurses asked if the boy had previously used the knife to cut meat.

'I don't know,' I said, wondering what difference that would make. He was bleeding, wasn't that enough?

Richard, who probably thought I was being a little melodramatic and could have helped the boy myself, stood up and walked into the albergue with me following close behind.

The boy was now sitting on his bed, still ashen faced and in a cold sweat. He had wrapped his thumb in toilet paper which was soaked in blood. I walked over to the boy and pointed towards Richard and said in my best Spanish: 'Doctore'.

The boy looked at Richard hopefully, and revealed his injury. Richard gently removed the toilet paper and washed the wound with water. After having inspected the cut, he asked me to fetch his brown toilet bag. He needed scissors and some Fixomull (a special kind of adhesive tape they use mainly in hospitals). The cut was quite deep, which made me comment that it probably needed to be stitched. A comment that immediately made the boy look even more apprehensive.

Richard, however, shook his head and smiled. 'No worries,' he said to the boy in a calming voice, 'you won't need any stiches. It's fine.'

Richard cleaned the cut with antiseptic liquid and smeared on some antibacterial cream. Then he pulled the edges of the cut together, and held them there by placing some Fixomull across the wound. He gave the boy two Panadols and told him to keep the hand elevated to prevent swelling. Richard then disappeared back down to the bar to finish his coffee and I went to my bed to rest. Several of the teenagers also went off to have a rest but only after they had checked that their friend was okay.

As the sun began to set, I decided to walk down the hill to a small old church to write in my journal. The rolling hills around the church were covered with crops, which shone like gold in the late-afternoon sun (no wonder I had been dreaming about gold-coloured hay). As always, I wanted to visit and view the churches I passed. But a service was being held so I had to wait. I went for a walk around the building.

In one line, in front of the church, stood three small, old-weathered stone blocks. On the first was carved a knights templar cross; another had a cross carved on it with a circle around the cross; and on the third block was a carved six-petalled flower. I wondered why the knights templar cross was depicted here. This church was not constructed like a knights templar church. And, looking at the second block with the gnostic cross, I remembered having read that this had once represented the goddess. The circle had symbolised that She gathered all the worlds into one: creating the perfect balance between earth and sky. The significance of the six-petalled flower on the third block, was however, a mystery to me, although I had seen it on many occasions, especially on this walk.

I sat down on an old stone bench beside the church wall and enjoyed the spectacular view. Waves of golden fields covered the rolling hills as far as my eye could see, and the sky was a crystal blue. Butterflies flew busily around, some landing on the sand in front of me and a tired dog was snoozing in the shade of a nearby bush. I lazily started to draw patterns in the light brown sand with my toes. A soft breeze came from behind the church and I thought that if paradise really existed, it would be right here. The tranquillity that surrounded this place was filled with the soft sounds of insects and birds, and the sounds were like healing waters to my ears.

Suddenly, as if struck by lightning, the worst-sounding chimes ever imaginable, rang out from the church. The noise from the bells hammered through the air, producing pain not only in my ears but throughout my entire head. Frantically, I tried to press my fingers as far as possible into my ears, but the the noise was too loud. By the time the bells finally stopped, my head was screaming in pain and my ears felt numb. The service was over.

With the painful noise still ringing in my ears, I quickly rushed to the now-open door and greeted the leaving parishioners with a *buenas noches*. I knew from experience that small churches were usually locked immediately after each service so I had to be quick. As soon as the last person in the group walked out through the door, I entered.

'Excuse me,' I said in a quiet voice, addressing the priest, 'is it okay if I have a quick look around your church?'

The priest smiled and nodded, whilst continuing a conversation with his two assistants. He seemed nice, and I would have loved for him to tell me about the history of the place. But as he was busy, I turned my full attention to the inside of the church. To my great disappointment the church looked rather empty. It seemed as if most of the original artwork, like the paintings and sculptures, had been removed some time in the past. The three carved stone blocks outside had indicated that there might have been a different story to this place. So I had hoped to find some more evidence inside; of Mary Magdalene, or other female figures, who might have been associated with pre-Christian spiritual worship.

As I walked around the sand-coloured church, I couldn't help wonder why the Catholic church had done so little to spread their important statement regarding Mary Magdalene, since her official title now was Apostola Apostolorum. The fact that the Catholic church admitted that Mary Magdalene had never actually been a prostitute, was of profound significance. As this change of narrative occured more than thirty years ago, the information should have been household knowledge by now. Yet, it seemed to be just another important issue hushed up by the Catholic church. I wondered what had made them admit to this to begin with? After more than a thousand years of suppressing the truth, it was as if they changed their story and didn't bother to inform anybody else about it. It appeared they were either reluctant to make the admission or were insincere. It definitely seemed as if the church was scared of Mary Magdalene. But why?

It was odd to me that women to this very day could submit themselves to an institution that so obviously, and aggressively, persecuted and degraded them. But more so, how could men accept and support such an institution when they saw what it did to their mothers, sisters and wives?

'Miss!' I turned around and saw a small woman, standing by the church door, looking at me. She held a set of ancient-looking keys in her left hand. 'We close now!' she said in broken English.

'Of course, I'm sorry,' I said, and began to walk towards the door. 'Thank you very much for letting me visit your church...hmm... do you know anything about its history?'

The woman ignored me and started to switch off the lights, making it clear that she wasn't interested in holding any further conversation. Too bad, I thought.

On the way out, I looked again at the three stone blocks – stones that possibly indicated an interesting story had been hidden in this place. If only the interior had been left intact, I sadly reflected.

It would have been so easy to just walk the Camino with my eyes closed and not see all the jewels of history that were there right in front of me. As I began to look, missing pieces of history started to become apparent, like missing pieces in a jigsaw puzzle. The only problem was, that there seemed to be a huge hole in the middle of that puzzle. And to me, the whole was connected to women and our innate spirituality.

When I returned to the albergue, I found Richard sitting outside by himself reading his guidebook. Earlier I had discovered that he was twenty two years older than me, something that had surprised me quite a bit, since he didn't look over fifty. However, it had been a relief to know about our age difference. Twenty two years meant that I didn't have to worry about any romantic or sexual misunderstandings. Instead, I could relax, enjoy his company and just be myself.

THE SECRETS OF THE VIRGIN MARY

When I awoke the following morning in Villamayor de Monjardin, I once again felt my need for space and silence. So I told Richard that we could only walk together if we stopped talking. I made it clear that I needed to walk in silence. I had to be brutally honest with him. The constant talking was just too much for me. My days at home were filled with constant talking and the never-ending noise of the city; I couldn't take it any more.

Richard looked at me with his deep brown eyes, and nodded in agreement. 'Okay, I can do that,' he said and smiled. I looked at him, not sure whether to believe him or not, but it seemed like he meant it. We agreed that we would only talk when we came to a town, or stopped to rest and, of course, at the end of the day when we had finished walking. Having agreed to this, we started off.

Apart from our good friend, Renate, Richard and I were the last pilgrims to leave the albergue that morning. Not that we were lazy or really late, because the sun had only just begun to rise. That was just the way it had turned out. The small group of Italian teenagers had left whilst it was still pitch black outside, about 4 or 5am. This kind of early movement usually woke up the rest of the pilgrims and, within an hour or so, everybody at our tiny albergue was awake. Some pilgrims liked to sleep in, although this wasn't the case in Villamayor.

I had begun to discover that leaving early meant a lot to me, since I walked best during the cooler hours of the early morning. The heat during the afternoon had a tendency to make me feel physically uncomfortable. Other pilgrims preferred to start walking later in the morning, after 'rush hour', as it allowed them to have more peace and quiet on the Camino. My friend, Ida, was one of those. So again, the time of departure was up to individual taste that worked best for each pilgrim. Truly, there was only one way to walk the Camino, and that was your way!

As the day progressed, Richard started to wonder why I always had to stop and visit every church we came to. He finally asked: 'Why do you visit all these churches? Are you religious or something?'

I could hear he was being careful about how he phrased his question.

'No.' I paused, wondering how he would respond to my answer. 'But have you ever noticed all the pagan, alchemistic and sometimes even Egyptian symbols that exist in the churches – especially in the Catholic churches?'

Richard looked at me, quite surprised, but remained calm and asked me to show him. And so I did. We walked into the first large church we came to. There I pointed out every single pre-Christian symbol I could find and explained what kind of tradition of knowledge they belonged to. By the time I had finished, Richard was speechless.

Silently, we walked outside and sat together on a bench, which was shaded under a large overhanging tree. Sitting there, obviously deep in thought, Richard looked at me as he tried to assimilate what I had just shown him.

'You know,' he said, 'I have been brought up in a very strict Christian environment, so I have been to dozens of churches, and I have never noticed these symbols. But you are right. How could I not have seen them?'

At first I did not comment, then I said: 'You haven't noticed them because we are brought up to be blind, seeing only what we are told to see.'

Richard then began to tell me about his disciplined, and painful upbringing in the church. He had left the church as a teenager, only to return later in life when he married. I could feel his pain and see how the memory of these experiences still hurt, but didn't say anything. I just sat and listenened.

'It wasn't just what the church did to me,' Richard said. 'It was also how it affected several of my school friends, girlfriends and most importantly my marriage. I lost all faith in organised religion. In later life, however, I felt deeply touched and inspired by the Dalai Lama and his Buddhist teachings about compassion and doing good for others.'

He looked at me with warmth in his eyes and continued: 'Here is a man who truly walks his talk. I believe that the deep truth of every religion is epitomised by the Dalai Lama himself.'

I nodded. I had also been inspired and touched by the teachings of the Dalai Lama, his compassionate personality and outlook on life.

Looking at the church, Richard continued: 'You know, during the time I grew up, and into my adult years, it has been very difficult for me to understand, and to see, the enormous wealth of the Catholic church, and the fact they hoard all their wealth, art, library and the knowledge they possess. Jesus was not like that. He threw the greedy money lenders out of the temple. He even declared how difficult it would be for a rich man to enter the Kingdom of Heaven!'

I nodded thoughtfully as he continued.

'There's also another thing I never liked about the church,' he said, 'and that is the way they looked at women. Either they are prostitutes or virgins, weak or aloof. The concept is really sick, now I think about it. It felt so odd as a child, looking at these absent and unreal women, thinking that this was the way they were supposed to be. It was so wrong in a sense and, yet, I was taught that this was the truth. So obviously, I thought it was me who had a problem, not the church.'

'What do you mean?' I asked curiously, rarely having heard a man oppose the church's view on women.

Richard thought for a second before he answered. 'Well, I can easily explain all of this from the church's point of view. That was the way I was brought up. But as a human being, in my heart, I found it difficult to understand. Why did Jesus' mother have to be a virgin, for example? Why couldn't He be concieved in the love between his mother and father? For me, the love between a man and his wife is one of the most beautiful and special things that we have. Why couldn't Jesus just be born into that loving relationship?'

Even though I didn't say it out loud, I agreed with Richard's point of view. One of the things that had always bothered me was the issue that Joseph never seemed to be a good enough father and had been removed from the scriptures. To me, Joseph seemed to be the beginning of 'the absent father' syndrome. An absent father and an aloof mother. Hadn't we all heard that story before? But the fact was, that the Virgin Mary figure had helped create a view of women and womenhood that we still believed in today.

'Maybe that's where the whole issue about women, motherhood and femininity comes from,' I said.

'What do you mean?' Richard asked.

'Well, a woman is still only considered a 'real woman' if she has children and, of course, is married,' I said. 'We are being brainwashed to believe that womanhood and femininity are based on motherhood alone. If a woman says: "My career gives my life meaning and I don't want to have children", she will be considered a cold, abnormal and monstrous person. If she says she just doesn't feel the call to become a mother, we think there is something mentally or physically wrong with her. If a man says that, we respect his honesty, responsiblity and maturity.

'Now, where do you think these attitudes originate from? And isn't it tragic that a woman's social worth, acceptance and self-esteem is entirely dependent on her bearing children and belonging to a man?'

At first Richard looked rather surprised, and then, after having thought about it, said: 'Yeah, I see what you mean. I have definitely been brought up to see women in that way.'

'Exactly!' I said. 'And those women who choose not to step into that stereotypical role are considered selfish and egocentric. However, with a world as overpopulated as it is, and orphanages around the world full of unwanted children, selfishness and being egocentric is definitely not the issue! Women have been depicted as having only two roles in society, thanks to the church; the Mary Magdalene (the sexualising of women) and the Virgin Madonna (the purity of motherhood).

'And the thing is, Richard,' I went on, 'the more I learn about what has been done to women throughout history, especially women with power and those who dared to step out of these stereotypes, the more obscure the issue has become. It's scary to see how maliciously it has been done.'

I paused for a moment to think, before explaining myself. 'The problem is, that up until very recently, most of our historical research has been undertaken only by males who have grown up in a culture with a negative and condescending attitude towards women and our innate spirituality. It doesn't take an Einstein to figure out how they will interpret their findings. For many centuries, female statues that were found around Europe were considered only the pornography of their time. The idea that a women could have been something divine was not even considered, thinking the female body could only be something sexual.

'Another good example relates to the coffins of both Queen Elizabeth I and Queen Christina of Sweden. Their coffins were opened in the 1960s, because they – the male researchers – thought there had to be something physically wrong with these two extraordinary women, simply because they didn't believe in getting married and having children. The two queens turned out to be perfectly normal, of course. But my point is, that history is so *entrenched, analysed* and *written* through these attitudes and understandings towards women, which is why Mary Magdalene and the origin of the Virgin Mary is so important!'

Richard looked at me, stunned. 'Er, why?' he asked.

I continued along my train of thought: 'You know, up until 431 AD, the Virgin Mary did not even exist in Christianity. Up until that time, the church had tried to eradicate goddess worship thoughout Europe, especially the widely popular Diana. Their attempts were not successful. So at the council of Ephesus – in 431 AD – it was decided to sanction the cult of Virgin Mary, which in reality was the cult of Diana, as well as the images of the mother and child.

'Diana was also connected to virginity and fertility, something quite similar to the virtues bestowed on the Virgin Mary. Diana originated from Artemis, who again originated from Cybele. And Cybele came from an area we now know as Turkey. She wore a crown shaped as a tower, or a citywall with towers, and she was seated on a throne of lions. Cybele was a mighty 'God' in her days.'

'Okay…' Richard said and whistled softly, 'But how does this relate to the church today?'

'Well, instead of resisting the goddess belief, the church gave in and included a women – but in a way that was totally controlled and shaped by them. The thing is that many goddesses had been worshipped in and around Europe, through so many cultures and for many thousands of years before Christianity.'

The topic was massive but extremely important, and since Richard showed interest in the subject, I continued to explain more. I told him that the very origins of the Virgin Mary and Mary Magdalene could be traced back to Cybele, the Mother of Gods, and the Semetic goddess, Asherah, The Mother of Heavens. The semitic mythology of Asherah and Elkunirsa was a mythology guarding the secret teachings of Spirit & Matter. Even the themes 'born of a Virgin and resurrected from the dead' were found in the mythical stories of Adonis, Mithras and even Osiris. So it was easy to see how the movement and immigration of cultures throughout history had blended and effected each other.

I also mentioned the council of Ephesus in 431 AC again because it was here it was decided that the Virgin Mary was to be considered only the mother of Christ, nothing more! Not a goddess, not the Creater of Life and certainly not a person in her own right. Everything spiritual, powerful and independent was stripped away from women by that council, even the spiritual understanding of fertility was removed.

Fertility, which represented the union between spirit and matter.

'Every season had a spiritual, mythological, practical and psychological purpose that embraced our connection to Life,' I finished.

'Wow! That is really interesting!' Richard said. 'And it certainly explains several things about the Virgin Mary.'

'I know…' I paused for a moment to sip some water, and looked at him. He clearly had an expansive knowledge about the Bible, which made it a lot easier for me to explain these matters. But most important of all, Richard wasn't caught up in the fear and hate that existed in many men towards women. This made it easier for him to listen and reflect on what I was saying. I put the lid back on my water bottle and continued.

'Consider all the violent attitudes and actions the Catholic church has perpetrated on women. These were carried out to ensure that both men and women never came to know about a different way of living, or about equality or the importance of our innate spirituality. The church made sure that we never came to associate the femininine principle with anything positive. If you wish to keep people ignorant, and under your control, you make sure that they don't learn to read, write, think or live independently. In this way, the church made women into slaves for men's needs, ergo, the mother to bear him children (and carry on his bloodline) or the whore to satisfy his sexual needs.'

I stopped and looked at Richard. Neither of us spoke for while. We just sat and watched a flock of small birds as they flew around a small well in front of us. I took out a juicy nectarine and began to eat, while Richard drank the rest of his soft drink. After thinking for a while, he said: 'What you have just told me is very interesting. It puts everything into a clearer perspective as to why the church has always had something against women. It is as if the church actually feared women; hence persecuted them. I think

I understand the reason better now!'

I nodded and said: 'And that's what I really look for when I visit all these churches – the traces of ancient wisdom and knowledge that the church has tried to erase or disguise.'

Richard agreed. He looked at me, still deep in thought. 'Tell me some more about what you are looking for,' he said. 'For example, what do you mean by disguise?'

'Well, let's look at Easter, one of the most important Christian festivals. The name Easter originates from the Norse goddess Éostre. She was the symbol of spring, the birth of new life. Éostre took the shape of a rabbit, hence the Easter bunny. I mean, even the egg symbolises the coming of new Life - and when you have grown up in Scandinavia, as I have, spring sure feels like life is returning after the long dark death of winter.

'It's a little bit the same with Christmas. When you look into the tradition of Christmas, which is the time of the winter solstice, you will also find many parallels with pre-Christian cultures which include a variety of goddesses of destiny and prophesy.'

Richard looked down at his boots, pondering. 'So, in other words,' he said slowly, 'the church took what they needed from these ancient cultures and assimilated this into their Christian practices. And what they could't assimilate, they called heretical and got rid of.'

'Yes, well, they tried to,' I answered. 'Many of these so-called heretical groups and their belief systems went underground and became secret societies, like the Alchemists and Freemasons. But what also happened, as Christianity began to violate the old ways of life, was that these cultures began to hide their spiritual beliefs and knowledge, even within Christian churches. They hid them in the interior design, such as in art and paintings and even in the architecture of the churches – simply as a way to ensure their knowledge survived. Actually, most of Christian mythology comes from pagan legends – like the virgin birth, for example.'

'Hmm, so the point you're making,' Richard clarified, 'is that these societies lived secretly alongside and inside the church? That sounds very Dan Brownish to me.'

'Yes, that is exactly what I am saying… and it is very Dan Brownish. It's all about having the key to reveal the hidden messages, and the key is knowledge and eyes to see it with.'

'Indeed,' Richard replied seriously, 'knowledge is therefore power.'

'You are very right on that one,' I said. 'Knowledge is power, whether you are giving it, hiding it or manipulating it.'

'But what about Magdalene?' Richard asked, 'You sound as if there is more to her besides the lies and manipulations of the church that changed her into a prostitute.'

I looked up at the sun, wondering if it was time for us to move on. The sun by now was high in the sky, and it was getting quite hot. It was time to stop talking and start walking. We had a long walk ahead of us, and time was passing us by.

'I'm sorry,' I said, 'but I think we need to start walking now.'

Richard shrugged his shoulders. 'Okay, but you will tell me later, right?'

I promised. We began to walk on whilst I thought about our conversation. It became clear to me how men throughout the centuries had been conditioned to fear women. In this process, they had also learnt to fear their own innate spirituality; a fear they projected onto women. When men had given into the church's concepts of women, they had not only lost the connection to their spirituality, they had also lost the connection to their own deeper emotions, sensitivity, diversity and inner knowing together with their ability to experience companionship, friendship and the freedom of equality with women.

In what I saw as human amputation, a raging war between the sexes had been created. A war we were still fighting, and a war that had created human beings deeply out of balance. It was, indeed, time for us to follow the scallop shell and take a different path. It was time to bring Her home, resolve the issues and pick up the parts of ourselves we had lost. To me, it seemed the only way to heal.

I realised, that just like the alchemists, I had to understand and find that place within myself, where dark and light, female and male, aggression and softness integrated into one. For as a wise person once said to me:

Just as the darkness is the shadow of the light, so is the light the shadow of the dark.

It was time to move on and explore what was beyond all of this separation. The question was: who was I when I wasn't any of these dichotomies? And who would I become when I rose above them and became 'one' within myself?

As I walked along, in the beautiful sunshine of the Camino, the answer came easily. It was about finding the golden middle way – a place of awareness, diversity and wholeness, where nothing inside of me had to be suppressed into separation and shadows. And, for some reason, I suspected this was the aim of the female guides in my dreams and the exact reason why I was led to walk the Camino.

THE POWER OF MARY MAGDALENE

Prior to leaving Villamayor de Monjardin, I had managed to convince Richard to walk all the way to Viana with me – a distance of about 30km, which, for me, seemed a very long way. By the time we arrived in Torres Del Rio, shortly before 2pm, the heat was unbearable. It was 40 degrees and not even the shadow of a cloud was to be seen, nor was there any breeze that could cool us down. The sun's rays were beating down on us, and even though I knew we ought to stop and have a siesta, we continued on. I felt that if I stopped, I would never get going again. Richard, however, seemed more or less unaffected by the heat and didn't need a rest.

We continued through the small towns only briefly stopping to see the churches. However, we did make a longer pit stop on the other side of Torres Del Rio to stock up on cold drinks and snacks – something that later turned out to be a very good idea. The pathway from Torres Del Rio to Viana passed through an area of rough cliffs that looked like something out of the Wild West. If an Indian or a cowboy had appeared, I wouldn't have even batted an eyelid.

The cliffs and dry earth reflected the intense heat of the sun. The air was so hot and dry that it felt like my skin was on fire. Sweat poured down my face and into my eyes, with the salt making them sting. My feet were paining, and my boots felt like they were three sizes too small. Even those parts of my rucksack that touched my body were soaked with sweat. It was, by now, the hottest time of the day, and the air was shimmering from the heat. We seemed to be the only people out walking. I pulled my hat down further over my head and spread my blue scarf across my neck and arms, protecting the most exposed parts of my body from being scorched by the sun.

Walking westward towards Santiago de Compostela meant that the morning sun was always shining on our backs. So the bright red sunburn on our necks and the backs of our arms and legs were as normal as blisters and painful feet. Richard appeared more accustomed to the heat and seemed to have a greater reserve of strength and energy, which enabled him to take many different short cuts amongst the sharp rocks and steep slopes. I, on the other hand, felt like I had to continually force my body to keep walking, despite a body temperature that was far from pleasant.

As I struggled to deal with the intense heat and burning sun, an unusual feeling suddenly came over me. I started to feel 'high' and full of energy. I felt for a moment that I could now walk on for hours. However, that feeling quickly departed and I was soon only able to focus on where I was walking. My head became 'light' and my body heavy. I sat down on a rock and slowly took my water bottle from my backpack, for a drink, and tried to dry the sweat from my face and neck.

Richard turned around, walked back and sat down next to me. 'This reminds me of the bloody Australian outback,' he mumbled, whilst wiping the sweat from his brow.

'Yeah, I could imagine that,' I mentioned in passing.

Richard took out his small travel guide and studied the relevant map. 'It can't be that far,' he said in a weary voice as he tried to locate Viana.

I sat and looked over his shoulder as he pointed out our position. 'We should be close now,' he said, and tapped on the map in an Indiana Jones kind of way. 'We are somewhere around here, and Viana is there, so we must be close.'

'Okay.' I was too exhausted to say more.

We got up and started walking again. Unsure of how far we had to go, it was a pleasant surprise to see Viana from the top of the very next hill. However, there was still a long way to go. Standing on the top of the hill, I started to feel better. Maybe it was the gentle cooling breeze, but I felt as if my head had cleared and my breathing had become somewhat easier.

Standing there, and collecting ourselves to tackle the last kilometres, I caught sight of a strange object in the distance. It was shaped like a person, lurching from side to side, carrying something that looked like an 'ET phone home' aerial. I pointed out the distant figure to Richard, feeling puzzled and even a little concerned. We started to walk, faster than we normally would have done, aiming to catch up with whomsoever it was. As we came closer, we realised it was a woman. Thankfully, she was walking very slowly, so it didn't take us long to reach her.

When we were about a hundred metres away, I started calling out, trying to attract her attention.

'Hello! Excuse me, ma'am!' I called out.

No response.

'HELLO!! CAN YOU HEAR ME?' I called out again, this time shouting.

Still no response.

The woman didn't seem to notice us until we were right alongside her. The 'ET' aerial turned out to be a broken umbrella, something she had tried to put on top of her head to create some shade but it hadn't helped much.

'Are you okay?' I asked, touching her arm gently.

The woman gave a garbled response. She seemed quite confused and I couldn't understand what she was saying, although I could tell from her accent she was an American.

'Could you please stop for a moment?', I asked, looking closely at her. I needed to make sure that she was actually aware of us.

The woman stopped. 'Have you got something to drink?' I asked her.

Still unable to understand what she was saying, I gave her my water bottle. 'Here, drink this. It might make you feel better.'

Without speaking, she accepted the bottle and drank slowly. After drinking half the contents she handed it back to me, but I told her to drink it all. I knew that Richard had more water in his rucksack if needed.

After she had emptied the bottle, we offered her a piece of fruit, which she also gratefully accepted and immediately began to eat. After a short while, she finally started to talk more coherently. She was even able to focus on us.

'What's your name?' I asked.

'Ruth,' she answered weakly. She sounded and looked absolutely exhausted, and her clothes were quite dishevelled.

At least she knew her name, I thought. That was a good sign.

'How are you?' I asked, rather concerned.

'I feel better now,' she said slowly, 'thank you.'

Richard and I looked at each other, convinced she had been dehydrated and suffering from the intense heat.

Ruth then set off again, talking to herself, without taking any further notice of us. At least what she said was now coherent and understandable, although her behaviour still seemed rather weird. To be on the safe side we decided to follow close behind her. Her state of mind seemed to be improving, and when she stopped at a well, where she drank some more water which she also poured over her head, she seemed nearly back to normal.

Afraid Ruth might have a relapse, Richard and I also stopped at the well under the pretence of some small talk. After about 10 minutes and feeling reassured, we said goodbye and walked on. The pain in my feet was, by now, excruciating and the pressure from my boots was sheer torture, but there was only one thing to do, and that was to keep walking and reach our albergue.

Just as we arrived in Viana, we came across the group of Italian teenagers we'd met earlier and who were standing waving to us. They were all hanging out in a small shaded square, enjoying their afternoon around a charming fountain.

'Hi!' they all called out in unison, and walked towards us with big grins on their faces.

The boy who had cut his finger the day before went straight up to Richard to show him his bandaged thumb. 'It's good,' he said, smiling gratefully.

'That is good,' Richard answered and patted the boy on his shoulder.

However, the girls started giggling, as they told me how they had teased the boys during their walk that day. This, of course, amused the boys. So they told me their side of the story, and everybody ended up laughing.

After a while, I began to wonder where their minder was. Looking around, I found him standing in the background, smiling peacefully, just like in Villamayour de Monjardin. Later I commented to Richard that the priest seemed to be good leader, as I had hardly ever seen such a harmonious and happy group.

The girls were sorry to inform us that their albergue was already full, as they would have liked us to stay with them. One of the older boys told us that he knew of another albergue further up the road.

'There!' he said, pointing towards a small paved road, 'you go there.'

Richard checked the information in his guidebook to make sure we took the shortest route possible. The albergue the boy had mentioned was the Albergue of Andrés Munos. Since it was fairly close, we decided we would stay there, and said goodbye to our newfound friends, who were returning home to Italy the following day. That was the last time we saw the teenagers.

The cobbled streets, which were terribly painful to walk on, led us upward to the Andrés Munos. A walk that felt much longer than it actually was, but it turned out to be a good choice. It was a large old monastery, situated beautifully in the older part of Viana. It was everything I needed at that moment: cool, airy, spacious and quiet. When we entered the big, open entrance hallway, I felt I could have collapsed on the floor.

A friendly man stamped our passes and informed us we would find our bunk beds upstairs on the first floor. Having struggled up the stairway, we arrived in a long hallway filled with huge windows, all facing south. On the northern side, doors let into several dormitories containing rows of bunk beds. Toilets and bathrooms were located at the very end. Passing the different dormitory rooms, we noticed many pilgrims were already asleep or just resting on their beds.

From our end of the hallway, we had an incredible view over the ruins of an old church, which exuded a warm charm of its own. To my excitement, some of the original frescos on the church walls were still intact. One of them especially caught my attention. But before I could go exploring, I first needed to find my bed, have a nice long cold shower and then get some rest.

Richard, as usual, fell asleep straight away and so did the rest of the new pilgrims who had arrived after us. Even the dehydrated 'ET' woman showed up in our dormitory. She looked a lot better that when we had last seen her, but she still looked like she had survived a day from hell. She, too, went straight to bed and immediately fell into a deep sleep, snoring loudly.

Despite the sound of her snoring, our albergue was relatively quiet and there was an air of tranquility that seemed to affect everybody. I tried to lie down for half an hour, but was unable to relax. My feet were still hurting and my legs restless. So I went downstairs, washed my clothes, and then walked out to buy water, fruit, almonds and energy bars for the next day.

Later, as I was walking out from a small supermarket I ran into my South African friend, John, who was sitting outside a nearby bar. He invited me for a beer, and soon I found myself in the company of a half drunk John and two pilgrims from Germany whom I hadn't met before. They were both very interested in the Knights Templar. John managed to drink several large beers before I even had finished my soft drink. When I commented on his drinking ability, John laughed in his typical fashion.

'That's the way I survive the pain these days,' he slurred.

I just nodded in sympathy. I suspected that John was pretty fond of his beer at any time, but his statement made me realise how much pain he was suffering. The two Germans, Carl and Rolf, were pleasant company, so we all agreed to meet up for dinner later on, together with Richard.

The minute I walked into the grounds of the church ruins, I immediately fell in love with its energy. I walked directly up to study a large damaged fresco that depicted a tall woman, with her arm wrapped around a magnificent tower, almost as tall as her. Next to her was a huge egg, with a symbol inside. It was similar to the ones I had seen in old astrological drawings. Even though the top of the egg was damaged, it seemed likely there could have been another symbol above the visible one.

I took several close-up photos so I could examine them more upon my return to Denmark and made some notes in my book. I knew the tower was a significant symbol, and I knew it was found in both alchemy and fairytales as well as seen in many places across Europe, such as the Glastonbury Tor and at Rennes-le-Chateau.

In my studies of alchemy, I had noticed that powerful women and towers were most often depicted together. This was important to me, because the symbol of the tower had to do with spiritual transformation and our inner spiritual power. Still bearing in mind my recent conversation with Richard about Cybele, I began to wonder if all the towers I had seen in churches, as well as in books on alchemy, were actually related to her spiritual tradition.

After all, the shape of her crown had been a tower, or a city wall mounted with towers. The symbol of the tower wasn't seen anywhere else! What made this even more significant was that the Hebrew name Magda meant *High Tower*, as in someone who is elevated above all others. Magdalene was considered an abbreviation of Magda. I had never given this information much thought, but now, it suddenly became important because Cybele wore a crown of towers, and she was indeed elevated high above Earthly life. Pope John Paul II had stressed that Mary Magdalene was *Apostle to the Apostles*. The belief system of Christianity was based on their faith in the resurrection of Jesus and this crucial information had been entrusted first to a woman, Mary Magdalene. Biblically nobody has explained why it was given to her and not Peter nor any of the other male disciples. Three women had been present at the time of His death, and one specific woman was the first to receive the Good News of Christ's resurrection. The term 'Apostle' means the bearer of good news and Magdalene had been chosen by Jesus to be that person! Yet again, I failed to understand why the Gospel of Mary Magdalene was still non-canonical? The Apolistic letter *Mulieris Dignitatem* had also mentioned, although very briefly, that Mary Magdalene, in her role as *Apostola Apostolorum*, was a teacher. But the letter never described what kind of teacher. Was this one of the many secrets the Camino was hiding?

A feeling of clarity descended upon me as I began to see several important links to a much greater picture – or should I call it 'the missing pieces of the hole' in our history? It seemed many people in the past had gone to great lengths to ensure that the true nature of our spirituality was not lost. Maybe they had experienced a glimpse of the future and seen that one day, we would once again be free to *see* and *hear*.

Needing time to process this new insight, I walked to a secluded corner of the ruins where I sat down to meditate. Tiredness was finally catching up with me, and it was time to process the experiences of my day. After having meditated for a while, I took out my notebook and began to write.

Every day I came to love this simple and meaningful life more and more. I literally felt how much the energy of the Camino nourished me, and taught me so much about myself, and the world I lived in. I had only one set of clothes to walk in and I didn't have to think about food or dinner because I was always eating out. I didn't wear any makeup and I loved my short curly haircut that needed no special care. Fashion, hair, weight, and all the other so called important things of life, became deeply irrelevant and uninteresting to me.

I wrote about all the women I had seen along the Camino and the visible traces of lost spiritual traditions; wisdoms, which slowly had ceased to exist. I wrote about the symbols and all the anonymous women who decorated the walls, altars and panels in the churches and museums. They had been depicted as scholars, leaders, writers and persons of authority. The more I saw, the more I started to understand, that the hole in our history wasn't an actual 'hole', it was just cleverly hidden from view. I wondered again and again; who were the people who had gone to such an extent to document our sacred past? But I also wrote in my diary about Richard and how good it was for me to meet an emotionally mature man like him. I often felt like pushing him away or just walking away, but he accepted me for who I was. He didn't need me to be anything or anybody in particular; he not only gave me the freedom to be who I was; he also met me there. That was one of the most beautiful presents anyone had ever given me.

As the evening drew near, clouds moved over Viana and with them came a refreshing breeze. Small cooling drops of water fell randomly without turning into actual rain. Quietly, I sat in the ruins and found harmony with the world in which I live.

'Louise!' Richard called out to me from where he was standing looking out a window of the albergue. He had just woken up. John was sitting on the window sill next to him, looking at his feet. I packed my things and walked inside, and met Scott halfway up the stairs. He was sitting, tending to his blisters with two young women next to him. They looked deeply in love. I shook my head. It surely couldn't be that romantic to watch people 'repair' their infected and blistered feet. However, I did understand why they liked Scott so much. He was a very gentle and warm person.

Scott smiled when he saw me and asked how my day had been.

'Ah, you know – good, but somewhat painful,' I replied. 'It was a hard walk today.'

Scott nodded knowingly, implying that his day hadn't been much different. I walked up the rest of the stairs to the first floor, where Richard and John were still talking together and looking out through the big open window. John's feet were wrapped in many layers of sticky tape and bandages. Only God knew how he managed to keep his flip-flops on. His two bulbous feet looked utterly tragic.

When Richard and John saw me, they slowly walked over and we made our way outside to meet Carl and Rolf. Together we wandered around the older district of Viana and were fortunate to find a small, local restaurant that was already open. It had about 10 tables and you could see the owners cooking in the kitchen. A sign outside told us that they served *Menu Del Dia*, the special discounted menu for pilgrims. A television was, as usual, present in the restaurant, broadcasting the latest news and sports results in Spanish.

The conversations during our dinner were lively and in good spirit. John seemed more at peace with himself, so I wasn't at all surprised when he announced he was going home. I supposed that decision was inevitable and had been coming for some time. His blisters by now were so extreme that he just wasn't able to continue.

After dinner, we decided to continue our leisurely stroll through Viana, as dark clouds began to appear in the sky, accompanied by the rumble of thunder. Ending up in the square in front of the big Iglesia de Santa María, Richard began to tell John and the two Germans the reasons behind my many church visits. Rolf and Carl were so excited that they asked me to show them the things I looked for. John would have liked to join us, but chose to wait on a bench outside. He needed some peace and quiet time to say his farewell to the Camino.

Iglesia de Santa María was one of the better churches when it came to its adornments. It seemed, to my delight, that most of the original art pieces and interior designs had remained. They even looked well maintained. As I walked around and pointed out the many different pagan artifacts and symbols, Carl and Rolf looked more and more amazed.

'Oh my goodness!' Carl exclaimed, looking around the church in disbelief, 'It's really true. You are right, but how on earth...'

Rolf was no different. He kept repeating; '*Mein Got...Mein Got*!' whilst running his hand through his hair.

Not knowing what to say, they kept staring at the paintings, symbols and figures I had pointed out to them. Some things needed more explanation than others, but most were pretty straightforward.

Richard, recognising their reactions, told them how he had felt the first time these things had been explained to him. While Richard talked with Carl and Rolf, I let my eyes roam slowly over the ceiling. I was so impressed with the building skills and inspirational architecture that existed in those days.

'Louise! Why are these symbols here?' asked Rolf.

'Sorry? What symbols?' I asked a little absent-mindedly.

'These!'

The German pointed towards the Knights Templar crosses that were visible all around the church.

'Why are they here?' he asked. 'The Templars were burnt by the Catholics. So why would they be here, in a Catholic church?'

Carl and Rolf discussed amongst themselves whether or not they had noticed this before, but came to the conclusion that, since they never went to church, they wouldn't know.

The truth was that I had no idea as to why these crosses were there, but I had noticed that they were apparent in nearly every larger church I had visited along the Camino. It seemed the bigger the church, the more crosses. The Templar crosses were even hung on pillars that surrounded the seating area. The largest cross would always, without exception, hang opposite Mary Magdalene or another female figure. This was something I found rather mysterious. What did the Templars have to do with Mary Magdalene?

Meanwhile, Rolf, Carl and Richard began discussing the history of the Knights Templar. Since I knew very little about them, I kept quiet and started to pay attention to what they were saying. Suddenly, all the lights in the church went out. We hurried to put a coin into the meter box, but nothing happened. We all looked at each other, rather confused, before putting another coin into the box.

Still no lights.

Again we looked at each other, quite puzzled. I was getting ready to put a third coin into the box when the costodian, who had been standing down by the entrance and clearly wanted to go home, signalled for us to leave.

'Church close!' he called. He sounded rather annoyed and did nothing to hide his irritation.

'I think it's time to go,' Richard said ,with a humorous look on his face.

'I think you're right,' the Germans and I said in unison.

We all marched politely out the door. As we passed, we wished him a good evening. One could almost hear him think 'stupid tourists'.

Back out in the square, we walked over to John and joined him on the bench. It had started to rain a little, but it was still pleasant enough just to sit and watch life go by. The square was filled with a lively energy from all the people there. There were Spaniards dressed up in stylish clothes, pilgrims recognisable in their usual attire and sunburnt faces, and children who were laughing and chasing doves. Everybody was enjoying the beauty of the early evening and each other's company.

Richard and the Germans were debating as to why the church had closed so early, and John sat quietly and said nothing, something that was highly unusual for him. For a change, I didn't think about anything in particular. I just cherished another evening on the Camino, loving every minute of it.

By the time we made it back to our albergue, it was dark, and heavy rain had started to fall, accompanied by loud peals of thunder. The thunder rolled over the sky making the walls of our monastery shake. Thunderclaps came in such a way that it wasn't hard to imagine how the idea of Thor and his wagon had originated. I stood in the large hallway window and looked out while the rain washed away the dust and emotional remains of the day. I deeply and sincerely hoped that these immaculate frescos would be well taken care of in the years to come.

It was still too early to go to sleep so Richard asked if he could have a look the weird red rashes that had appeared on the back of my legs. He must have been thinking about the rashes for a while, because he had decided on a rather unusual way to treat them. Looking down, I could see how red they had become, but thankfully, they didn't bother me. Firstly, Richard soaked some kitchen paper in ice-cold water and then he placed it over the rashes, followed by layers of clear plastic wrap to keep the kitchen paper in place. It didn't seem to help much, but it was nice of him to try to help.

THE LITTLE QUIRKY THINGS

Bedtime for pilgrims was 9.30pm, and 10pm meant lights out. Many pilgrims began to prepare their bags and clothes for the next day when they returned from dinner. That was a ritual that tended to suit many of us – a peaceful way to end each day and a transition to the next. The road to Viana seemed to have been one of the harder walks because most of the pilgrims in my dormitory went to bed shortly after nine, absolutely worn out.

I had to admit that I was also more tired than usual this evening. My feet were still burning and sore, and I feared they would be the same the following day. Richard, on the other hand, had slept for a couple of extra hours, having his siesta, which meant his body was more rested. Looking at him and how well he felt, I understood how important the midday siesta was. It really did make a big difference to how one's body recovered and how it felt the following morning. Organised rest times were indeed important on the Camino.

Back in Denmark, when I had prepared for the Camino, I had decided from the very beginning that I wanted to enjoy my walk. That meant not rushing ahead, and not measuring my day's achievement by the distance walked. Now, during the day, when I stopped for a break, I would always take off my socks and boots so that they, and my feet, could dry in the sun – a theory Richard didn't quite agree with. However, I followed Ida's advice, feeling that it not only helped prevent blisters, it also lessened the swelling in my feet.

Richard, who had observed me performing this ritual for well over a week, continued to be openly critical. But it only lasted until, one day, his feet felt really hot and sweaty. He then gave up and took off his boots and socks. By the time we were ready to walk on, his feet weren't only dry, the swelling in his feet had also gone down.

'I have to admit,' Richard said, while enjoying his now dry socks and aired boots, 'that it feels so much better. I thought it would be so much harder getting the boots back on again, but it has actually helped!'

He laughed and mumbled something about the fact that Ida's idea wasn't so bad after all.

Men! I thought, and rolled my eyes. What a cost it must be for them to accept other people's advice. Especially for Richard, who rarely thought other people's opinions were right. Which, of course, I felt I had to comment on. Richard grinned and said, half-kidding and half-confessing: 'I am a doctor and spend all day telling people what to do, not the other way around!'

'Sure,' I said, laughing.

I think Richard was able to hear what he had just said, because he immediately began telling me one of his many stories from the operating theatres. As usual, I kept waiting for the juicy after-work store-room details, but was again disappointed. It turned out they didn't use those any more; they had moved to the doctors' private sleeping quarters. And then, of course, there were all his funny stories from university and medical school. I had to admit that I found amusement in this doctor's wicked sense of humour.

UNEXPECTED CHANGES

Despite the difficulties of the previous day, the walk after Viana was surprisingly comfortable. My feet felt a lot better than I expected, and the day was blessed with a fresh breeze and many small clouds which provided some shade. Richard and I talked constantly during our rest breaks but, after that, I disappeared into my own world and thought about the history of the Camino and all the things I was seeing. I was often so engrossed in my own thoughts that, at times, I forgot Richard was even with me. But then, at other times, I couldn't help but think how lucky his girlfriend must be. I had to admit, that even considering our age difference, warm feelings towards him had started to grow. We had a good chemistry together, and I felt extremely comfortable with him.

After having left Viana in the morning, we arrived at Pantano de La Grajera about lunchtime. La Grajera was a lake, about 13km before Navarette, and it was surrounded by lovely grassy areas. Here we decided to take a well-deserved rest under some large trees. Richard rolled out his sleeping bag next to a small creek that ran down into the lake. A welcome cooling breeze was blowing through the trees, making it a perfect spot to have our first long break for the day.

Everybody around us was eating ice-creams from the parlour close by. So, in a moment of inspiration, Richard walked over and bought some for us, too. While we sat and enjoyed our strawberry-flavoured ice-creams, a squirrel raced around in the branches above our heads. Richard had never seen a squirrel before, and found it both funny and cute, especially its big bushy tail. As I was finishing my ice-cream, the Dutch nurses showed up and joined us under the trees. One of them also went to buy an ice-cream, whilst the other took off her boots and socks. Shortly after, Ditte, Søren, Scott and Pierre appeared. Everybody stopping for a chat and a rest, well, except for Pierre. He could stay for a only little while since he was meeting someone nearby.

It was becoming really apparent now how the demands of the Camino had begun to take their toll. People looked tired, had pains throughout their bodies, and disabling blisters were a common problem. Most couldn't keep up the distances they had planned to walk each day. Any expectations above 25km a day rarely lasted. Basically everyone, even the most ambitious pilgrims, had by now realised that they had to walk more slowly, have more breaks and keep to shorter distances. If they didn't realise this by themselves, circumstances would force them to. Injuries had also become more frequent, as experienced by my Danish friends Ditte and Søren. They had started with an aim to walk 30km every day. Due to their blisters and pains, they actually had not travelled any further than we had.

Richard and I agreed, that a distance between 22–24km a day was the best, taking into account that on some days we were able to walk further; on others, less. This made it difficult to pre-plan and control the distances for each day. If the body told you to stop, it was best to stop. Ignoring the signals from our bodies brought only hardships.

By the time we reached Navarette, we both felt really tired. I was, for a change, also quite mentally tired, and Richard's back had been hurting for most of the day. From time to time, Richard had stayed at hotels along the Camino. He thought that it was cosy staying at the albergues, but every now and again, he needed a hotel room with a bath and a good bed to ease his sore back. Reaching Navarette, he said it was, once again, time for him to check into a hotel. So we stopped in a small square opposite a bridge that led us into the main part of town. Richard took out his beloved guidebook and decided on a small hotel, close to an albergue that I had chosen to stay at.

'It's only a few streets from here,' he said, and showed me the map.

'Okay. I'll drop you off on my way then,' I said.

All I could think about was to reach my albergue, have a shower and go to bed.

Richard's hotel turned out to be quite quaint and very pretty. I especially liked the long emerald green curtains. Too tired to really care, I simply walked into the foyer and dropped down onto the nearest soft chair. I could hear Richard say 'okay, okay' in Spanish a couple of times to the receptionist before turning to me.

'The only room they have available is one containing two single beds. You can have the other one if you want to?'

I looked at him rather suspiciously, but when the lady mentioned that the room had a bath, I said 'okay'. It was the mention of the bath that did it! Richard just nodded and paid.

A bath! With hot water! What a luxury! I walked straight up to the room, filled the bath and soaked for an hour or so. I didn't even unpack my backpack or wash my clothes – the things I would usually do immediately after walking. I didn't care. I just wanted a long hot bath to soothe my aching body. Richard only wanted to lie down to rest his back.

Later, as I drifted off into dreamworld, on my large, soft comfortable bed, it occurred to me that this was the first time, in a long while, I didn't have to sleep in a hot enclosed room with lots of other sweaty, noisy pilgrims. The stillness of the hotel room was surprisingly pleasant and the cooling fresh air from the air-conditioning was such a relief. I actually managed, for the first time on the Camino, to have a good rest before dinner.

When I awoke, across from me on the other bed, Richard was looking thoughtfully up at the ceiling. I realised then that I had become quite attracted to this man. I had initially thought that he had been happy, but I had recently discovered that he was in the midst of making some very large changes in his life. He had heard about the Camino from a radio interview with an Australian High Court judge who had previously walked the pilgrimage.

The judge had talked about his need to get away from the elevated role of being a high court judge, into a place where he felt free to relate to others in a more down-to-earth way. This had touched something in Richard. Many changes had been knocking on his door, but he had ignored them persistently for many years. After hearing the interview, Richard knew he had to travel to Spain and walk the Camino. He felt this might be the way of dealing with the changes he needed to make, but it took two years before it became possible for him to go.

As I lay there, watching him on the other side of the room, I thought it would be cozy for us to lay arm in arm. So I asked if that would be all right.

Richard just shrugged and said okay, if that was what I wanted. And so, against my better judgement, one thing led to the other and I discovered Richard felt the same about me. Cuddled up next to him, I didn't expect anything and I didn't want anything, either. We had both had our share of affairs and made wrong decisions when it came to relationships. The fact was, that any romance between us was unrealistic from the very beginning. Not only due to our age difference, but also because he lived in Australia and I in Denmark. We couldn't have lived further apart.

The next morning, by the time we left the hotel, the sun was starting to appear on the horizon. I walked out onto the street feeling things had a changed a little bit, although I wasn't sure how. Richard seemed to be his usual calm self. On the small street outside our hotel, old paper cups, bottles and rubbish were strewn everywhere. They were leftovers from the town celebration the night before. But not all had made it home, as there were still people sitting around on the pavement, drunk and half-asleep. We had passed the partying crowds on our way out to dinner the night before, but hadn't heard any noise from them during the night.

At the end of our street, was a large town square. Turning the corner, I noticed the albergue where I had intended to stay the previous night. There were still colourful flags and party leftovers scattered over the square, whilst an old church made a home for the many storks and their nests. A familiar sign on the footpath, told us that the Camino continued up the hill behind the church.

'Good morning!!' two well known and energetic voices called out from behind us.

Ditte and Søren were two typical Danish students, both in their twenties. They had backpacked across most of the world, worked as volunteers in Africa, whilst of course studying at university. They were a guarantee for a good laugh and also a long talk. Their words always fell with impeccable enthusiasm, many at the same time.

'Well, good morning!' I answered with a big grin.

'Did you hear all the noise from that street party last night?' Ditte asked in a rather annoyed fashion.

The always super-energetic and positive Søren, was surprisingly in a foul mood this morning. Ditte just stood and looked rather tired with big bags under her eyes and, before I had a chance to ask, Søren exploded angrily.

'You are not going to believe this!! It is outrageous! Unacceptable!'

He was so upset, that his short hair stood up all over his head and his large blue eyes bulged abnormally. I looked at him, wondering what possibly could have upset him that much.

In very demonstrative language, Søren told us about the night they had spent at their albergue. It turned out that a group of young pilgrims had been partying all night in the kitchen, keeping everybody awake. Several of the larger male pilgrims had walked out and asked them to go somewhere else. The young people had ignored them, and continued partying. There hadn't been anybody in a position of authority at the albergue, so the sleeping pilgrims weren't able to get any help and ended up with very little sleep.

'When we came out into the kitchen this morning,' Søren said angrily, 'it was all dirty – a real mess and gross – I have never experienced anything so inconsiderate!'

Many other details of the night followed, while Ditte stood there silently nodding along the way.

'And now!' Søren cried out in a tired voice, 'we have to walk all these kilometres today. We'll never make it.'

My first reaction was to feel rather relieved that I hadn't slept there. My second reaction was to feel somewhat upset about what had happened. Unruly behaviour at an albergue was simply not acceptable. It made me think that some people were too immature and irresponsible to walk as pilgrims. Otherwise, they would have gone somewhere else to party.

After Søren had finished telling about the night, Ditte began to entertain us with stories about Søren's amazing blisters. In my head, I recalled John's blisters, thinking that nothing could top those. Søren, however, didn't find the blisters so much of a problem. His real concern was that he wasn't able to come up with the ultimate theory on how to treat them.

'Let me show you,' Søren said and walked over to a bench, where he sat down and took off his boots and socks.

As we looked at his multiple blisters, it was clear he needed to see a doctor, or at least rest for a day or two, to allow them to settle down.

'Tell them about your morning ritual,' Ditte said, whilst quietly giggling to herself.

He went on to tell us that he spent 30 minutes every morning, wrapping every toe, one at a time, in a soft bandage, followed by tape over the top. Richard stood listening to Søren's explanations with a humorous look on his face, but remained impressively silent. Søren was determined to prove his theories correct, and there was no room for a doctor's advice. Ditte and I looked at each other, laughing to ourselves.

After spending some time watching Søren dress his blisters, which seriously looked like hard work, we decided to walk on. Passing the church to reach the green hills, I once again turned my attention towards the many storks and their nests, perched high on the church towers. If a stork ever settled in Denmark, you would hear about it on the news. That was how scarce they had become at home. Here, in the north of Spain, they were everywhere! I had taken at least a hundred pictures of them, and I made sure to add more to the collection that morning. Richard just seemed to have fun with the way I pronounced the word 'stork' in English. I told him to 'zip it'. If he was able to understand how I pronounced it in English, there was no reason to make fun of me.

MORE TRACES

Navarette turned out to be a very interesting place when it came to finding more traces of ancient goddess worship and the Knights Templar. We had again met up with Carl and Rolf, the two Germans. After Viana they had been so inspired by the things I had shown them in the cathedral, that they had since visited several churches. Now, after drinking our coffees and catching up, they asked what I had found in the churches here in Navarette. When I finished sharing most of my discoveries, they immediately raced off to have a look for themselves. And what I had found, was indeed interesting. I had seen several objects that included an Egyptian obelisk, beautiful towers depicted together with female saints who, by the way, usually held a feathered pen signalling they were writers. I had also seen a significant painting that linked the Knights Templar to the worship of female dieties. I was now beginning to have several questions about the Knights Templar. They consistently appeared in contexts I hadn't heard of before, contexts that, without exception, had to do with The Virgin Mary, Mary Magdalene and other unnamed madonnas. Why would artists repeatedly describe scenes, that were so direct in their symbolism and meaning – and which, were so different to the history most of us were taught? Once again, I returned to what appeared to have become the recurring theme of the Camino; it was for those with ears to hear and eyes to see…

There seemed to me two groups of *Magdalenes*. There was Mary Magdalene herself, often depicted with a skull, a book and sometimes a grail chalice. Then there were all the other women with towers, but without any of the usual Mary Magdalene symbols. Once again I began to wonder who Mary Magdalene had been before Pope Gregory's edict in 591AD? And what was her connection to the other women holding towers?

Richard and I were having a break on our way to Najera, when I asked him the same question. He looked at me for a while, quite perplexed.

'I seriously don't know,' he replied.

Will and Susie, who had overheard some of our discussions about the relics and Mary Magdalene, were keen to learn more. Will, it turned out, was a walking encyclopedia when it came to the history of Britain, so he had something to say regarding the topic.

'Louise!' he said in a teacher-like kind of tone, 'you have to understand that many of these Christian symbols come from the Celts.'

As it turned out, Will was an Englishman of the old school. And however knowledgable he was, his parsimonious attitude towards others seemed to drain the energy from his audience as well as their attention. Now, when I looked around, I noticed that Richard and Susie looked quite bored. I hadn't really noticed this attitude in Will before, since we had always shared the same interest in England, supposedly because I was thinking about moving there. But Will did actually have something very interesting to tell.

He told us that the skull was a Celtic relic, even a sacred one, that had symbolised spiritual knowlege and the source of wisdom. The human head was considered 'the seat of knowledge' and the reason why the Celts chopped the heads off their enemies in battles and kept them. In this way, the person who chopped off the head would inherit the powers from the person they had just beheaded.

'Well okay,' I mumbled, thinking it sounded very much to me like the cult movie *The Highlander*.

As Will explained more about the Celts and the skull, I came to understand how, as a symbol, it had been used in Europe decades before Christianity. I had always been taught that the skull, which was depicted with Mary Magdalene, was really the head of John the Baptist. But, as with most Christian symbols, they belonged to spiritual traditions that had existed before and during the earliest times of Christianity. I didn't manage to hear much about the rest of his story, because I found it so much more interesting that Mary Magdalene was depicted with sacred relic's within Celtic culture.

THE SMALL THINGS

We walked from Navarette to Najera and the following day on to Santo Domingo de Calzada. By the time we reached Santo Domingo, I had been walking without a break for 10 days straight, and Richard for nine.

Life on the Camino seemed to bring peace and stillness to many, which increasingly created a community based on openness and consideration. Many had been forced to realise that issues such as blisters and other physical pains, could neither be avoided nor completely prevented beforehand. The best prevention against blisters lay in the individual's prior preparation at home, and in realising that the pilgrimage was a lot harder than most had been led to believe. It wasn't just a stroll in the park.

In the Middle Ages, the Camino had been used as a means of punishment. If a person had committed a serious crime, the punishment was often death or being lashed. The convicted would sometimes be given an option: they could either accept the punishment or walk the Camino. The convicted would then have to walk from their town, wherever it was in Europe, all the way to Finisterra via Santiago de Compostela. This walk could take a year or two to complete, as they also had to walk all the way back again, and the walk was extremely dangerous. The countryside was alive with bandits, they often got sick and had to fend for themselves, with no albergues around. As evidence of having fulfilled their punishment, they were required to bring back a scallop shell from Finisterra. Modern pilgrims wear fancy high-tech footwear, but in the Middle Ages, they wore only thin leather sandals over very rugged terrain. Looking at how many pilgrims suffered nowadays, it wasn't hard to imagine just how difficult it must have been in the Middle Ages.

Richard was starting to treat other people's blisters more and more. It seemed to me that the method he used was the only one that really worked effectively. Many blisters quickly became infected and grew to such a size that forced the pilgrim to rest for several days. The realisation that we just couldn't treat our body as if it were a machine was slowly starting to dawn on us. Richard's method worked in several stages; Large blisters were punctured with a sterilised needle and emptied of liquid. Then the pilgrim was sent out to wash their feet carefully with soap and water. Once completely dry, a small amount of anti-bacterial cream was gently rubbed onto the area to prevent infection. The blistered areas were then covered with Fixomull (an adherent stretchy dressing tape). The Fixomull was to stay on for several days to protect the skin from further rubbing and to allow healing. Usually, the pilgrims' feet would feel better and less painful by the following day.

Richard told me he had begun removing all the dead skin and callouses from his feet at least three months before starting the Camino.

'And after having a shower each day,' he said, 'and removing dead skin with a pumice stone, I would rub lanolin into my feet to keep the skin soft and smooth.'

'How does that prevent blisters?' I asked rather bluntly, not quite seeing the point.

'Well, blisters are created when something rubs repeatedly against the skin. So, when there isn't any hard calloused skin on your feet for the boots to rub against, there is a reduced risk in developing blisters.'

'Ah,' I said, 'that sounds logical.'

But Richard also gave them Ida's advice, which was to remove their socks and shoes when having a break, allowing their feet and footwear to dry in the sun. Richard always gave me an ironic look when giving that advice. I suppose my suggestion wasn't so bad after all.

A few days prior to reaching Najera, I had discovered that it was possible to have chorizo and egg, as in bacon and egg, for breakfast. Now, I insisted on stopping for breakfast only at those places that served lovely big portions of fried chorizo, egg and white bread. It was incredible how much this breakfast changed things for me. Before discovering chorizo and egg for breakfast, I would usually have great difficulty going to sleep, or even just resting, in the afternoon. Now, however, I had no difficulty at all. I also felt less hungry during the day and had more energy, both physically and mentally.

One day, whilst I was eating breakfast, Richard sat and looked at me with an amused look on his face.

'I have to say, Louise, it is such a pleasure to see how much you enjoy your food!'

'Mm-mm,' I mumbled, while stuffing a piece of tasty fried chorizo into my mouth.

'It's so tiring when women don't eat anything and only sit and move the food around on their plate. It seems as if they are afraid of something, and not enjoying life.'

I looked up at him and nodded, while contentedly chewing on my food. I found my breakfast to be much more interesting than talking about women's annoying eating habits. I continued, without saying anything further, and scraped the last of the egg from my plate with some bread. As I lifted my cup of tea, I discovered that it was empty.

'Oh, damn it! I could really drink another cup of tea,' I mumbled to myself.

Not realising that Richard had heard me, I was quite surprised when he suddenly got up and walked back into the kitchen.

'What were you doing?' I asked, when he came back and sat down.

'Just ordering some more tea and coffee,' he answered, with a big grin on his face.

I felt very touched by his consideration when two minutes later we sat and enjoyed our hot drinks together.

Richard's and my daily routine consisted of walking for one or two hours before stopping for breakfast. After breakfast, we usually walked for another two to four hours before having another break for lunch. In between, we would often have short stops to have a drink or to admire the views and take photographs.

This rhythm varied little from day to day. It depended on how one's body felt, the energy levels and the kind of paths we encountered. Lunch, on the other hand, became the meal I dreaded the most. The only choice seemed to be sandwiches (boadillas) or tortilla (eggcake with white potatoes). None of them satisfied my hunger or nutritious needs for very long, so I always had to carry fruit, almonds and muesli bars which I ate whilst walking.

Richard had purchased a blue hiking pole in Roncesvalles. Not the old-fashioned type, but a super modern one in a neon blue colour. And, because Richard was a sports physician, I often had to listen to his commentary about people's footwear and the use of hiking poles. His comments taught me a lot about the importance of the gear a pilgrim used. Having the right kind of footwear and the right kind of backpack, with the right kind of support, meant everything.

We often met pilgrims who suffered from ankle and knee problems because their footwear hadn't been worn in, or their backpacks adjusted properly before arriving on the Camino. This issue led to Richard giving me a longer speech about how great his hiking pole was.

'Here!' he said one day, 'try my pole while walking up this hill. It's a really great support.'

I didn't even bother looking at the stick as he offered it to me. I despised them and thought the people who used them looked really stupid. And then there were those who used two sticks, one in each hand, which made them look like spiders. I had, in other words, great difficulty understanding other people's love for these hiking poles.

'Come on, just try it,' he said again, as he held it out.

'No, thank you! I prefer to let my arms hang freely,' I answered.

Eventually I gave in, just to discover that he had to show me how to use it properly. Thankfully, I mastered it quickly and walked with the stick for a while. As I returned it to Richard, he asked what I had thought of it.

'It's not so bad,' I mumbled.

'Don't you feel it helps you?' he asked kindly.

'Nope,' I answered and immediately proceeded to stumble over a rock.

'It's my best friend,' Richard said, looking very pleased with himself.

'Good for you!' I replied.

After this little incident, Richard sometimes offered me his hiking pole when we walked uphill, which led to a further discussion of its merit that went on for the following two days. Eventually we agreed that I would use it when walking downhill and Richard uphill. For as Richard said: 'You seem more insecure on your feet when walking downhill – especially when you're tired. Then you often slide or stumble over the loose rocks. I need it most when I walk uphill since it helps my back.'

The truth was that I did it mostly to make him happy since it seemed to mean so much to him. It wasn't like Richard had tried to impose his hiking pole on me, but he had noticed that it could help me. This was, however, one of the many considerations he showed me.

On the morning after Najera, and as the morning progressed, I began suffering from stomach cramps. I had felt some during the night, but they didn't start to bother me before then. The cramps prevented me from walking comfortably and I began to feel really tired. It had been a good thing that I had been able to eat breakfast, since the energy it provided was essential and enabled me to make it to the next town. Richard and I had decided to take 'the road less travelled', as suggested in Brierley's book. A detour that led us through a tiny village called Ciruena. As we approached the place, we discovered the village consisted of a large brand-new golf course, many newly built houses with perfect lawns and newly paved roads. But the area was completely void of any activity! The houses seemed to be empty and there weren't any people to be seen, other than Richard and myself. Not even a car. It was like walking through a ghost town.

All the energy had been drained out of the area. The nature we had walked through up until now had been so beautiful, but the starkness of what confronted us we found offensive. What was meant probably to be a luxurious golf resort for wealthy pensioners, now looked like one hollow echo of artificial emptiness. Richard commented that it reminded him of the movie *The Truman Show*. We simply walked through without even stopping to take a picture. On our way out, I noticed a little arrow-shaped sign saying albergue. Richard and I looked at each other and said at the same time: 'Who would want to stay here?' But who knew. Maybe this place would change for the better in the future, and life, with all its trees and unspoilt nature, would be allowed back to where it had once been before.

SANTO DOMINGO DE CASZADA

Once again, I was convinced, that my boots were several sizes to small. With growing irritation, a blister was beginning to appear on my left big toe. So when we arrived at Santa Domingo de Calzada, I needed to get out of my boots, which led us to check in at the first albergue we came to. The albergue was a part of an old convent, Abadia Cisterciense, and was just my style. It was, to be honest, quite fortunate that Richard also preferred staying at old local albergues and monasteries. I just felt that staying at these places gave a more authentic feel to the pilgrimage.

Abadia Cisterciense turned out to be very cozy place run by friendly Cistercian nuns. The first nun we met, sat and greeted us as we entered through a massive old wooden gate. She smiled warmly at us and managed to explain, in very few words of Spanish, where to leave our boots and how to find our beds. She looked with interest at the many stamps I had in my pilgrim's pass, at times smiling when she saw one she recognised. Then, she carefully placed her own stamp in the next available empty space. Returning my pass, she gave us a warm, personal welcome.

Richard and I walked upstairs, via a stone staircase, and in through a hallway. All the walls were painted white, in the old-fashioned style, with very few things hanging on the walls. A number of the dormitories had interconnecting doors, and each room was filled with bunk beds made of wood. We chose our beds in the very last room. Each bed was made up carefully with neatly cleaned and ironed white sheets. A warm woollen blanket was carefully folded at the foot end of each bed. The care and work that seemed to have been done, to make it comfortable for the pilgrims, was very heartwarming.

I emptied my backpack, took out the clothes and toilet gear I needed and headed off for a shower. We were still the only pilgrims to have arrived, so it was nice and quiet as I walked back to have a rest. I really loved the old-fashioned bunk beds and my warm orange-coloured blanket. Some of the blankets on the beds even looked hand-knitted, a detail I thought was really sweet and homely. I imagined how the nuns had sat and knitted the blankets, by the light of the fireplace, so that tired pilgrims could sleep warmly and comfortably in their beds. This albergue certainly had that warm atmosphere about it. I smiled, quite contented, and closed my eyes to have a rest.

Two seconds later, Richard leant over and looked down at me from the top bunk. 'Louise…'

'Hmm,' I said sleepily.

'I really love your idea about not talking when we walk. It makes me think more about things – it gives me time to enjoy all of the Camino, to take it in and reflect upon it.'

'That's good…'

'I just wanted to say, that I really like the idea. It's a good thing you insisted on it. As a sportsman, I would have missed out on this, and instead focused on walking to Santiago as quickly as possible. I now realise that I would have missed the entire point of the Camino – as well as having collected a few injuries and many blisters. I also like the slower pace you walk at. It's quite comfortable and relaxing.'

'You're welcome,' I responded wearily, still with my eyes closed.

An hour or so later, a cu-cu-ru-coo call filled the room, waking me up with a start. It was Susie, and she was accompanied by Will, our all knowing Englishman. They had claimed the two bunks opposite us. Susie stood smiling at us, dressed in her bright orange T-shirt. Richard, who was wide awake, greeted them from his top bunk. Susie and Will sat down on their beds, and immediately began to tell us about their experiences in Ciruena. Susie, who also had developed a stomachache earlier that day, had become quite unwell upon reaching Ciruena. When seeing a sign pointing towards an albergue, Susie had decided to stop and stay there for the night.

However, that was not going to be the case. The man who had opened the door into the albergue had told Susie to get lost as the place was closed. Susie, quite taken aback by the man's rudeness, then politely explained her situation and asked if he would call her a taxi.

'No, I can't!' he had yelled, slamming the door in her face.

How Susie had managed to make it all the way to Santa Domingo wasn't quite clear, but here she was. And we were relieved and happy to see her. They then settled down to have a well-deserved sleep. I, on the other hand, got up and placed a dressing on my new blister. Then I gathered up my laundry, together with Richard's, and prepared to take a look around town and see if I could find a laundromat. Richard, who also wanted to go sightseeing, accompanied me. Outside the albergue, we took a left turn and walked down to a small square where I found a laundromat on the corner. After putting our clothes on to wash, we walked into one of the nearby bars. I ordered only water since my stomach hadn't settled completely yet and Richard had his usual Cortado. The barman said it was okay to take our drinks outside with us, as long as we returned the empty glasses. So we walked out, took two chairs and sat down to enjoy the last sunshine of the day.

Sitting there, I couldn't help but think how my life on the Camino highlighted the superficial way we interacted in the Western world. Maybe it was because we all seemed so indifferent to each other. There seemed to exist an ever-present power struggle. It was always about *me* and my needs for acknowledgement. There was now an 'if you don't give it to me, you're gonna get it' kind of attitude at many workplaces. Or maybe it was just a sign of our times. So, really, it wasn't surprising that people felt insecure and threatened in one way or the other. Here, on the Camino, we actually liked getting to know each other and give of ourselves, instead of constantly defining others by what, and whom, we thought or needed them to be. Maybe we were able to actually hear and see others, because we experienced enough freedom and silence to actually hear and see ourselves. There definitely seemed to be many important lessons we could learn from walking a pilgrimage like the Camino.

After the laundry was finished, I left Richard and went to explore Santo Domingo's cathedral, which proved to be a place that held many surprises for me. The altar in the cathedral was absolutely exquisite! As well as being enormous, it was also ornately lined with gold. Above the altar was an enchanting window with an egg-shaped circle in the middle. It was such an incredible piece of art that it just took my breath away. Directly under the window was a painting of a women who was looking down on what, I assumed, was the head of John the Baptist. Right beneath his head was a huge golden chalice, placed in such a way that the base of it touched the head of a goddess-like looking woman dressed in gold. There she was again, my unknown golden goddess. Beside her right foot was a small sun. Beside her left foot was a small half-moon. They were made in a most artistic and skilful way. Finally, beneath the sun and the moon, was an image of Jesus sitting on a throne.

In the smaller side scenes of the altar were many interesting figures, such as the lady with the tower, Mary Magdalene and many scenes from the Bible. The most incredible thing about the altar was that it had been created with a window above it. Extraordinary couldn't even describe it. When I was finally able to avert my gaze from the altar, I continued to explore the rest of the cathedral and the exhibition.

As I walked through the cathedral, I saw the most exquisitely carved wooden relief, which depicted two women, one holding a tower and one a sword, all blazed in gold. However, the more I walked around, the more amazed I became. There seemed no end to the presence of pictures, relics and wooden carvings, with stories belonging to ancient spiritual practices. The sun and moon appeared in many places, even on a huge pyramid-shaped chandelier.

When I finally walked out of the cathedral, I felt quite overwhelmed. Whether it was because of the priceless collection of artwork or the many references to Mary Magdalene, the tower, the golden goddess and the Knights Templar, I couldn't say. But in the end, what seemed to stay with me the most, was the image of the egg. Through the window with its inner egg shaped pattern, light radiated into the church and lit up the golden altar. The beauty of it inspired me in a way that I only had felt twice before. The first time was in Cattedrale de Santa Maria del Fiore (Basilica of Saint Mary of the Flower) in Florence. The other time was in the room devoted to the Virgin Mary in the cathedral of Orvieto, Italy. It is said, but others deny it, that it was this room that inspired Michelangelo to create the paintings seen in the Sistine Chapel. People in those days surely knew how to combine architecture and divine inspiration.

Early that evening, after dinner, a strong wind swept through Santa Domingo. As Richard, Renate, Will and I walked back towards our albergue, paper rubbish, leaves and dust swirled through the air, and shutters slammed into the walls every time a gust caught them. I had to zip up my fleece to stop it flying up into my face, and I had to squint to keep the worst of the dust out of my eyes. In the middle of it all, Ditte and Søren appeared.

'Louise! Richard!' they called out, waving to us.

I could see that they had something particularly interesting to tell us, because they had grins from ear to ear. Their walk was also more energetic than usual for this time of day, for a pilgrim anyway.

Ditte and Søren told us they were staying in a brand new albergue that had only recently opened.

'It is so cool!! You must come and see it!' Ditte and Søren burst out, overfilled with joy.

So we said goodnight to Will and Renate, and followed Ditte and Søren to their 'heavenly abode'. Once at the albergue, Ditte and Søren gave us a guided tour. 'It's incredible,' Ditte said, her eyes sparkling with excitement. 'It's huge, spacious ... they even have several food, snack and drink machines. Look!'

'And huge leather sofas,' Søren added, whilst throwing himself down on one. He stroked his hand gently over the new leather. 'Isn't it just neat?'

The brand new albergue did indeed offer every single comfort a pilgrim could dream of. They had even made separate rooms for certain types of pilgrims. Søren pointed towards a door with a sign 'For snorers' on it.

'Is that cool or what!?' he said excitedly.

'That's brilliant!' I said. Thinking about it for a second, I came to the conclusion that this was absolutely a stroke of genius!

'So let's hope that snorers are actually aware of the fact that they do snore!' Ditte wisely commented.

The truth was that the infamous snorers could keep an entire dormitory of 30-plus pilgrims awake for an entire night. It was really amazing how loud some people were able to snore. The worst ones were so loud that it sounded truly painful for them. This was the very reason why I had brought my ear plugs with me and they saved me, night after night. However, it wasn't only the snorers who were noisy and woke people up. There were also a few inconsiderate pilgrims, who usually set their extremely loud alarms to go off at four in the morning. After allowing their alarm to ring for way too long, they would get up, turn on their torches and start organising their backpacks, seeming to make as much noise as possible. There was a constant rustle of plastic bags, the sound of people falling over their boots and dropping things on the floor. They repeatedly blinded the sleeping pilgrims with the lights they usually had strapped on their foreheads.

Whilst still wearing the torch, of course, they then made several trips between the bathroom and their bed, making sure to bump into people's backpacks and beds along the way. When they finally left the albergue, a collective sigh of relief washed like a wave through the room. Everyone could go back to sleep for another couple of hours.

To avoid this scenario, after my own lack of thoughtfulness in St Jean, I always organised my backpack before going to bed. I would also have a shower upon arriving in the afternoon, so as to avoid the hassle in the morning. I always prepared my clothes and toilet gear ready on the top of my backpack, so when I woke up in the morning, I could grasp them in one hand, and my sleeping bag in the other. In this way, I could leave the room as quietly as possible and without needing a torch. Once out in the common room area, I would fold up my sleeping bag, and then change in the toilets. Simple and easy.

FOR THOSE WITH EYES TO SEE

There were so many exciting things and places for me to see along the Camino: amazing cathedrals, churches, Knights Templar castles, ruins from old pilgrim hospitals, museums with priceless historical art collections and the ever extraordinary and changing scenery. For me, it was a paradise! It often felt like I was walking through a living museum.

As for Richard, one of his most memorable experiences was when we met an old, elegantly dressed Spanish lady, out on her daily morning walk. She spoke very little English and understood even less. The woman stopped on the road when she saw Richard and began talking to him. Richard struggled to understand everything she said to him but, from what he understood, the women told him all about her familiy who had lived in the area for many generations. She also told him how the modern day pilgrims had changed the Camino for the worse. By the time the lady departed, she was so enamoured with love for Richard that she gave him a warm hug and a kiss on both cheeks.

Due to my inquisitive nature, I would always pay close attention to the places I passed by, and read the signs along the way. In so doing, I was astonished to discover that there was an incredible acceptance about the legend of Saint James, although it wasn't the way most people thought. One of the signs actually said that the church had created this special pilgrimage as a way to earn more money. This was an issue that seemed to fit with what we knew about the Catholic church in medieval times, where they always seemed to be in need of money because they had to finance the greedy power brokers of the church, their families, mistresses, their luxurious lifestyle and the constant wars they were waging. The Knights Templars never seemed to be far away, either, when it came to making money. Rolf and Carl mentioned that the Templars had arrived in the area shortly after the church made it into a Christian pilgrimage.

I read this sign twice before I believed what I saw. This was, however, one of the many surprises the pilgrims came across, if one paid enough attention. As I saw more and more, there appeared to be a growing gap between the real living history of the Camino and the Christian story of the Camino. Surprisingly, these two realities seemed to co-exist quite peacefully, side-by-side, and gave pilgrims a freedom to choose which path they took. The locals understood, somehow, that actual history and actual faith were two completely different issues. One couldn't look at them as one and the same, a wisdom the locals seemed to have grasped a long time ago.

One of the places I came to, by pure chance, was Monasterio Santa Maria de la Real, a convent where many of the queens and kings of Navarra were buried. What really excited me here was the burial site of Dóna Blance de Castile y Navarre. There was something quite majestic, almost divine, about her burial site. Before experiencing my dreams, I would most likely have skipped this kind of place. Why spend time looking at people who had been dead for hundreds of years? But things had changed, and I had come to discover that our history was really important, especially to me, from a psychological point of view.

I kept thinking about how the burial site of Dóna Blance stood out from all the others. But then, who had ever heard about Dóna Blance de Castile y Navarre? I could recall several incredible women, from several countries in Europe, but only one woman from Spain, and that was Marguerite of Navarra. But here was Dóna Blance, resting as if she had been the most powerful queen of that region. Why hadn't I heard about her before?

I had actually thought a lot about Marguerite while I walked through Navarra. It had been really weird not to see a single sign or statue of her because she had been a woman of significance in the years she lived. As I reflected on my own history lessons, during my senior years at school and in college, it occurred to me that I had never once been taught about any women in history or power. We would only hear about all the important men and their wars. I had grown up believing that women didn't exist in history, and that women were usually hopeless leaders, stupid, crazy – or all of the aforementioned. So one might be able to imagine my surprise when I learnt that this wasn't the case at all, and it was certainly not the reality I was seeing on the Camino either.

The frescos from the older churchs often depicted females as leaders and as the ones being worshipped, even by monks. They were pictures that, without doubt, would disappear with time. It was just the same in Villamayor de Monjardin, when I realised there was so much more to European history than I had ever been told. And again, there was no doubt in my mind, that the hole in our history was primarily related to women and the way scholars and religion had treated them. Could we even trust these scholars, I wondered?

From 591AD to 1969, the church had portrayed Mary Magdalene as a prostitute and repentant sinner. However, that was not the Mary Magdalene I experienced in the churches and museums along the Camino. The Magdalene I saw here was both mystical and powerful! So somebody had disagreed with the prostitute version from the very beginning! I suppose I shouldn't have been surprised about the apparent contradiction, as I later found out that the bones buried in the cathedral of Santiago de Compostella were reported to really be those of Priscillian of Avila, and not St James. Priscillian was, funnily enough, a Catholic priest, who had been executed by his own church for having believed in the equality of women and in the belief that priests should be able to marry.

I was starting to realise that history had to be seen, felt and experienced in real life. It could not be understood only from books in a library. There were so many layers to how history had been documented, described and manipulated through time. Many famous and important libraries had been burnt and documents stolen or destroyed. Researchers, with hidden agendas, had sought to destroy historical evidence they didn't like or agree with. Even the issue that many (elderly) male scholars today refuse to accept responsibility for how they had chosen to support the suppression and degradation of women throughout history is just tragic. As a result of these issues, I came to consider the Camino a treasure trove of invaluable art, and something, consequently, that seemed to be teaching us about different ways of life and how to live with our our innate spirituality.

Moving along the pilgrimage, I experienced how the hidden meaning of the Camino stepped out from behind the shadows: one step at a time, and a little more every day. Too much authentic and beautiful history had been walked over, and covered in the dust from our boots, only to be forgotten with time.

But times were changing.

THE KNIGHTS TEMPLAR AND MARY MAGDALENE

On the way to Burgos, we had to cross another mountain, Sierra Atapuerca. As we were walking, I recalled a funny story I had heard the previous night while we had been dining with a newlywed couple from Germany. After dinner, Ingrid, who seemed rather shy, told us the story about her first date with her husband, Kurt. Kurt had been sweet on Ingrid for a long time and made many attempts to invite her hiking. Ingrid, who wasn't particularly keen on this kind of activity, had repeatedly declined.

Eventually, Kurt managed to organise a hike that was to be safely guided by two of his most experienced hiking friends. Ingrid had finally accepted! Together they planned a lovely day out in the mountains, and he made quite an effort to reassure Ingrid that it would be perfectly safe. Kurt remembered the situation as being rather stressful, since there had been a lot at stake for him. On the day of departure, Ingrid recalled feeling rather nervous, but somewhat reassured by Kurt's presence and the presence of his experienced guides.

The first hours of their walk had been perfect with a clear blue sky and lots of sunshine. Everybody was enjoying it, but then the weather changed dramatically. Suddenly, a storm blew up, together with heavy rain and strong winds, which forced them to run for shelter. The map they were using to guide them blew away in the strong winds, and even the experienced hikers found themselves lost. The storm eventually abated and left the mountain cloaked in a wet, dense fog. Ingrid had been terrified, Kurt devastated and his friends shocked. Everything that could go wrong, did go wrong.

Richard and I looked at each other and laughed.

'Well, I must have done something right!' Kurt said, and blushed as he took Ingrid's hand, 'she ended up marrying me, didn't she?'

'And now he's convinced you to walk the Camino!' Richard said with a loud laugh. Now it was Ingrid's turn to blush.

'I've only gone wrong once!' Kurt exclaimed, looking like an embarrassed schoolboy.

Even though this wasn't the German mountains, many of us here on the Camino, at one time or other, took a wrong turn or missed a yellow arrow, or, as in my case, several of them. The thing was that these stories were often the funniest, when told after the event. And so it happened, that very morning, Richard and I arrived in a tiny square, at the very outskirts of a village, not knowing whether or not we were lost. We weren't quite sure what to do, but figured we would sit at a bar for a while and watch out for any passing pilgrims.

As we sat with our cold drinks, I looked around and wondered if I could take off my boots and socks. Richard wondered the same, but felt it was rather inappropriate. I agreed, but since we were the only guests, I took them off and tucked them under my chair, out of sight. Lining the square were many beautiful trees covered in pink blossom. In the middle was the small bar and some white plastic tables and chairs. A couple of parasoles stood spread amongst the tables, offering some shade from the strong sun.

'Isn't it weird?' Richard said, after we had sat silently for a while, 'that we both came with plans for the Camino. Now I realise that it is the Camino that has plans for you! Not the other way around.'

Although his comment came a little out of the blue, I knew exactly what he meant. So I continued the thread of thought and said: 'We came because the Camino called us! And when the Camino calls you, you have no other choice than to stop, listen and surrender.'

'Precisely!' Richard answered excitedly.

We sat and philosophised about the Camino until we saw a tall man carrying a huge backpack and wearing a dark Basque hat come sauntering down the road. He came from another direction than we did (so maybe we had been lost) with an easy and untroubled gait. The high curb leading into the square didn't even bother him. Some people walk straight into one's heart. Peter was one of those. He had walked all the way from Switzerland.

He had large blue eyes and spoke English with a charming French accent. He smiled often and seemed to be a person at peace with himself. As it often was on the Camino, we quickly settled down together and began to share our personal stories about how we had ended up in this part of the world.

We learnt that Peter camped out each night, and cooked his meals on the gas burner he carried in his backpack. I then began to understand why his backpack was so large, as it also contained his tent, the small gas burner, cooking appliances, clothing, food and a sleeping bag. In his life outside of the Camino, Peter owned a luxurious B&B with his husband.

'One day the workload and never-ending business stress became too much for me,' Peter told us openly. 'I couldn't take it any more.'

He had asked for a time out, which had been granted. For six months! An emergency work plan at the B&B, with help from friends, had been put into place. So one morning, Peter farewelled his husband and began his long walk to Santiago de Compostela, dedicating his pilgrimage to a time of stillness and reflection.

Suddenly, his phone rang. Peter looked up apologetically and answered it. It was his husband who needed to ask something about the B&B booking system. Peter had a short conversation with him in French, before hanging up. He smiled at us, as he put down the phone, and apologised again. 'I might have been given six months off, but it was part of the deal that people could ring if an urgent problem arose at work.'

We all laughed about the irony of life. Peter was, however, quite happy with the situation.

'Don't you miss your husband?' Richard asked.

'I do, but we have a very special relationship, and speak together on the phone every day. We give each other space whenever something is important to us – like when I needed this time away.'

As Peter told us about his B&B and life, he somehow managed to mentioned Orval, a monastery close to where he had once lived in Belgium. I looked at him, surprised. 'Orval, you know Orval?' I asked.

Peter looked at me just as surprised. 'Yes! You know of Orval? Do you also know about Matilda of Tuscany?' he asked.

'Sure! I loved Michéle Spike's book about her.'

'Wow, you really know about that little place?' He seemed impressed.

Richard felt somewhat left behind in the conversation, since he had never known about Matilda or the monastery she had built there. The monastery was called Orval: The Valley of Gold. He did, however, find the topic fascinating and listened attentively. The famous symbol of Orval was a fish with a gold ring in its mouth. The legend had it that a fish had returned Matilda's gold wedding ring when she had lost it in a pool of water. After experiencing this miracle, Matilda exclaimed: 'This is indeed a Valley of Gold. Here, I will build my church.'

Following our inspiring conversation with Peter, it was time for us to move on. As we stood up and put on our backpacks, he signalled for us to go on ahead.

'Sorry, but I always walk alone,' he said politely.

We said our goodbyes, put on our hats (and I, my socks and boots) and began walking the rest of the way to Burgos. The day was hot. Really, really hot. A few pilgrims had warned us about a 10km stretch that went through the industrial outskirts of Burgos, and then into the centre of the city. We were forewarned that this specific stretch would be exhausting and tiring. Brierley's map showed us an easier alternative route we could take around this. Unfortunately, we failed to take the correct pathway and ended up walking alongside the busy highway, on concrete sidewalks, for the next 10km and in 40-degree heat. The walk was absolutely killing. There was no shade at all and, for the first time ever on the Camino, we started to look for a taxi or a bus, but there was nothing! It was Sunday and siesta time, so no buses, no taxis. Nothing. Resigned to our fate, we put our heads down and plodded on, one foot after another.

Sweat poured down my face as the sun burned my skin, and I began to feel like a barbequed chicken. My body started to feel heavy, as the heat from the concrete radiated up through my swollen feet. All I could do was to try to think of something different. When we finally reached the city limits, we saw Peter, looking up at a large roadside map of Burgos. By then, I had no idea how many hours, or kilometres we had walked. Peter, who didn't look at all tired or sweaty, greeted us with a big smile. Our own smiles, by comparison, were quite small by this time. It was really great to meet up with Peter again, but we just didn't have the energy to show it. Richard commented, ruefully, that we had missed the arrow for the alternative pathway, and how terrible it had been to walk in the heat and the traffic. Peter just shrugged his shoulders. For him, that experience, was just another part of the Camino.

We stood talking together for a few minutes, before Peter again headed off by himself. He had seen a camping area nearby and wanted to check it out. With Peter gone, Richard and I tried to make sense of the large map next to us.

'There has to be an albergue close by!' I sighed, but apparently there wasn't.

The map didn't make much sense at all, and nobody we asked could help. It was the hottest time of the day and, according to Brierley's map, we were still a fair way from the centre of town. We were, in fact, so far out, we weren't even located on his map. We continued to walk for another 20 minutes without seeing a single scallop shell to confirm we were going the right way. When we finally came to a cafe that was open, we decided to go in. Maybe a rest and something to eat and drink would help restore our energy, but it didn't. Resting in the shade, I noticed how the well-dressed city folk looked at us, in our sweaty hiking clothes. Our boots, socks and legs were dusty and brown with dirt, so we clearly stood out in the posh crowd. But I was in a state far beyond caring. If they had a problem, they could either offer to help us, or they could ignore us all together.

My feet felt like I had been walking on hot needles, my knees were stiff, my leg muscles hurt and my head couldn't take any more heat. I just wanted to get to a fucking albergue as soon as possible. It was Richard's faulty directions that caused us to take another hour before finally finding an albergue. He had been so sure that he knew better than Brierley's map. Apparently, he didn't.

The moment I walked into the elevator that was to take me up to my dormitory, I could have cried in relief. My entire body was in such pain and agony that I barely made it to my bunk. The moment I lay down, however, the first stomach cramps appeared. Before they got any worse, I hurried out to have a shower and wash my clothes. Once back in bed, the pains returned even worse than before. Richard decided to go out by himself that evening to eat with the other pilgrims, while I stayed in bed suffering and trying to sleep.

Later, when I woke up, I noticed, resting on the bunks opposite us, was a Spanish family consisting of Mum, Dad and their eight-year-old son. The woman was a nurse and the only one in the family who spoke any English. She and her husband had spent a week of their annual holiday walking the Camino with their son. She told me that their son had been little bored at times during the walk but, even so, he enjoyed the time he spent with his parents. By now, Richard was back in his bed and reading a book. He had eaten dinner at a local tapás bar and had met some nice people there. Other pilgrims in our room were also slowly making their way back after dinner. My stomach cramps were wearing off, although I still felt rather unwell.

While the nurse and I talked, I attended to my one old, and one recent, blister. I now had one on each big toe. The older one had appeared several days ago, so I had put a Compeed dressing on it, just to discover, that sweat made the dressing loosen. When I tried to pull the dressing off, it had pulled even more skin off the toe, and made things worse. So now I sat looking at my bandages and toes, wondering what to do.

'Would you like me to fix those for you?' the nurse asked and pointed towards my feet.

'That's really nice of you. Yes, thank you,' I answered.

She immediately found a tin box in which she kept all her medical supplies. When she had finished, my two toes were wrapped up in the most beautiful way like Egyptian mummies. Without saying a word, Richard had followed the procedure, very suspiciously, from his bed above me. I ignored him and thought the nurse had done a great job.

Yes! It rained all that night, and as most of the windows in our dormitory were open, a wonderful cool breeze swept through the room. By the time I awoke the next morning, the little Spanish family had gone and Richard was resting on his sleeping bag, reading a book. Thankfully, I was feeling much better now.

Twenty minutes later, as I sat down to put on my boots, I discovered, that the bandages were too big. My toes didn't fit into my boots! There simply wasn't enough room for my feet together with the huge bandages. I looked over at Richard. 'Would you mind changing them?' I asked.

It wasn't that I couldn't do it myself, it was just really important to me that it was done correctly. It was now or never for these blisters. As Richard changed my bandages, he couldn't help but say, with a humorous glint in his eyes: 'Never let a nurse do a doctor's job.' I couldn't help but laugh. It was just so typical of Richard to say something like that.

Just as my stomach was getting better, Richard was starting to feel sick in his, and said: 'On our walk today, if I suddenly disappear, it's because I'm sitting behind a bush. Just keep walking, I'll catch up with you.'

He tried to smile, but he looked tired and his otherwise tanned skin was pale. Richard hated being sick.

'Doctors don't get sick,' he grumbled, as I noted out loud on how pale he was.

'Whatever,' I replied, and walked towards the elevator. It was time for fun! And a fun time meant exploring the huge cathedral in Burgos. Richard didn't feel like going in and he didn't feel like walking either, so he made himself comfortable on a bench outside and waited for me.

After having spent a significant amount of time exploring the outer facade of the cathedral, I finally made my way inside, having no idea I was up for a great surprise. Was I really seeing what I was seeing? Because if I was, I would have to go somewhere and faint! I didn't faint, though, but I remained utterly speechless as I moved around the enormous church. When I came walking out more than an hour later, I couldn't wait to tell Richard what I had seen. To my surprise, Pierre was sitting on the bench talking with him. Richard still looked sick, but seemed happier in Pierre's company. When the two men saw me, Pierre reached up and gave me a hug.

'How are you?' he asked.

'You're are not going to believe this!' I exploded.

'Believe what?' they asked. Pierre looked curiously at me.

'I have just spent more than an hour inside that cathedral, and I deeply and sincerely believe that what I have just seen, is proof linking the Knights Templar to Mary Magdalene.'

'What?' Pierre jumped up from his seat, nearly choking on the coffee he had been drinking. He quickly contained his surprise, but continued to stare at me. Richard, however, took it quite calmly and asked, what it was that had made me come to that conclusion.

'I can't possibly tell you all of it at once, since that would take forever – but I can tell you this!'

I then proceeded to tell them how the Knights Templar, ancient spiritual teachings, women and Mary Magdalene were major recurring themes throughout the church. It was as if the church had been especially built for this reason; I had seen the most priceless Hieros Gamos relief in marble, a painting with Mary Magdalene in a golden dress, the grail in different shapes, many Tree of Life paintings, the Venus Temple, numerous eight-pointed stars (the Star of Venus) and ancient signs representing both the masculine and feminine.

Above a small entrance door, was a plaster figure of a Madonna with a crown of stars above her head. Surrounding her were two different temples of Venus, a tower, a the Tree of Life (again), a well and a water fountain. The Madonna was standing on a dragon, and to her left was a stone wall with a towered gate leading into a beautiful garden. I also saw an incredible fresco that depicted a monk kneeling before a pregnant women. In this fresco, the blood from Jesus' wounds sprayed down on the monk, as he worshipped the pregnant woman who held a half-hidden book in one hand and what looked like a closed lotus flower in the other.

The fact that the Templars were repeatedly depicted together with Mary Magdalene and her children showed me that a close relationship once had existed between them. In fact, they were depicted together so often, one practically had to be blind not to see it. Another thing I found puzzling was that alongside Mary Magdalene and the Templars, were many other pagan spiritual symbols belonging to different spiritual traditions – even Jewish ones. And then there was this ever present symbol of the six petalled rose in all the large cathedrals. I had no idea what it meant, but it must have been significant, because it was one of the most prominent symbols displayed. Inside, to the left of the main entrance, I found two rooms dedicated to many different and unnamed female figures. Always unnamed. In the first room, in front of its altar, were four busts of an elderly and three younger women. Each had a mirror placed on their chest.

The second room, which appeared to be the most important of the two, was unfortunately closed. So I had to stand and peek through the bars of the locked gate. Of course, the closed room contained the larger collection of female deities and many seemed somewhat more controversial than the typical Madonnas. The significance of the mirrors, seen on the female busts and in many other places, such as the Hieros Gamos relief, meant 'seeing the soul inside' or seeing into other worlds.

Just as I had finished telling about my experiences, two of Pierre's friends appeared. They stood, as usual, at a polite distance and waited for him. Pierre, wanting to hear more, looked rather disappointed he had to leave. He said a reluctant goodbye before walking off with them.

Richard and I put our backpacks on and prepared to leave while I told him more about the different rooms I had seen in the cathedral. He didn't completely buy my theories, which was fine by me. I didn't have any hard evidence for them, either, but everything I saw on the Camino and in this cathedral was telling me a very different story – an untold story that I had never heard before. It was so incredible, to once again, stand face-to-face with the living history of the Camino, which indeed contained hidden treasures beyond my wildest imagination.

Richard still looked rather unwell, so I asked if he wanted to stay in Burgos another day and recover.

'No!' he said. He just wanted to moved on since he wasn't that keen on Burgos anymore. Richard sighed with a sad expression and said: 'While waiting for you, I was watching this sick elderly women, who was sitting begging in front of the cathedral entrance. The way her poverty contrasted with the wealth of the Catholic church just made me feel sick inside. Very few who entered the church gave her any money at all.' Eventually Richard had walked over and given her a donation.

I looked at him and nodded acknowledgement of his emotions. We walked on in silence for a while, until Richard stopped in front of a shop to look at the window display. The windows were filled with souvenirs related to the Camino and Spain.

'You know,' he said, in a quiet voice, 'The patroness of the Templars was the Virgin Mary.' He had a knowing smile. 'Come on, let's go inside.'

I followed Richard into the shop and wondered why he hadn't mentioned this before? It sort of explained quite a lot to me. But Richard just shrugged his shoulders and walked to the back of the shop to examine some jewellery while I wandered around and looked at the many things on the shelves. Suddenly I turned around, and walked over to where Richard was standing.

'Richard!' I whispered.

'Yeah?' he answered absent mindedly.

'I just remembered the painting I saw in Navarette!'

What painting?'

'The painting of the Templar ship, where the people on the deck stood looking up into the sky at an image of the Virgin Mary – worshipping her.'

'And?' Richard looked at me quizzically.

'But didn't the Catholic church accuse the Templars of heresy, torture and kill them because of that? Well, if they belonged to the Cult of the Virgin Mary, a Catholic Saint, how could they be heretics then?'

'Well, it probably had more to do with the power of the Templars and their extreme wealth rather than their actual beliefs. The same happened to the Cathars, and, by the way, do you like any of these bracelets?'

'What?'

I looked first at Richard, and then at the bracelets. 'Well, I like both the brown and the black ones,' I said, pointing to them.

'Good.'

Richard then walked over to the counter and, unbeknown to me, bought them both. Outside the shop, he handed me a little box. 'They are for you.'

Richard had bought me the two beautiful bracelets. One in brown leather with a silver scallop shell on it, and one in black, with three small discreet scallop shells engraved into its metal band.

YELLOW BUTTERFLIES

If anyone asked me if the Camino had its own special sound, I would say the sound of a cloud of yellow butterflies as they flew up around me and followed for a while. But the truth was, the Camino was filled with wonderful sounds. There were the sounds of my boots striking the gravel pathway as I walked along, and the clattering of stork beaks as they looked down on us from their nests. There was the sound when a fellow pilgrim said a heartfelt, kind word, and the joy of Susie's cu-cu-ru-cuu call. There was the unspoken closeness when Richard had given me the bracelets, and the absence of sounds when Richard had walked off the path to collect me a beautiful rose.

The Camino was, in truth, filled with sounds of the heart and I listened.

THE MESETA

It was still early in the afternoon when we stopped at the albergue, Liberanos Domine, which was located in Rabé de las Calzados. This was the last village before the feared plateaus of the Mesetas. Since Richard was still feeling sick, we decided to stop here. Being some of the first pilgrims to arrive, we could choose a quiet room to ourselves at the end of the hallway.

Richard fell asleep as soon as his head hit the pillow. Meanwhile, I made up my bed, collected my laundry and then went off for a shower. When I returned to our room, Susie was quietly unpacking her gear on a bed opposite us.

'Susie!' I whispered excitedly and gave her a big hug.

She looked over at Richard who was deeply asleep.

'Is he sick?' she whispered.

'Yeah, he's got stomach pains and diarrhoea,' I replied. Susie and I had just recovered from ours.

After having completed my laundry together with Susie, I went to bed to rest for while. My body was beginning to feel rather bruised and battered. I had thought that if I walked shorter distances, it would be equivalent to easy walks and easy days, but that wasn't the case. We constantly found ourselves walking up and down hills and mountains and, in some places, encountered ascents of 12 and 18 degrees. My legs were continually fatigued and my knees stiff by the end of each day. Now, I would happily pay a person to do my laundry for me – something that firstly had been against my pilgrim 'principles'. Instead of feeling love and respect for my body, and the great effort it had made so far on this pilgrimage, all I felt now was its limitations. It had also crossed my mind that my days with Richard were passing quickly. He had to be back in Barcelona in ten days to catch his flight home to Australia. The time for saying goodbye was lurking somewhere soon. I knew the goodbye would be painful and the thought of this filled me with sadness. Even so, I knew I would always treasure and appreciate our time together and our resulting friendship. He had indeed become a very special person to me.

Richard woke up after dinner, feeling a little better. Richard, Susie and I were lucky to have the room for ourselves that night, and during the evening the three of us sat cosily in our beds, talking. One of the conversations inspired me to use one of the shavers Susie had given me, and I removed all the dead calloused skin from my feet. This activity was so nice and relaxing, I became totally engrossed in doing a very thorough job.

The alarm clock rang at 4am. It was dark in our albergue and also outside, and not as much as a snore was to be heard throughout the quiet hallway. Susie, Richard and I got up and silently gathered our things. Richard, although still looking rather sick, said he was feeling better and wanted to walk.

Without a sound, we crept down the stairs and into the kitchen. Richard and Susie had ordered breakfast the day before. Upon seeing the table, I understood why I hadn't ordered anything. On the table were jam, dried biscuits and the kind of sugary food so typical at the albergues. Once again, I had to eat my almonds and fruit for breakfast. Tip-toeing out of our albergue and into the sleepy village, Richard and Susie turned their torches on. It was now 5am and still pitch black.

Of all the places on the Camino, the Meseta was the most feared. It had a reputation of being one, long never-ending nightmare. Richard and Susie's major concern was the heat, which is why we decided to leave very early, and make the most of the cool morning hours. Leaving the village behind, we began to walk along a rough, tyre-marked roadway. I had never walked this early before and felt rather excited. There was something magical about walking in the dark under the stars, slowly witnessing how the world around me unfolded itself as the sun rose. At first we hadn't been able to see anything, except for a few steps ahead of us. The corn could just be glimpsed growing in the fields alongside the roadway. The only sounds to be heard were those of our boots hitting the path, or when one of us spoke. The world around us was completely silent.

The narrow road up to the top of the Meseta started with a sharp climb where we had to tread carefully to avoid loose stones that we could slip on. Once we reached the top, we stopped and turned around, just in time to see the birth of the first light of day. The light revealed such a breathtaking view that the three of us just stood in awe. None of us had expected this. With the sun's appearance, birds and insects suddenly woke up and began to fly and buzz around, while the lavender and golden-coloured morning sky surrounded us with its endless space and beauty. It was quite an experience for me to see how the plateau was transformed in the passing from night to day, and continued to change as the sun rose higher and higher in the sky. Moment by moment, it unfolded the ever-changing beauty of huge golden fields and the endless crystal-clear blue sky. It felt like I was raised above the rest of the world, in a place that stretched out into an eternity of beauty and bliss.

I wondered many times, as I walked the Meseta, how anyone could describe this place as an never-ending nightmare. This was certainly one of the most beautiful and enchanting places on my pilgrimage. And for anyone who knew just how spectacular the scenery was on the Camino, it said a lot. However, I had no doubt that the walk across the Meseta would be tough as soon as the heat of the day set in. The dust from the corn fields, the dry air and the total absence of shade would make it hard in the burning sun. It was important for pilgrims to be prepared for the Meseta.

We all walked at a different pace, taking the time we needed to soak in the magic of the Meseta. Sometimes we walked together and at other times apart, and continued to do so all the way through. By the time the first heat of day was felt, we had walked the Meseta for three or four hours. Thankfully, Richard was feeling much better. I, on the other hand, had developed an infection in my little toe as a result of all the skin I had removed the night before. A few kilometres before we reached Hontanas, the pain in my toe became so bad that I had to stop. So when we came to a nice grassy spot beside the road, we had a break. I took off my boots and socks so Richard and I could have a look at the toe.

'Well, Louise,' he said in a matter-of-fact manner, 'removing too much skin yesterday was not a good idea. Now you have no protection – only underlying soft skin, damaged from the heat and sweat, and the constant rubbing from your boots.'

'Oh, damm it,' I mumbled as I looked down. I had even developed a new blister under the infected skin.

Richard repeated his usual dressings, and gave me two paracetamol for the pain.

'The pills will help you make it to the next town,' he said, 'but no further than that.'

I sat, feeling rather annoyed with myself. Wasn't that just typical? I hoped it wouldn't cause me too many problems. As I moped there, feeling sorry for myself, I suddenly heard sounds coming from the field behind me. It was Richard, who had thrown himself down in the corn field. He had needed to lie down and rest his back, surrendering to the healing energy of the Camino. And why not do it in the oceans of golden corn fields?

In the meantime, Susie was sitting on the opposite side of the road meditating. Since there wasn't much else to do, I also lay down to rest. Once in a while, distant sounds of an aeroplane could be heard amid the stillness of the Meseta. A short time later, it may have been five minutes or thirty minutes, two cyclists appeared, travelling down the road. I turned my head, and watched them as they slowly drew closer. Richard who also had heard the sound of the bikes emerged from the field, and Susie opened her eyes to see what was happening.

'Look!' she said, 'we have visitors.'

Now, we were all watching the cyclists, wondering who they were. One of them, a young, blonde female, turned out to be Australian, and with her was a very good-looking Spanish man. Before taking off again, the Australian woman told me she had met another Danish woman a few days earlier. Like so many other pilgrims, the Danish woman had bought her boots the day before starting the Camino, and had no time to wear them in. As a result, she had quickly deveoped blisters that had become so bad that a local Spanish doctor had told her to stop the pilgrimage immediately. If she didn't, the blisters would never heal properly. Proper footwear was serious business here.

As the painkillers started to work, we put on our backpacks and began walking again. Watching the two cyclists disappear in the distance, I wondered if cyclists being allowed on the Camino was a good idea. The problem with the cyclists was becoming an increasing concern for the walking pilgrims. However, I quickly realised I had to concentrate on walking in a way that irritated my toe the least, so I had to leave my worries about the cyclists behind. When we (finally) arrived in Hontanas, we stopped at the very first bar we came to, and threw ourselves down on some chairs in the shade. A friendly woman came and asked if we would like something to eat or to drink?

'Both!' I exclaimed.

'Same here!' Richard agreed.

Susie ended up translating the menu, as well as ordering the food and drink for us all. There were freshly made sandwiches on the menu, as well as Cortados for Susie and Richard. Everything was so much easier on the Camino if one spoke Spanish. It was my luck that Richard knew enough for us to get by during the day. The freshly made sandwiches were fantastic. Some were filled with tuna and others with delicious meat. Richard and Susie ended up eating three each. I managed four, of course!

Our walk that morning had been about 19km with only one stop, so we stayed at the bar for quite some time. There we met Renate, who also thought that walking the Meseta had been a really great experience. We all agreed that the Meseta had to be walked well before noon, or else late in the afternoon. Otherwise, the heat and lack of shade would be intolerable. I thought to myself, that walking the Meseta during sunset, would also be quite a memorable experience.

I suggested to the others that we should take a taxi to Castrojeriz. I couldn't walk any more (my toe was beginning to hurt enormously) and I wanted to get away from the dry heat. Susie was tired and Richard was starting to feel sick again. Renate, however, wanted to stay and check out the albergues in Hontanas. Once again, Susie saved us and, with her fluent Spanish, a taxi arrived in no time at all, seemingly from nowhere.

THE PAINTING IN CASTROJERIZ

From Hontanas to Castrojeriz, the pilgrims' path was alongside the road our taxi took. The pathway was flat and shaded by many large trees, providing welcome relief for the walkers. As we drove past the walking pilgrims, I hoped they wouldn't spot us in the taxi, but they were quick to notice us. The look in their eyes when they saw us, made me feel as if we had betrayed them. Richard and I tried to duck down, hiding our heads in shame. A real pilgrim walked, no matter how hard it was. They didn't cheat.

Once in Castrojeriz, Susie walked off to do her own thing while Richard and I checked into a nice little hotel, where he immediately went to bed. I followed my usual routine, had a short rest and then put on my flip-flops and went off to explore the new town. It was peaceful and quiet as I walked out of the hotel and up a little road to Plaza Mayor. Castrojeriz was a quaint old village. It seemed very sleepy, and one of the places to which pilgrims had brought much-needed business. After finding a newspaper for Richard, it was time for my real passion, a visit to another church. The name of the church in the village used to be the Church of our Lady of the Apple, but it was now called Iglesia Santa Maria. The original title, however, sounded very promising.

I knew the Welsh word for 'apple' is Avalon as in the 'Island of Avalon'. It was a place mostly known from the legends of King Arthur and had functioned as a sacred place for the Celtic priestesses. But this island had indeed existed, and was located in Somerset, England, which has always been famous for its apples. The apple was also a symbol, known from the story of Adam and Eve; a bite of the apple killed ignorance, and gave one wisdom and eyes to see with. The term 'Our Lady', dated back to ancient goddess cultures and none other than Cybele and Asherah. In the village church was a large colourful rose window. This didn't surprise me, as the rose, in the Middle Ages, had become a symbol for the divine, feminine principle. There was, in other words, a strong connection between the symbol of the apple, the rose and goddess worship.

The church was delightfully cool inside, and gave me a break from the strong sun. As I walked around, I suddenly saw a painting that took my breath away. I stopped, transfixed. Was I really seeing what I was seeing? I couldn't believe it and walked closer. The painting was called *El Triunfo de la Iglesia* and was painted by Rubens between 1626 and 1628. The title meant either 'the victory of the church', or 'the triumph of the church', depending on its context. In the painting, a powerful woman was depicted draped in a massive scarlet papal robe. Underneath she wore a flowing royal blue and emerald green dress. She was seated in a beautiful golden chariot, which was pulled by three strong white horses with long golden manes. Angels and humans celebrated her coming and, together, they helped by pushing the chariot and horses forward. There seemed to be a great celebration about her coming.

One of the most important details in the picture was that an angel was placing the papal crown on the woman's head. In front of her, the woman held a large lantern, the light from which illuminated the dark sky, indicating that the women was the deliverer of enlightenment, healing and divinity. The fine details and symbolism in the painting were extraordinary, and the more I looked, the more I discovered. There was also a woman in a golden dress, holding a sword in one hand and the reins of a horse in the other. The chariot crushed what seemed to be darkness and sickness.

I kept staring at the painting for a long time, feeling overwhelmed with what I saw. A woman, being crowned as a pope? I immediately thought about a theory I had heard, that Jesus had appointed Mary Magdalene to take over the ministry of his teachings after his death, and not Peter as we had been taught. However, the title of the painting left me even more puzzled. Here was obviously a woman being crowned as a pope, and the painting was called 'the success, or victory, of the church'! What success? And why would a woman symbolise that? Could this painting have anything to do with my dreams about the Church of Mary Magdalene?

I spun on my heels and walked straight over to where I could buy a postcard of Rubens *El Triunfo de la Iglesia*. Having purchased the postcard, I walked back and looked at the lantern in the painting for a while longer. I was quite sure I had seen this before, and I knew it was somehow important. I just couldn't remember where. Scratching my head, I kept looking at the painting. Then it dawned on me that Cybele, The Mother of Gods, would always arrive amid great celebration, in her golden chariot, and that was pretty much what I was seeing here. Yet, there seemed to be so much more meaning to this painting. In fact this painting seemed to be telling me a lot of important things, and yet everything seemed to point back to one important detail; a glorious women, the bringer of Life and Light, being crowned with the Papal crown.

I slowly moved on and noticed several other interesting objects and tapestries in the church. All of them revealed the important roles women played in areas such as astronomy, academia, knowledge, art, leadership and teachers. On the way out of the church, I bought more postcards that depicted some of the things I had seen inside. This was too good to forget. I needed to study the postcards more closely, especially that of Rubens' painting. Later, I had no doubt that this 'invisible' little village and it's church, were indeed a very special place. The church in Castrojeriz was a true treasure chest of sacred art, or should I say, sacred art related to Cybele and other pre-Christian spiritual traditions. The question was: what had inspired the artist to paint this scene? And why had they chosen Ruben's painting (the original one is in Madrid) to hang in their church? Hidden, but at the same time, very prominent.

Returning to the hotel, Richard was awake and feeling much better. 'Feel like going out again?' he asked.

'Sure!' I said, and took my little green bag with me.

We ended up at a bar named after the Knights Templar. It was filled with swords, shields, armour and other pieces of knights' attire. Richard, whose fascination with the Templars had grown whilst walking the Camino, strolled around to have a look at the displays. After ordering our drinks we went outside to sit and enjoy the beautiful weather and a good coffee. A cu-cu-ru-coo suddenly echoed through the air. It was Susie, hiding behind some bushes. We could hear her laughter before we even saw her.

'Hello there!' she said, full of energy, and walked over to our table and sat down next to me.

'Hi Susie,' I said. 'Richard was just telling me that he would like to buy one of the Templar shirts hanging on the wall inside.'

'Well you go and ask the barman then,' Susie said with a laugh.

I did, but the owner didn't speak any English. Richard tried with his limited Spanish, but that didn't work either. So we had to ask for Susie's help again, which she happily gave.

'Susie, could you please ask the barman if he is a Templar?'

'Okay,' she said and asked him.

The barman broke out laughing when he heard our question.

'No, he's obviously not,' Susan translated back to us.

'Well, if he's not a Templar,' I said, 'why does he have all this Templar paraphernalia then? Could you please ask him?'

'Seriously?'

'Yes, seriously. Ask him, please please!'

Susie sighed and asked the poor barman. She looked back at me as he shook his head.

'No, they are not antiques – but he does have some originals.'

'Well, aren't originals antiques? Especially if they are from the Templars?' I asked. 'Oh, never mind.'

I looked over at the barman who seemed to be enjoying himself with the confusing three-way conversation.

'If your things aren't antiques, then why won't you sell me that shirt there?' I asked, smiling at him.

The man laughed again. I had a sneaky suspicion that he understood and spoke more English than he actually let on.

'No, no sale,' he answered.

'Oh, that's a shame,' I said, 'but thank you anyway.'

'You welcome!'

He certainly understood what I had said then!

We walked back outside and sat down at the table again, looking at each other for a little bit, wondering what we should do next.

'Why don't we take a taxi around town and see the sights?' Susie suggested.

Richard's eyes lit up. 'Yeah, that's a great idea!'

In reality that was also the only way we could get around. I was barely able to walk with my sore toe, Richard still had stomach cramps and Susie had done her walking for the day. The barman called us a taxi, and, judging by the look on his face, seemed rather relieved to get rid of us.

Ten minutes later, a taxi arrived. The driver was a local man and at least 70 years old. Susie showed off her brilliant Spanish, and became our translator. She immediately connected with the taxidriver, who turned out to be a kind and considerate person. With Susie in the front seat, we began to discuss where to go. The obvious place was to a Templar ruin located on the very top of the hill overlooking Castrojeriz. However, none of us felt like going there. It was too hot and demanded too much walking up a very steep and winding pathway.

'How about the convent of Santa Clara?' I suggested. 'I heard somewhere that they make these really great cakes.'

The taxidriver turned around and looked at me. 'Monasterio de Santa Clara – good place!' he said and smiled.

We all looked at each other in agreement and off we went in the taxi. The driver had lived in this area all his life, and obviously knew what was worth seeing. With the refreshing cool breeze blowing through the open windows of the taxi, we had the most marvellous journey through the tranquil countryside. I could almost have been in one of those wonderful feel-good movies from France or Italy. But good things don't only happen in movies; they also happen in real life.

The convent turned out to be much smaller than I had expected. A lot smaller actually, but it was very romantic and beautiful. It was also very closed.

'Darn it!' Susie said, when we saw the closed gate through the taxi windows.

'*Uno momento*,' the taxidriver said and got out of his car.

He walked across the small parking area and rang a doorbell next to the gate.

Susie, Richard and I watched him curiously, commenting on everything.

'Oh, he's ringing the doorbell.'

'Do you think he knows them?'

'That's really nice of him.'

'Look, a nun just opened the door!'

'They're talking.'

'Shh, he's coming back.'

It turned out that the taxidriver was old friends with the nun and had asked if she would let us in, even though the convent was officially closed. The nun had most kindly agreed and stood waiting for us at the gate.

Inside, behind thick protective stone walls, was a small pebbled courtyard and a number of buildings. It looked very much like an idyllic scene from a medieval movie. There was a small house where the nuns lived, and a much larger building, which included the church and their bakery. In between these buildings was a well-kept garden, with colourful flowers and a small cobblestoned pathway.

The nun smiled and greeted us warmly as we walked through the gate. She locked it carefully behind us and led us to the main house where they had the bakery. The bakery was a bit different as it was hidden behind a thick wall, and the cakes were delivered through a rotating hatchway. Apparently, most of the nuns wished to have no, or only little, contact with the outside world. To respect their wishes, the hatchway had been installed to prevent outsiders from actually seeing the nuns. To no one's surprise, I suggested we buy some cakes to support them. Richard and Susie heartily agreed, and Susie asked the taxidriver if it was possible to buy any. He turned around and asked the nun, who smiled and nodded.

'*Uno momento*,' she said, as she went off to find a list of the cakes they sold.

We ended up ordering a large box of almond cookies, together with four fancy cream-puff cakes. The nun took our order and walked off into the bakery. Meanwhile, we walked around the adjoining and sparsely decorated rooms.

'Look at this cross above the doorway?' Susie said, pointing to a piece of wood, with a T engraved into it. 'I have never seen that before?'

I shook my head. I hadn't either.

'Try and ask the taxidriver?' I suggested.

Susie then asked the taxidriver, who then asked the nun, who then told us in her cute broken English that it was the cross of Santa Clara. The cross was called *La Tau*. I had never heard of it.

Clank! Clank! Clank! Puzzled by the noise, we turned around. The sound came from the hatchway. Our box of cookies and the four cakes had arrived.

The extra cake was for our taxidriver, who looked extremely happy when we offered it to him. He told us it was his favourite. We also shared some of our cookies with him.

After a while, the nun returned and told our driver that she had opened the church especially for us, a gesture that really touched me. The church was a most sacred place for them and, yet, she didn't mind opening for us, even on a closed day. I entered the church full of excitement. I had never visited a church before that was devoted to Saint Claire, but I was in for a disappointment. The church had very little decorations and there was not one single picture or art object of Saint Claire! Saint Claire was non-existent in her own church. I didn't say anything as I didn't want to offend the nun. Maybe it was a part of their belief system. I didn't know, but I had been to churches devoted to Francis of Assisi and there had been many pictures of him in them.

When we left, I thanked the nun profusely for letting us visit her convent. I wished her, and all the nuns, the very best for the future.

'Thank you,' the nun answered kindly. She stood at the gate, waving to us as we drove away.

During our visit, Susie had bought a *La Tau* for each of us.

'As a memory,' she said, 'of our friendship, of our journey on the Camino and as a token of this special day.'

SPIRIT AND MATTER

The walk from Castrojeriz to Boadilla del Camino was extremely peaceful, as it was free from cars and the increasingly scary cyclists. The path on which we walked was actually a dirt road covered with many sharp rocks. It was the kind of surface that made one's feet really sore. The rocks would also puncture a bicycle tyre, which might have been the reason cyclists didn't come this way. The absence of cyclists that day made it clear to me just how big a problem they were; they didn't seem to understand that the Camino was actually a pilgrimage and that their presence often stressed the pilgrims.

They always cycled at high speeds, approaching from behind. They never bothered to warn about their presence until the very last moment, yelling out or ringing their cycle bells for you to get out of the way quickly, or risk being run over. For most, the pilgrimage was a place of peace, contemplation and stillness, something the cyclists did not seem to understand. It was a great shame, since there were millions of other places the cyclists could go, but there was nowhere else where we could safely walk an actual pilgrimage. Even Richard, who was a keen cyclist himself, found them to be a real nuisance and distraction. Riding a horse wouldn't be a problem here, but a bicycle seemed totally out of place. For these reasons, I really enjoyed my walk that day.

As we came closer to Boadilla del Camino, I noticed my fellow pilgrims were walking very carefully, concentrating on the path ahead of them. It was strewn with even more sharp uneven rocks than before. I could actually feel them through the thick soles of my boots. At first, I gingerly picked my way through them. Then, when I looked up, I noticed a winding trail that meandered between them. As it turned out, this pathway was in the shape of a snake, and had been created by all the pilgrims trying to avoid the rocks. As a result, they had flattened an easier path for me to follow.

There was something amusing about following a 'snake trail', and I felt quite at peace as I pottered along. It was impossible to walk even at my normal slow pace on this kind of surface. However, walking the snake trail reminded me of walking in a large labyrinth. It became, for me, a form of meditation.

When we reached the outskirts of Boadilla del Camino, Richard and I came across a beautiful yellow-painted hacienda with an expansive green lawn in front. Close to the road, there were several benches and a water tap for the pilgrims' convenience. This was the first albergue on our way into the village. Four pilgrims were already resting there when Richard and I arrived, and one man was filling his bottle from the tap. A small stream flowed along the edge of the lawn and disappeared behind the house. Everything about this place looked extremely inviting.

Unfortunately the gate into the hacienda was closed, and a 'closed' sign out near the road made its meaning clear. Richard and I took our backpacks off and sat down on one of the benches, wondering when this lovely place would open. We didn't have to wait long for an answer. A few minutes later the gate suddenly opened with such a loud bang that we all jumped. From behind the open gate we could hear heavy metal music, at maximum volume, from poor-quality speakers. An unpleasant looking man in his 40s walked out with a bucket in his hand. His long dark hair was all over the place and looked like it hadn't been washed for days. We all stood up and stared at him, not sure what to make of what we saw. Ignoring us, the man walked over to the stream, into which he emptied his bucket full of rubbish, all the time mumbling angrily to himself.

On his way back towards the hacienda, his eyes fell on other pilgrims who had walked past us, and he started yelling at them. 'Come here! Come and stay here! Come, now!' he yelled aggressively in poor English.

The louder he yelled, the more aggressive his behaviour became, and the more the pilgrims tried to ignore him. Thankfully, he quickly ran out of energy, stopped yelling, and walked back to the house, slamming the gate after him. We all stood stunned and open mouthed at the closed gate.

'What a sodding nutcase,' an English pilgrim said, which of course made us all giggle.

'He's a raving luni,' his mate added.

'Not wrong,' said a third.

Still shaking our heads, we all agreed we would not be staying there, so we picked up our backpacks and walked off. Following the scallop shells, Richard and I continued on the same road for a while, before turning up an old cobblestoned street. Halfway up the street we noticed a large, old wooden doorway with its gates wide open. We looked in, expecting to see either a messy garage or a dirty backyard. But to our surprise, what we saw was an oasis! A large, beautiful green garden stretched out before us, adorned with pretty trees and organic art sculptures. It even had a swimming pool!

Richard and I looked at each other in amazement. 'Wow!'

We were so surprised by what we saw it took a few seconds before we realised this place was actually an albergue. We were so busy looking at the garden, we missed the sign on the gate.

'Let's go in,' Richard said cheerfully.

We walked in and followed a small stone path. As we rounded a corner next to the pool, we saw a small outdoor dining area shaded by parasols and surrounded by colourful flowerbeds.

'I think this is a small restaurant,' I whispered to Richard.

And so it was. Birds flew around everywhere and a sweet-looking white golden retriever walked over to greet us as we sat down at one of the tables. Had we reached a pilgrim heaven? A charming young man approached us, and asked what we would like. His eyes were dark brown with a warm glow, and his long dark hair was thick and curly. His name was Begona, a true Spaniard and, as we soon found out, a perfect host!

'Well, what do you have on the menu?' I asked, not knowing what to expect.

Begona then listed a whole lot of dishes they served all day. I was quite amazed and decided to go for the salad with tuna. Richard and I ended up spending many hours relaxing in the dining area. This made it possible for us to catch up with many of our Camino friends, who called in for something to eat and drink. Even Peter and Pierre stopped by, and, whenever Begona had a spare moment, he would come and sit with us. He told us that his familiy owned the place; Mama ruled the kitchen, Papa took care of the finances, Begona the pilgrims, and everybody else helped wherever needed. It was also his artwork we could see spread around the garden.

Later in the afternoon, I mentioned to Richard that we had to decide on whether to stay or move on.

'Stay!' Richard said, without any hesitation. 'This place is perfect and, besides, it is too late in the day to walk to the next village.'

'I agree!' I said.

Richard walked in and asked Begona if they had any rooms available for the night. Beside an albergue, Begona also ran a small and very cute hotel.

'Of course!' he replied and, after having booked us in, he took our backpacks and carried them up to our room.

The next morning, Richard tried to wake me up at 6am, but I fell asleep again before I had even really opened my eyes. He tried several times, but I just couldn't wake up. All I did was to mumble that I felt so tired. Eventually he gave up and walked out to find Begona. I didn't wake up until after 9am and hadn't been aware of anything that had been going on.

'Good morning!' Richard said, as I finally surfaced.

'What time is it?' I asked, a little confused.

'It's after nine but don't worry,' he answered. He then told me how he had tried to wake me up repeatedly, but seeing how tired I was, he had gone down and asked Begona if we could stay one more night.

'*No problemo,*' Begona had answered in his usual carefree way, although we had to sleep in the dormitory. All the private rooms for that night were fully booked. Even though I felt quite mentally rejuvenated after my long sleep, my body was still exhausted and sore. So I stayed in bed for another half-hour before making my way out to the bathroom for a shower. I wondered why I was so tired, but it was then I realised that I had been walking for 16 days straight. And this day my body had said stop!

For breakfast, I ordered two portions of eggs and toast, and two large cups of tea. Richard was so happy to get his toast, with jam and butter, that he also ordered a double portion. I could hardly believe it. After breakfast, Richard headed to the pool, and I walked over to keep the dog company in the shade of a big tree. Together, in the warmth of the morning, the dog and I had a long snooze.

It was way past noon before I found myself strolling randomly through the small streets of Boadilla. I came by a tiny area that looked like a misplaced, abandoned garden. It was only one to two square metres in size and was covered with long grass. There was even a tree and some flowering bushes along the edges. Looking at it, I figured there were just enough room for me to squeeze in next to the tree. The peacefulness of the village was comforting. From time to time, a pilgrim would pass close by to where I was sitting. It was fascinating to see how wonderful the pilgrims looked as they walked on by. It had never occurred to me, but there was actually something really beautiful about pilgrims and they fitted so well into the scenery.

As I sat quietly under the tree, I leant back and looked up into the sky. I thought about how much I had fallen in love with the lifestyle of a pilgrim, my friendship with Richard and the excitement of finally moving to England. I took out my journal and looked back though the notes I had written. I also looked at the postcards I had bought and the photos I had taken along the way. Soon, my head was filled with the thoughts and images of towers, important female figures, Templars and the many other things I was seeing along the Camino. Why was this iconography so strong here? I had visited an unknown number of catholic churches around Europe and I had never seen it so intense, as I did here! What had made the church chose this specific path as their second most important pilgrimage, and not the one in England? Which, for all it's history, would have been a more logical choice.

I felt overwhelmed by all the unexpected religious and historical connections I kept encountering – connections that stood out in such a way that the stories they were telling just couldn't be ignored. The things I experienced caused me to reflect more and more about the present-day roles of women and men, the issues that surrounded the concepts of femininity and masculinity, and how we viewed these in our modern society.

The research of Marija Gimbutas revealed that many ancient cultures, in and around (olden day) Europe, had been cultures of equality, where the relationship between men and women had been a natural partnership. Everything we had discovered from these times revealed societies that cultivated spirituality (not religion), creativity, peaceful co-existance and the pursuit of knowledge. Then along came the Roman Catholic church, with its extreme form of patriarchy, and there was no longer any room for partnership and equality.

I realised that the Catholic church's madonna/whore syndrome (the

Virgin Mary/Mary Magdalene) was still deeply ingrained into our modern society, disguised as the glorification of motherhood and pornification of women. The church considered there were only two ways to look at a woman; and you were either one or the other. In that respect, one could wonder how much has actually changed over the last 2000 years. But with the extreme pornification of our modern society, women's bodies were constantly exploited for the satisfaction of men's sexual needs and fantasies, at the same time teaching us that these needs and fantasies were also those of women. Hollywood and the music industry were great examples of how women's bodies were used to sell a product. But it wasn't only there; it was also in advertising. Brands such as Dolce&Gabana had used advertisements that suggested group rape of a woman, and other major brands glamorised violence towards of women.

Violence towards women today was becoming 'acceptable' and 'their own fault'. In this regard, even our concept of what a normal healthy woman should look like had been distorted. Maturity and womanly curves had been removed, and women were pressured to look like anorexic teenage boys, largely due to the fashion industry and how women were portrayed in the media. This exploitation had been so extensive that people had become numb to it and blasé about it. The horrific consequence of this was that we had lost touch with our humanity, and didn't see that the media and porn industry had now locked eyes on children and adolescents.

The irony of it all was that where sex used to be a sacred and beautiful thing, it had evolved into something deeply destructive and abusive – behaviour that unfortunately had also been acted out in large in the Catholic church (as well as others). It seemed to me that the split between women and sexuality (the Virgin Mary and Mary Magdalene), which had been created by the church, had come back to bite us. And now our children were paying for it. It wasn't hard to see how the damage from this split reached far into our society today. One had to remember that a large part of the church's power was based on the supression of women and humans' innate spirituality, whilst elevating the position and power of men.

Thankfully, this behaviour is gradually changing, but the psychological and social effects are still being lived out in the deepest layers of our society. If one thought the patterns from our childhood were hard to change and heal, think of a 1500 to 2000-year-old pattern. Not even Rome was built in a day!

All of this made me think of the New Age movement, and its role in all of this. The New Age movement was to be a new path towards the liberation of our innate spirituality and the equality of the sexes. A part of this emancipation was to change the negative connotations attached to femininity and masculinty. So new terminologies such as 'sacred femininity' and 'sacred masculinity' appeared, and almost created a new religion. The problem was, however, that they still clung to the same definitions Christianity had given us. One sacred side apologised to the other sacred side, but nothing really changed, because nobody looked at the causes behind our loss of identity and spirituality.

Many missed the point that 'man' and 'woman' were biological terms, and 'femininity' and 'masculinity' were man-made definitions. Such definitions we had created in the past in an effort to understand the human psyche and the forces behind the divine powers of creation. Whether we cared or not, we were an integral part of our cultural and historical inheritance. It was a part of who we were, our roots and collective experiences. We couldn't separate ourselves from the past any less than we could run from the future. Past, present and future were all a part of the same breath, which could explain why new definitions hadn't changed anything at all, and why we kept acting out old patterns of suppression and destruction.

So now, in 2011, men struggled to discover what it meant to be a man, and women struggled to find out what it meant to be a woman – all of us still suffering in the roles that had been given to us 1500 years earlier. I paused, and stopped writing for a moment, wondering ...?

Could it be that the idea of masculinity and femininity originally had been a way we humans had tried to describe *spirit* and *matter*? The feminine being the *spirit* (divine energy), and the masculine being *matter* (the physical manifestation of energy). If the feminine symbolised divine energy, did this explain why divinity had once been manifest in the shape of a women and her many aspects? It could certainly explain why Mary Magdalene and the belief in goddesses couldn't be destroyed. You simply can't destroy spirit!

The Great Goddess had existed since the dawn of time through many names, cultures, symbols and shapes. But the church had castrated the meaning behind the Great Goddess (that is our divinity), and all we have left are the figures of Mary Magdalene and the Virgin Mary. The deceit and manipulation involving these two women was shameless and premeditated

– something that very much mirrored the church's attitude towards women, both in the past and present. Could this be the reason the Vatican keep the knowledge they hold in their library so secret?

I sat and stared up into the sky. My head was spinning. So many pieces of the scattered puzzle were now coming together and making sense. I looked down at the last words I had written and read them again. I felt really sad. It seemed that men and women were lost in a maze, unable to get out. The whole idea of masculine and feminine was not only a great illusion; it was also a great tool to keep us in a wheel of sorrow and spiritual suppression. It was time for us to get rid of these two terms and go back to the concept of 'spirit and matter'.

Spirit and matter are at the very heart of our innate spirituality. We are all, both men and women, a part of the divine energy of creation, and we all have the power to manifest this through our actions. We were all both spirit and matter. The whole idea that masculinity equalled men, and femininity women, was nothing but an illusion we used to hold each other down. This divine energy wasn't hateful or violent, as many of our religions had shown us. It didn't give us power to abuse others; to feed on other's energies like vampires; or to turn ourselves into gurus. What it did was to give us true freedom together with real responsibility, and this could not be controlled or owned by anyone or any institution!

As I walked in the light of the scallop shell, I realised we had to support each other in order to experience and explore the diversity and incredible depth we each had inside us. Essentially, it was all about having the courage to take the journey into one's real self. As Carl Jung once said:

There is no coming to consciousness without pain. People will do anything, no matter how absurd, in order to avoid facing their own soul. One does not become enlightened by imagining figures of light, but by making the darkness conscious.

Jung's concept of darkness wasn't only about evil and pain as portrayed by the church. It was so much more. It was about our spirituality; resources and talents we had been born with; our creativity; our wisdom and power. Our inner darkness was, in fact, a true treasure box with an abundance of gold and riches; it was that which was hidden beneath the tip of the iceberg! By bringing issues out into the light and dealing with them, true healing, transformation and inner emancication could occur. The Camino was giving me so many answers to questions I had been struggling to understand since my twenties. Now I understood why nobody had been able to answer them.

Hearing the pealing of bells nearby, I collected my things and slowly made my way over to the old church. I went in and, after having inspected the interior, I sat down in one of the pews. Once again a feeling of sadness overcame me as I stared up at the altar, feeling regret that these incredible buildings were the home of an organisation that had been the instigators and perpetrators of so much violence and hate in the name of a 'loving' God. Who did they insult the most, God or humans?

As I passed a nearby stand filled with candles, I stopped and put a euro coin into a moneybox. Then I took a candle, lit it carefully and whispered:

'I light this candle in loving memory of all the women who have been disgraced, simply because of their gender. I light this candle in memory of all the beauty and resourcefulness we humans have inside of us, and I light this candle to illuminate the darkness.'

After adding my light, three small white candles stood and shone brightly. Ironically, in a church, three seemed to be a good number. As I turned around and walked out of the church, passing another Madonna with a tower and a book, I knew the path I had to follow. I knew, of course, the way back to the albergue, but I also knew what pathway to take in life. I knew that one day we humans would make it out of the loop of hate and violence – probably not in my lifetime, but one day. We had too much beauty inside us not to.

Outside, small clouds danced across a clear blue sky. I dreamt about buying the yellow hacienda and I knew exactly what kind of albergue I would make it into.

THE SINGING NUNS

After our restful stay in Boadilla, Richard and I walked on to Carrión de los Condes. The first part was the most boring stretch we had walked so far. Fortunately, the 27km to Carrión was easy, without any physically challenging sections. After about 15km we noticed a large stone wall that had been erected beside an old dirt road. It seemed to go on endlessly, as far as the eye could see. There was nothing behind it, except for some small trees and bushes leading out into the fields. We discovered that pilgrims used the small gaps in the wall to hide from view when nature called, because there was lots of used toilet paper scattered around on the ground.

At the end of the wall, I was pleased to find a typical pilgrim's bar, seemingly located in the middle of nowhere. It was in a remote rural area, with only one or two farmhouses to be seen. This was a recurring pattern on the Camino. No matter where the pilgrims were, a bar magically seemed to appear. It could be in someone's driveway, a small garden or in front of someone's house. It often seemed that the locals enjoyed the contact and the chance to talk to pilgrims. This was again one of the many examples of how the constant flow of pilgrims along the route had brought locals some welcome income.

As we turned into the bar area, I immediately spotted Peter, who was resting on a chair with a look of absolute bliss. When he saw us, he broke into a huge smile and waved us over.

'Louise!' he called out as we walked towards his table, 'you've got to see this!'

He took out his big camera and started flicking through some of his photos.

'Remember we talked about Mathilda and Orval? Well, look what I found the other day!' Peter turned his camera around so we could see the screen. 'I actually saw a picture of Orval's symbol, the fish with the ring in its mouth. Here on the Camino!'

'Wow, that is so cool!' I said with surprise. 'What would that symbol be doing here on the Camino?' I wondered out loud.

'I don't know.' Peter laughed and shrugged his shoulders. 'But I thought it was funny, since we had only been talking about her the last time we met.'

And so once again, Peter and I immersed ourselves in a discussion about Mathilda and Orval. Whenever Peter and I met after this, we would always spend a minute or two discussing Orval and Mathilda, as it turned out Peter knew a lot about Belgium's history. After this discussion, Peter went on to tell us about his camping experiences of the previous day.

Back along the road, before the wall, Peter had passed a newly built toilet facility designed for pilgrims. It had been rather late in the day and the sun had begun to set. Only cyclists were out on the roads at that time of day. As the last group of cyclists had moved on, Peter decided to stay and had walked around the area to find a suitable site to erect his little tent. It was too late for him to try to reach a formal camping ground, and with a toilet facility this was the best alternative.

Like a Lucky Luke story from the wild west, Peter described how fantastic it had been to camp so far away from any other people, and how he had watched the sun go down as he cooked his dinner over his gas stove. I could almost hear the banjo playing in the background. As the last pink and red colours of sunset disappeared over the horizon, a blanket of shining stars had rolled out above him and covered the sky.

'So there I sat, under the beautiful night sky and ate my dinner. Alone in nature – except for when my husband called to say goodnight – and I thought to myself, that I am in the most beautiful place in the whole world. I felt so happy, just so incredibly happy!'

He looked at us for a moment, tears appearing in his eyes.

'Then this morning, I woke up while it was still dark, and as I stood outside my tent, in the first morning light, I noticed a large concrete tank full of water in the field behind me. So I took off all my clothes and jumped up into it! And here, in my own jacuzzi in the middle of nowhere, I sat and watched the sun come up.'

Peter's eyes sparkled as he told his story, and on his lips rested that very special smile, that only a pilgrim who had experienced the magic of the Camino, could smile. None of us really said much afterwards. We just sat and smiled at each other, maybe because there really wasn't anything to add, for experiences like these could only be felt. When the Camino touched our souls like this, the only place we could be was above the earth and beneath the stars. That very place where one discovered that life could be so much more than we would ever be able to understand.

Peter then picked up his Basque hat from the chair next to him, put it on, and farewelled us: 'It's time for me to start walking again.'

Richard and I looked at him and nodded knowingly. 'See you around,' we said.

'See you around, and *Buen Camino*!'

Peter's big blue eyes sparkled with life as he turned around and departed with a glorious smile on his face.

Richard and I left shortly after Peter, and by the time we reached Carrión de los Condes, we had walked a total of 27km – an exceptionally long walk for me. However, due to the previous day's rest in Boadilla and the flat easy walk that day, I felt remarkably well. Richard still wished for the comforts that a hotel could provide, so once again we located a small charming hotel. Neither of us needed a lengthy afternoon rest, so we continued with our usual after-walk activities, gathered up our laundry and walked out to find a laundromat. The woman in reception said we could find one in an old albergue, just up in the town square next to the church.

The town square turned out to be located very close to our hotel. It also turned out to be just my style; romantic, rustic, full of atmosphere and history. I would never become tired or bored with all these old villages and their sand-coloured cobbledstones – stones that, when the sun hit their surfaces, changed into a warm glowing yellow. I felt so nourished from the warmth that radiated from them. Upon reaching the square, we turned right, as the receptionist had instructed us, and soon found the old albergue. What the receptionist hadn't told us was that the albergue was a part of a functioning convent. When we arrived at their doorstep, a nun stood at the entrance and greeted us. I asked her if they had a place where we could wash our clothes.

'Yes, we have laundry,' the nun answered kindly and pointed inside, 'over there.'

Richard asked the nun if they would let us use the washing machine although we weren't staying there, but we would of course pay for it.

'No no!' the nun answered, whilst laughingly shaking her head.

'Sorry?' Richard said, not sure of what she had said 'no' to.

'No no, we wash for you!' she replied happily.

In the back of my mind, I couldn't help but think, that just as grumpy and cold the men at Roncesvalles had been, just as happy, cheerful and caring the sisters were here. However, there seemed to be four nuns 'on duty' that afternoon with only one aim, and that was to provide love and care for every pilgrim. It didn't matter whether they were just passing by on the street, or actually wanted to stay at their albergue for the night.

As the nuns' care was so sincere and authentic, I insisted on paying.

'No no,' the nun said as she broke into another huge grin. She kindly, but firmly, took my green laundry bag out of Richard's hand, and told us to come back about 5pm. Then she disappeared with our laundry and a satisfied smile on her face. Not being fully clear on what had just transpired, I looked at Richard rather blankly.

'How much is this really going to cost us?' I asked, worrying that we could end up with a huge bill.

'I don't know,' he said just as blankly, 'but whatever they want, it will be worth it with all the love and effort they put into it.'

'Yeah, you're right,' I agreed, and stopped worrying about the cost.

We continued down the street, and spent the hour we had to spare exploring Carrión. To my great irritation, the church I had planned to visit turned out to be closed. So did all the other ones in town, which resulted in Richard having to listen to a long line of my complaints. At exactly 5pm, we arrived back at the convent. All four nuns were now standing outside, busily greeting and talking to pilgrims. Everybody was received equally with the same care and attention. The nun who had disappeared with our laundry recognised us immediately.

'*Uno momento*,' she said and disappeared back inside.

A few moments later, she returned and handed me our finished laundry. Instinctly I looked into the bag, just to discover that our clothes not only looked very clean and dry, they were also neatly folded.

'How much do we owe you?' Richard asked politely.

The nun laughed again. 'Nothing!'

'Nothing?' I questioned.

'Nothing!' she replied. 'But if you like, you donate some money to our Convento.' She pointed towards an old money box that hung on the wall inside.

She then asked: 'Would you like to stay for afternoon sing-along?'

Richard looked at me rather anxiously, but how could we say no when they had been so kind to us.

'Oh, come on, Richard!' I said. 'We will just stay for one song!' How bad could that be? Well, bad.

We put 10 euro in the old moneybox, walked to the very back of the common room and sat down on a hard wooden bench. It was surprising how quickly the room filled up with pilgrims. The nuns quickly handed out little song booklets, then one nun picked up her guitar and all the nuns began to sing. Their well-trained voices blended with those of the pilgrims' somewhat tuneless and rusty voices.

After a half-hour of singing, I looked over at a pilgrim's watch, wondering when the sing-along would be over. As if they had read my thoughts, one of the nuns began talking about a special group song we all could join in. One of the pilgrims knew the song, and introduced an international version where the short chorus of the song was to be sung in a different language each time.

The nuns found the version very funny, and laughed so hard that tears ran down their cheeks. They agreed that we immediately had to try it out. After having gone through the song a few times, so we could all learn it, the nun with the guitar started to ask where each pilgrim came from.

'Where do you come from?' she asked a man sitting next to her.

'From Quebec!' he answered, and proceeded to teach us the words of the chorus in French, so we all could sing it together.

'Where are you from?' the nun asked the next pilgrim.

'Germany!' said the woman, and so we all sang the chorus in German.

After we had been through Norway, Argentina, Korea, Portugal, Russia, New Zealand, Greece and many, *many* more countries, I started wondering if there were any countries we hadn't mentioned. My bottom was starting to feel numb. We had been singing for over an hour now and I couldn't take it much longer. Just as I was getting ready to lean towards Richard and mention that it was time to leave, the nun with the guitar looked over at me.

'Where do you come from?' she asked enthusiastically. Every head in the room turned to look at me and, unlike myself, they all looked to be happy and excited about continuing.

I forced a big smile and said: 'Denmark!' And so we all sang the chorus in Danish and everybody laughed and clapped their hands – even me (although I might have looked somewhat tense).

After having sung the chorus in Danish, I was convinced the song would be over, but the nun happily continued, looking over at Richard. 'Where do you come from?'

'Australia!' Richard said with a smile, and once again, everybody broke out into joyful laughter before singing the chorus in English, for at least the fifth time.

By now I had suffered enough, so as soon as all the eyes in the group moved on to the next candidate, I leant over to Richard and said: 'I'm leaving. Are you coming or staying?'

He looked at me and asked teasingly: 'I thought you wanted to stay to the end?'

As I stood up, I mumbled that he should zip it, smiled politely at the nuns and quietly walked out, trying not to draw to much attention to myself. We walked into the first bar we came to and ordered some well-earned drinks. Then we went outside to relax in the late afternoon sun.

'Cu-cu-ru-coo!'

That was Susie's call! Surprised, we looked around to see where it came from. Susie was hiding around the corner and laughed when we spotted her. She looked very tanned and dressed in a bright blue T-shirt. Our five-minute drink break turned into a couple of hours, with wine, juice and tasty Spanish tapas. The simplicity of life filled the evening as we enjoyed each other's company.

It was way past Susie's usual bedtime when we finally said goodnight and went our separate ways. On our way back to the hotel, Richard and I stopped at a restaurant to order homemade hamburgers, french fries and beer. It would take something special to recover from that seemingly, never-ending religious singing, no matter how much I loved those nuns.

TERRADILLOS DE LOS TEMPLARIOS

I knew Richard was leaving the Camino in five days time. I also knew, that I wanted to continue my pilgrimage after that time, but I wondered what it would be like without his company. Richard had also begun to think more and more about leaving the Camino, leaving me and what it would be like to return home and face the many life changes he couldn't put off any longer.

We never talked much about what would happen after the Camino, and what would there be to talk about anyway? Our time together would end the very moment our paths separated, and we would go back to where we had come from, adjusting our lives to the changes that had occurred during our pilgrimage. I also felt a little unsure of how to best spend our last days together. Should we try to reach Leon and spend the days there? To get to Leon in time would force us walk an increased number of kilometres each day. I knew neither of us wanted that as it would only cause more physical pain.

After Carrión de los Condes, the cyclists became a problem again. They were more aggressive now, and did nothing to show any consideration towards the walking pilgrims. All of us who walked had, at times, to jump for our lives if we didn't want to be run over, literally. There were even certain stretches of our walk where the cyclists completely ruined that special mental and spiritual space that made this pilgrimage so special.

Having nearly been hit by a cyclist, who rode up on the sidewalk so he could ride faster, I came to the conclusion that cyclists should be totally excluded from the pathways the walking pilgrims used. It was ridiculous, and it wasn't fair that they ruined this special pilgrimage, when they had millions of other places around the world where they could ride their bikes. The Camino was one of a kind, and should be kept as a place where it was safe to walk, especially for women and the many pilgrims who walked alone.

Richard shook his head as he checked the scratches from when the cyclist had pushed me into the wall. 'Tsk tsk tsk,' he said iritated. 'This is not the right place for adventurous cyclists!'

Also feeling angry, I nodded in agreement. It just wasn't fair. However, the cyclists must had known that a dirt road, filled with stones, was coming up, for a short time later they all disappeared. As a result, the rest of the walk towards Caldadilla de la Cueza was wonderfully peaceful and again we were free to enjoy the beautiful countryside. When we arrived at Caldadilla, about lunchtime, we finally sat down to rest and talked about how we would spend our last days together. It turned out Richard had one dream, and that was to stay at a Knights Templar albergue. Looking through the different albergues in Brierley's book, we found one in Terradillos de Templarios. The albergue was named Jacques de Molay albergue. Jacques de Molay was the last grand master of the Knights Templar, so it couldn't have been better. We decided to take a taxi to Terradillos, and 15 minutes later we were on our way.

I had expected that a Templar albergue would be an old castle filled with secret rooms and interesting objects everywhere. Well, upon arrival, I discovered that this was certainly not the case. The albergue looked just like most of the other ones along the Camino. But it had a small very cosy central garden, and a large roofed terrace with pleasant views. The woman who worked there stood behind a little counter, where she registered the incoming pilgrims. She had a particularly serious look on her face. Unaffected, I just smiled and talked to her like I would anyone else. I asked if they had any smaller rooms available, which she confirmed they had. Without changing her facial expression, she wrote our names down in the registration book, stamped our pilgrims' passes and collected her money.

As this all transpired I stood silently watching her. I wasn't sure what I had done or said, but as the women returned the passes, she suddenly gave me huge smile. After that, she smiled at me every time we met, even though she continued to receive all the other pilgrims with the same introductory grave look.

While Richard went to bed to rest, I sat down in the garden and talked to a Dutch pilgrim. It seemed we had walked much the same distance each day, and stayed in the same villages without ever meeting up. His name was Aalt, and was a very down-to-earth and easy person to be with. Aalt had travelled a lot, which led us to talk about the problems associated with tourism. We had both experienced how too much tourism had ruined the authentic culture and nature of different places – something we both feared would also happen to the Camino in the near future.

At dinner time, candles had been lit and white tablecloths had been spread over the round tables. The previously dark dining room had now come to life, and a small bar had been opened for the pilgrims. Richard and I came to share a table with Renate, her two German friends and Aalt. Smiles, laughter and inspired conversations danced across our table in spite of the usual tiredness as our traditional Menu del Dia was served. First we had a salad, then a delicious tasting fish with a few vegetables, and last of all, a small dessert. The food here tasted better than average. However, in spite of the nice surroundings, the good food and the good company, this village made me feel uncomfortable. There was something about it that made me feel uneasy. I felt it wasn't a good place to stay and I just couldn't wait to get moving the next morning.

So we got up early the next morning and were quickly out the door. The woman, who had been so serious when I had arrived, was now standing outside. Her kind eyes followed me as I walked out of the albergue. As I reached the street, she called out a 'Buen Camino!' and waved me goodbye. Putting on my hat, I looked back at her, wondering why her behaviour had changed, but thought one should never judge a book by its cover. She was such a good example of that. If I had responded to her with my own negativity, I would never have seen that warm-hearted, kind person she turned out to be. I smiled and returned her wave before walking on. If we had lived in the same town, I felt she could have become a good friend.

A long time later, reflecting on my meeting with this woman, I realised she had illustrated to me a really important point. This was that when I was able to meet another person from a grounded feeling of who I was, positivity and realness often was the result. In that way, I was able to meet other people with a neutral openness instead of expectations for them to fulfil certain needs in me.

We departed the village in silence, and at a faster pace than usual. Once out of there, Richard gave a huge sigh of relief. 'God, what an uncomfortable energy that village had!'

I looked at him with surprise. 'You noticed that too?'

'Did I? I mean, our albergue was fine – good food, great company – but, wow, am I glad to be out of there.'

'What do you think it was?' I asked.

He thought for a minute, before answering. 'Louise, have you noticed that every time we plan to stop at a Templar site, we just walk on – without even discussing it.'

I thought about it for a moment and tried to recall a specific instance. 'Yeah, you're actually right, except for San Juan de Ortega, although I didn't even visit the Templar church there, which is highly unusual for me.'

Richard nodded, lost in thought. 'True, and it's not that these places felt haunted or anything like that. It's more like they had been totally drained of energy. It was the same thing with the last village; it just felt empty of anything positive.'

The more I thought about it, the more I could recognise what Richard had sensed. Then Richard, who apparently also had been thinking about this, said: 'Have you noticed, how we do so many things intuitively here on the Camino? We never really thought about why we just moved on, nor really spent any time discussing it. The energy of these places just didn't feel good. They weren't in harmony with the energy of the Camino – or maybe, just not in harmony with how we felt on the Camino.'

I thought about this for a while, before replying. 'In reality, that's also how we've chosen where and when we stop. Then, when we walk into our albergue, many of the pilgrims we feel in harmony with have also chosen to stay there for the night.'

We both laughed at this new insight. For a person like Richard, this kind of thinking and experiencing, was way out of his comfort zone. Now he seemed quite matter of fact about it for he continued: 'It's true, though, because when we meet up at the albergues, we all seem equally surprised to see each other. Out of the many albergues to choose from, we all end up at the same place. It's like there is an invisible email service along the Camino!'

'Isn't that true!' I said laughing. 'The Camino is really about listening, isn't it?'

'It sure is,' Richard said. 'It sure is …'

'For *those with ears to hear*….' I thought to myself.

We continued walking in silence. Now that we had shaken off the uncomfortable energy of Terradillos, the day seemed to take on a new beauty. The walk was also fairly comfortable – no cars and no cyclists, only the lush vegetation and vast scenery surrounding us.

I found myself again wondering how Richard and I could get the best out of our last days together. Should we go to Leon and play tourist for a couple of days? It felt like a good idea, but I was not sure if that was what Richard really wanted. Maybe he just wanted to stay on the Camino and enjoy as much of the walk as he possibly could? Which I completely understood of course, but I didn't feel comfortable bringing it up. I felt it was up to him.

Between Terradillos and Sahagún, on the top of a steep hill, stood two lounge chairs sculpted out of concrete. As well as being works of art, they were also a gift to the pilgrims as a place to rest. The place was quite desolate, so it was a rather unusual and surprising sight that met our eyes. When we reached the hill top, the two pilgrims who had been sitting in the lounge chairs saw us and signalled that we could use the chairs.

'How lucky is that?' I said cheerfully and walked towards them.

It was absolutely great to sit on those chairs, looking over the panoramic vista. It was funny to see the surprised expression on people's faces as they arrived at the top of the hill and saw us sitting there. The great thing was, that no matter how tired they were, the sight made every pilgrim break out into a huge smile.

I put on my fleece as it had become quite cloudy and a little chilly. I was again thinking about Leon and decided it was time to talk to Richard about the subject.

'Richard,' I said, looking at him, 'I've been thinking about how we should spend our last days together.

'Ah, me too!' he replied, sounding quite relieved that I had initiated the discussion.

'Well, what have you been thinking?' I asked.

'No, you go first. You started.'

'Well, I was wondering if we should skip the walk into Leon and take the train instead? Then we could spend the last days together there, and just be tourists. It will be easier for you to find transport to Santiago from there, as well.'

Surprised, Richard lifted his head and looked at me.

'That's exactly the same idea I had! It's incredible how often we think the same things,' he said, looking quite pleased.

He sat down and found Brierley's book in one of the front pockets of his backpack.

'Let me see,' he mumbled, as he flicked through some pages. 'Yes, here it is. There is a railway station in Sahagún, so we should be able to catch a train to Leon from there.'

'Sounds good!' I said. 'That's settled then.'

I put on my backpack and tightened up the straps. Two pilgrims arrived at the same time, and just as the pilgrims before us had done, we signalled for them to use the chairs. It was their turn now.

'They're great and quite comfortable!' I told them.

They both seemed excited about their unexpected luck, but who wouldn't be?

Sahagún turned out to be a large picturesque town. Many of the buildings we passed on our way had an authentic old adobe look about them. Sahagún also had a quiet, relaxed feel about it; it wasn't overly busy or crowded like some of the other larger towns and cities we had passed through.

As we came closer to the centre of town, we reached a T-intersection in the road. Across from us, on the right, was a bar that seemed to be perched on top of a high stone wall. We stopped to look at the map in Brierley's book, hoping it would show us the quickest way to the train station. As we tried to find our present location on the map, we heard a voice call out.

'Hi there!' A woman was trying to attract our attention.

We both looked up, and saw a couple of pilgrims waving at us.

'If you are looking for a place to rest, you should try this café. Their cakes are fabulous!' The man next to her nodded enthusiastically in agreement.

Richard looked at me. 'What do you think?' he asked, looking positive about the suggestion.

'Yeah, that sounds good to me – we needed a break anyway,' I replied.

Richard looked up towards the couple, and asked if there was any room up there.

'There's room at our table,' the man said, and then explained how to find our way up to the café.

With a little bit of luck and a lot of huffing and puffing, we made it over to their table without tipping over too many glasses or stepping on too many feet. Our modest backpacks and big boots suddenly seemed rather clumsy in such a crowded place, so it was quite a relief to finally find a safe haven and a seat.

The couple, who turned out to be Canadian, smiled and also made room for our backpacks on the floor, under their table. After having introduced ourselves, Richard stayed at the table, watching our things, while I walked over to what was actually a little bakery, and not a café. All the cakes looked mouthwatering and it took me forever to decide. I knew Richard liked cakes with apple filling and whipped cream. I preferred strawberries and light custard. Thinking back and forth, I decided on three different cakes that we could share. One of them had been specifically recommended by the Canadian couple. They said they had each eaten two of them because they had been so good.

When I returned with our cakes and drinks, Richard and the couple were in deep conversation. It turned out, that Lorrena, the woman, was completing part of her PhD scholarship in Europe, whilst Michael stayed back in Canada working on their new house. They had recently organised a holiday together and decided to walk the Camino. Lorrena, however, had sadly developed the pilgrims' affliction – terrible blisters. Her feet had become so sore that she needed transportation to get from one town to the next. Michael, however, had decided to walk each day and then they would meet up later at their albergue.

Discovering that the three of us, minus Michael, were taking the same train to Leon, we all walked together up to the railway station, to buy our tickets. We had roughly four hours before the train departed and agreed to meet back at the station later on. Richard suggested Lorrena buy some adhesive plaster and anti-bacterial cream for her feet. Michael and Lorrena thanked him and headed off to find a pharmacy. Richard and I went off to explore the many wonders Sahagún had to offer. In fact, I liked it so much that I decided I wanted to stay there on my next pilgrimage.

Almost as soon as the train to Leon left the station, I fell asleep. The calm rhythmic movement made it impossible not to. Lorrena, Richard and Susie (who had surprised us by showing up at the railway station) either sat, looking out the window or dozed off like me. Soon, it would also be time for Susie to return home. She didn't talk much about it, though, and seemed eager to enjoy her last days as a pilgrim. She, too, had come to love the Camino deeply. I wasn't quite clear on when or how Susie would be leaving. I only knew it was in a few days time, and that she was also going to spend those last days in Leon with a friend.

Richard woke us up as the train arrived in Leon. I looked out the window and was immediately overwhelmed by the large crowds of busy people and colourful billboards, all competing to attract our attention. Once outside the train, Susie and Lorrena said goodbye, and headed off to their respective meeting places. The other pilgrims who had been on the train with us avoided looking at each other. Shame was written all over their faces, and everybody rushed to get out of the station. All the noise, the commotion, the people and limited space felt rather claustrophobic. Out on the busy street, one could breathe again, and the other pilgrims quickly disappeared into the anonymity of the city. Nobody at the albergues would know that you had arrived by train, and the chance that somebody would 'kiss and tell' was very remote.

After the Camino, it occurred to me that the shame might not have been about the judgement from the other pilgrims. To me, to really be transformed by the Camino, one had to walk, touch and breathe in the energy of its sacred pathways, day after day. So I wondered if the shame was actually about cheating themselves, rather than the unspoken pilgrims' rule.

LEON

Oh Leon, I had heard so much about you. It was truly a beautiful city, sparkling with life and history. I had heard from many that the Camino would change dramatically after Leon because of the vast numbers of new pilgrims who started their pilgrimage from here. The kinds of pilgrims who started here would be very different from those I had come to know. Many would travel in larger groups, they would be noisier and they would fight to get to the albergues first. And worst of all, the tranquil pathways would from now on become very crowded with those I called the commercialised pilgrims, with and without bikes.

I just couldn't believe that my Camino could be anything else but sunny days filled with happiness and tranquillity. It had been so since my very first day, and I couldn't imagine it changing. But I had a lot to learn. Initially, I didn't really like being back in a city again. From the moment I got off the train, I missed the freedom and space of the Camino, but upon arriving in the old part of the city, I started to change my mind. It was filled with many incredibly beautiful old buildings, cobbled streets full of atmosphere and a magnificent cathedral. Judging from the outside, I knew I would find many things of interest in there, but that visit would have to wait for now.

Richard, in the meantime, had spotted a small hotel where he thought it would be romantic for us to stay. It was located in the main walking street that led up to the Plaza Regia, in the old centre of town. It was called the Hotel Paris. After checking in, we went out to find something to eat for lunch. Walking through a maze of small streets, we ended up at the Plaza San Martin, an extremely cosy square filled with many small restaurants.

The square echoed with the sounds of happy voices and had a lively atmosphere about it.

We decided to eat at a lovely restaurant that served Italian food. It advertised a Menu del Dia, for both lunch and dinner, and had comfortable seating outside. Although the pictures displaying the different dishes didn't look particularly attractive, it turned out that this little Italian place was a good choice. It was owned by a great cook who just loved his guests. My spaghetti bolognaise was simply fantastic, and so was the salad. Even Richard, who usually survived on a Cortado and a croissant for lunch, ordered the same meal for himself, and ate every bit of it.

While sitting and enjoying our food, Pierre happened to pass by and stopped to join us. This time he was alone and, following our recommendation, he also had the spaghetti bolognaise together with a Cortado. He seemed quite happy to talk about trivial things and having a break from whatever he was doing. He too, knew of the changes that were about to occur on the Camino. He looked sad and disappointed thinking back on how it had been the other time he had walked the Camino.

After Pierre left us to find his albergue, Will then appeared. He had been trying, in the maze of little streets, to find his albergue for quite some time, with no luck. He too joined us for a Cortado and spaghetti bolognaise. Will had previously been quite helpful with my plan to move to England. He had also offered to be my 'contact person' there and help me out whenever I needed it. However, we quickly ended up talking about the Celts again. Amongst several things, Will talked a lot about how the area of the Camino and Finisterra had been very sacred to them. There was something about the Celts that felt really important to me, and I wondered what pieces of the puzzle I had yet to discover about the Camino.

Our host was just wonderful! He took such good care of us and whomever stopped at our table. He was quick to serve whatever we ordered, and he would always ask if we needed more parmesan cheese with our meals. It always annoyed me when restaurants were cheap with their parmesan. The owner had this warm caring energy, a great attitude and his prices fitted a pilgrim's wallet.

A few hours later, as we were about to continue our stroll through the old part of Leon, we ran into several other Camino friends including the newest ones, Ingrid and Kurt, the German couple whom we had been dining with in St Juan. They radiated abundant energy, and smiled from ear to ear when they saw us. They had, without a doubt, a fabulous time and looked very much in love. They, too, were going to spend several days in Leon. For me, it felt like a luxury, knowing that I wouldn't have to walk for the next few days.

Whilst in Leon, Richard and I talked a lot about the Camino and life in general, but, as usual, we talked very little about what would happen after leaving. Again, what was there to say? Even if we had wanted more than just friendship, it wasn't possible. But either way, I hoped that we could continue to be good friends. Returning home by myself, with all the experiences of the Camino, just seemed too much to bear. The days we spent together in Leon were filled with immense joy and good times. We met many of our pilgrim friends, who either stayed for a day or two or moved on straight away.

Like a true Mary Poppins, Renate suddenly showed up one afternoon just as a massive rainstorm hit Leon. Chairs and tables from the small bars were blown across the big, but now completely empty, Plaza Regla. Umbrellas flew out of people's hands and joined the chairs and tables as they danced wherever the wind and rain took them. Richard and I were forced to run for shelter under one of the many archways that led into the various buildings that lined the square. A few fearless pilgrims, completely covered by large rain jackets, were the only ones who dared to cross the open square. One of these pilgrims stopped just in front of the archway where Richard and I were standing. As she peered out from under the hood of her rain jacket, we recognised Renate's face.

'Renate!' I called out. 'Hey, Renate!'

Renate looked around to see where the voice came from, but I had to walk out from our shelter before she could actually see me. It turned out that Renate wasn't bothered by the rain at all!

'It'll pass,' she said. 'It's just rain.'

However cold and wet Renate looked, she still seemed happy, and as usual, on a mission. Nothing was going to hold her up, not even the bad weather. So as soon as the rain eased a little, we said our goodbyes, not knowing that this would be the last time we would see her.

Sadly, I knew that Susie would be leaving the day before Richard. We all agreed not to say formal goodbyes as it would be too painful. Instead we enjoyed and appreciated the many spontaneous and wonderful times we experienced with Susie, as we constantly ran into each other during our time in Leon. We exchanged email addresses and double-checked them to make sure they were correct.

Richard and I spent our last days together walking around and exploring the many wonders of Leon. Every day, we would pass by the grand cathedral where I walked the tiny labyrinth that was laid out in front of it. Richard loved to sit on a nearby bench, listening to a man playing his harmonica. We bought books from a little shop (which had a surprisingly large selection of English books), and ate ice-creams from an ice-cream parlour on the corner in front of the church. It was such a great place to just sit and watch life go by. For a short time, we had left the harsh life of the pilgrimage behind us.

Sitting outside in the sun, we saw many pilgrims passing by, some never even looking up. They seemed absorbed in their own world or maybe it was because they were afraid of missing the scallop shell in a busy city and losing their way. I knew what that was like. Or maybe it was because they wanted to get through Leon as quickly as possible, and get back out into the countryside. I had the impression that pilgrims were like an invisible stream of life that ran through this old city.

Catedral de León was an outstanding piece of Gothic architecture, and it was huge! The rosetta window inside the cathedral was enormous and much prettier than the famous one in Notre Dame. I was literally in art heaven. What impressed me the most, were the vast numbers of magnificent stained-glass windows that filled the cathedral with colourful light. The ceilings were so high it felt like they reached up into heaven, and the lights from the many windows created a fantastic larger-than-life effect, creating a divine presence in the building.

There was so much amazing iconography throughout this church, even many symbols I understood as Jewish related. But what stole my attention was a statue of the Virgin Mary holding the infant Jesus in her arms. Three large towers were suspended above her head, resembling a gigantic crown. There was no doubt. Both Mary and the infant Jesus were holding an egg in their hands; the pagan symbol for rebirth and new life.

However, the serpent-dragon creature she was standing on left me somewhat puzzled. In Christian settings, the serpent-dragon was usually slain by the Archangel Michael or Saint George. Then why did I seen so many females in church settings along the Camino, standing on a serpent-dragon, not killing one?

Studies of many indigenous, ancient cultures throughout the world, including their shamanistic practices, showed that the serpent-dragon as a symbol had been around since the earliest of times (Narby, J. (1996) The Cosmic Serpent – DNA and the Origins of Knowledge.) What was interesting here was that all these cultures, independent of each other, described meeting serpent-dragon shaped creatures, during their shamanistic journeys. When the drawings of these creatures, as well as drawings from other shamanistic experiences, were later studied, it became obvious that what they were really describing was the helical pattern and make-up of our own DNA. But these cultures didn't have the scientific technique to understand this, so the DNA took a shape that was well known to them; the S shape of a serpent. And so the snake came to symbolise the seed of all knowledge and spirituality.

Somehow, many diverse ancient and indigenous peoples were able to tap into a kind of collective spiritual consciousness and experience a higher intelligence of life. Sadly, this ancient symbol of our innate spirituality was made evil by Christianity. So when Saint George and the archangel Michael killed the serpent-dragon, they illustrated, in fact, the very aim of the church. The serpent-dragon had to be made evil, dangerous and be killed so we learnt to fear one of the strongest powers we held: our spirituality and the knowlege of it.

If Mary had been standing on the serpent, without Cybele's crown and the egg, it could have represented the same notion as Saint George killing the serpent-dragon. But seeing Mary with both Cybele's crown, the egg *and* the serpent-dragon, pointed me towards the secret teachings of ancient (goddess) cultures in Europe (where the snake also had been an important symbol). This again pointed towards the origins of the Virgin Mary.

Were all of these women I had seen along the way, holding the original purpose and teachings of the ancient Camino? Were they behind the dreams that had led me on this pilgrimage? And was this what the legend of Saint James was really trying to hide? I was very much beginning to think so!

The following day was our last together before having to say goodbye. Richard was travelling by train to Santiago, where he would fly on to Barcelona and then home to Australia.

A former pilgrim had told me, that the way out of Leon could be compared with our exhausting walk into Burgos. I therefore decided to catch a bus for the short trip to Astorga. If the way out was only half as bad as they had said, I wasn't in the mood. I knew that it would be hard enough in itself to walk out of Leon without Richard. But for unknown reasons, going to Astorga felt extremely important to me. There was a tingling, knowing feeling in my body every time I saw that name written in Brierley's book. I wondered why?

The next morning, as we were packing our things and getting ready to leave, Richard looked at me thoughtfully and asked: 'Louise, if you could have any wish come true, what would that be?'

I looked at him for a moment. 'My wish would then be that you could be in Denmark, with me, on my birthday, which is on October 14.'

Richard smiled, said okay and shrugged his shoulders, seemingly satisfied with my answer

He then turned around and picked up the guidebook from his backpack, and tore the book into two halves.

'Here!' he said, and gave me the second half. 'Take this with you, so you can find your way. You can write about your experiences under 'Reflections', and then post it to me after you return to Denmark. Then, when I read it, it will be as if I had walked the last part of the Camino with you.'

We both had tears in our eyes. Richard quickly glanced away, trying to hide his emotions. Then he bent down and picked up his blue hiking pole and passed it to me. 'Here, take this with you, too. It has helped me a lot, and it will help you, too.'

Without a word, I reached for his hiking pole. I knew how much it had meant to him, and I knew how much it would help me in the mountains that were to come.

As Richard finished his packing, he also gave me the leftovers of his Fixomull and anti-bacterial cream.

'Even if you don't need them, I'm sure others will,' he said and closed his backpack.

He stared thoughtfully at it for a few moments, before making eye contact with me again.

'Is there anything else that I have you would like?'

'Um, no, not really, but thank you. All of this is really great!'

'You know,' he said quietly, 'for many years, I have dreamt about going back to England and seeing where I grew up. I could stop by and visit you in Denmark on the way?'

'That would be lovely!' I said, feeling hopeful. 'You would be welcome any time!'

The thought that we might be seeing each other in the future was comforting; however, it didn't ease the pain of our imminent separation.

My bus was due to leave shortly before Richard's train, so he walked me down to the bus station to see me off. Neither of us said much. We had shared so many experiences along the Camino and discussed so many deep topics, but now we seemed to have run out of words, unable to share the deep sadness that welled up within us.

While we waited for the bus, I kept wishing that Richard would change his mind and continue the pilgrimage with me. I knew this was unrealistic, since he had to go back to his work at the hospital and I had to go home and proceed with my own plans. However, life sometimes works in it own mysterious ways.

The bus arrived on time and people quickly entered. Richard put my backpack in the luggage compartment under the bus, and then we double-checked each other's phone numbers, email and skype addresses. Tears kept welling up as we stood there, holding each other.

'I promise I will ring you before I fly back to Australia,' he whispered to me.

As the bus driver called out for the last passagers to enter, we reluctantly let go of each other.

'Goodbye, and take care,' I said quietly, realising this might be the last time I would ever see him.

'You too, Louise … you, too.'

I had wanted to tell him how dear he had become to me, and just how much our friendship meant to me, but because he lived with another woman, I felt it was inappropriate. So I turned around without another word and walked into the bus. By the time I had found my seat and looked out through the window, Richard had left. Immediately after, the bus backed up and then drove quickly out of the station, keeping to its schedule.

I kept looking for Richard from my window seat, but couldn't see him anywhere. I figured he had walked straight to the railway station. But, as we turned the corner, I saw him leaning against a tree, looking for me in the bus. I could almost have jumped out through my window. Instead, all I could do was to keep waving and waving, hoping he would see me.

A few seconds later, we were out of sight.

JESUS CROWNING THE GRAIL QUEEN

Twenty minutes after I had left Leon, my bus stopped outside the beautiful surrounding city wall of Astorga. Here I had a clear view of the grandiose Palacio Episcopal and the back of the Catedral Santa Maria. I felt relieved being here, having made it safely, and in one piece, out of Leon. But however sad I felt upon arriving in Astorga, I immediately fell in love with the town.

I quickly collected my backpack and walked through a lovely park, up an beautiful old stone staircase and through an opening in the city wall. This led me directly into Plaza Catedral, where Gaudi's *palacia*, together with the magnificent cathedral and its museum, were located. For someone who loved Gaudi as much as I did, it was hard to admit that I didn't like his *palacia* at all. It looked like a Gothic nightmare.

I walked over to the huge fence that surrounded the cathedral and found a place to sit. Here I searched for Brierley's book to see where the town's albergues were located. I decided to stay at San Javier Albergue because it was located only two minutes from the cathedral. I had a feeling that I would be spending a lot of time there; I could actually feel it in my stomach. I wanted to go and see the cathedral then and there, but as it didn't open until later in the day, I walked directly to San Javier.

The moment I opened the door into the albergue, a storm of loud voices accosted me. There were masses of pilgrims everywhere, yelling and pushing each other so they could all get through. The two hospitalarios, who were sitting and registering the vast number of pilgrims, looked blown away by all the chaos. At this place, nobody even bothered to look at each

201

other or even say hi. I just shook my head and walked down the stairs to join the line for registration.

As soon as I had registered and received my stamp, I found an available bed where I left my backpack and immediately walked back out into Astorga. I felt very lonely as I walked through its streets. I visited Museo Chocolate, the different city squares, the back streets, smaller churches and even some local shops, but it still felt like there was something missing. And that 'something' was Richard and his companionship. It was also sad knowing that I wouldn't bump into Susie anymore. I felt as if I had left so much sunshine behind in Leon.

Later in the day, shortly after the cathedral opened, I walked excitedly through its gates and entered. I had been waiting for this moment all day and I knew something important was going to happen. And I was right! I ended up spending more than two and a half wonderful hours in the cathedral and its museum, and I was amazed – absolutely blown away by what confronted me! Firstly, a most unusual sight was that of a massive tower in the middle of the altar wall. Of all the churches I had visited over the previous years, this was the first time I ever saw a tower as the very centerpiece of the altar wall.

There were also many powerful madonnas throughout the cathedral. Several madonnas were pictured with towers and books, serpent-dragons under the madonnas' feet, Venus temples and, most incredible of all, a statue where Jesus was placing a huge golden crown on a woman's head. At first sight, there was no clear indication of who the woman was but then, when I looked closer, I saw that the woman was holding a small chalice between her hands, something that strongly indicated she was the Grail Queen! In later times, the cup used by Christ at the last supper became known as the Grail Cup – a legend in its own right. But in the Grail stories that arose in the Middle Ages, the Grail was always carried by a woman! When I had looked into various histories around Europe, even in Christian tales, Mary Magdalene was every so often considered the Grail Queen. It was a detail that again connected her to the ancient teachings of the goddess cultures.

The museum wasn't much different. It was filled with huge, priceless silver crescent moons, which stood either by themselves or were shown in paintings together with the Virgin Mary, who was dressed in scarlet red! Often two silver crescent moons were depicted together, so that they either made a full circle of the moon or the meeting place between the upper and lower worlds (heaven and earth). Both symbols referred to the ancient spiritual teachings of Oneness and Wholeness, which again originated from ancient goddess cultures. A significant detail was that the cresent moon was a symbol of the goddess Diana, one of the several goddesses who derived from Cybele.

After leaving this impressive museum, I walked back into the cathedral to sit for a while. It was incredible to experience the beauty of the art in these places, and the hidden knowlege contained in them. This was, in so many ways, a legacy of a craftmanship that was dying. I was now convinced that there had been people and societies, throughout history, who had remembered and preserved this inheritance. An inheritance that had been forced into secrecy by the onset of Christianity.

The moment I left the cathedral, I again felt Richard's absence. I missed him deeply, but I also felt the flow of the Camino moving on, like a mighty river as it winds through the landscape. Nobody knew what would or could happen in the future, but as long as I followed in the light of the scallop shell, I knew I would be fine.

After having wandered aimlessly through the streets for a while, I ended up in a bar at Plaza San Bartolomé. I ordered a late lunch, went outside to sit, took out my half of Richard's guidebook and began to write:

Astorga has a very beautiful, and very old, city wall surrounding it. There are heaps of pilgrims and groups at my albergue. They are all extremely noisy. I have bought food so I can make my own sandwiches for tomorrow as well as some almonds and a vegetarian lasagna for tonight. Things are very different after Leon. Pilgrims I have known since St Jean look so tired now and not happy like we were used to…What will my next 17 days be like? I can't feel them. I want to walk all the way to Manjarin tomorrow as I would like to stay at Tómas' place. I think I will like him. It's about 30 kilometres from here.

As I looked up from Richard's guidebook, I saw Søren walking through the square and waved to him.

'Hello!' he called back, and walked over to me. 'Good to see you again,' he said with a smile and gave me a big hug.

We were both quite surprised to see each other, as it had been a while since we last met.

'I thought you and Ditte would have finished the Camino by now, knowing the long walks you had planned for each day.'

Søren rolled his eyes and sighed. 'No. Ditte is really sick and has been having problems with her knees and ankles, and my blisters are still a really big problem. We had to stop here yesterday because neither of us could walk anymore. We also had to cancel our walk today. I hope we will be fit enough tomorrow.' He sighed again and looked really worried as he ordered a cold drink. The waiter quickly returned with his lemonade and a glass filled with ice.

We sat and talked for an hour or so about the Camino and life in general. Søren explained his newest theories about how to treat his massive, multiple blisters. I just listened and nodded in a friendly manner. He was still not open to advice on the use of Fixomull and anti-bacterial cream. As he spoke, I quietly began to wonder if he and Ditte would ever make it all the way to Santiago on foot.

Søren's typical optimistic nature had cooled a little now, and he looked pensive as he finished his drink and made ready to move on. He had to go to the pharmacy and pick up some medicine for Ditte.

'See you around, Louise. It was really good seeing you again,' he said.

It seemed our chat had been of some comfort to him.

'Good to see you too, Søren. Give my love to Ditte.'

'I will.'

After he left, I sat and looked around at the empty square, thinking that it mirrored how I felt. It had been really good to see Søren again, as it had brought back some of the lost feelings of sunshine and happy days. I found it comforting to know that they hadn't disappeared completely. Feeling a little bored, I began to walk slowly back towards Plaza Catedral, taking a detour through the back streets. Since I had nothing better to do, I might as well just go back and spend some more time at the museum. However, shortly after entering the plaza, I heard a voice calling out my name.

I turned around and saw it was Aalt. He was sitting in a restaurant, outside the Hotel Gaudi, drinking coffee. I waved and walked over to him.

'Hi Aalt,' I said and smiled. 'What a surprise.'

'Would you like some tea or coffee?' he asked and pulled out a chair for me.

'Yeah! Tea sounds good!' I said and sat down while he ordered tea and cake for both of us.

'How are you?' I asked, 'I haven't seen you since Terradillos de

Templarios.'

Aalt was doing really fine and was taking it easy. He had taken two days off in Leon to meet up with some friends who lived there, and was now slowly making his way to Santiago. He had more than a month at his disposal. I was distracted from my sadness for a while and enjoyed my tea with Aalt. I felt rather touched by his kindness and generosity. He was so easy to talk to, and wasn't at all put off by my sombre mood. He just let me be and, without noticing it, two hours had passed by the time his friend came to pick him up.

The cathedral and its museum had closed by the time I left the restaurant and so, with reluctance, I walked back to my albergue. To my relief, it was now almost empty as everybody had gone out to eat. I walked into the kitchen and put my lasagna in the oven, feeling much better in myself. A petite Hungarian woman sat quietly at the dinner table reading her book, and a young blonde German walked up the stairs to the open kitchen where I was standing. We quickly started talking and ended up sharing our food with each other.

I discovered they had both been walking the Camino for quite some time, which to my mind explained why I felt so comfortable in their company. One could say we were on the same wave-length. A little after eight that evening, just before the other pilgrims returned from dinner, Richard rang me from Santiago. He was feeling really sad and quite indifferent about being there. He said it wasn't any fun being there without me. He hadn't even bothered to go and pick up his Camino certificate.

'What do I need it for anyway?' he said. 'And there wasn't even anything interesting to see in the cathedral,' he complained, sounding very disappointed.

He said he really missed me. I missed him too.

UP INTO THE MOUNTAINS

I woke up about 5.30 the next morning and again felt the call of the Camino. People were still asleep, but it was time for me to start walking. I quickly climbed down the ladder from my bunk bed, collected my gear and quietly sneaked out, closing the door behind me. In the hallway, I tip-toed down to the bathroom where I washed, dressed and brushed my teeth. Once downstairs, I quickly rolled up my sleeping bag and put it into my backpack.

It was 6.10 when I opened the front door and walked out into the empty street. It was still dark, and very quiet. I stood stationary for a moment, getting used to the idea of walking alone, before turning around to look at the beautiful cathedral one last time. As I walked out of Astorga, in the quiet of the morning, my head felt clear and my body energised. It had been extremely comforting to meet old and new friends the previous day. I felt reassured that everything from now on would work out fine.

From here on, the path would take me up into the mist-covered mountains, and I felt excited about meeting Tómas, whom I had heard so much about. Tómas was a modern-day, self-professed Knight Templar, and had built his albergue in a remote place called Manjarin. There he lived his own monastic way of life, serving the pilgrims.

As I walked further and further up into the mountains the weather started to change; the sun was losing its heat and the cold could be felt more and more. I didn't mind, though. It was far easier to walk in the cooler temperatures than it was in the heat – something that explained how I was able to walk as far as I did that day. Even though my walk from

Astorga to Foncebadón was quite demanding, it was also extremely beautiful. I walked through a never-ending landscape of mountains, large green forests, mysterious dense mists and along rough rocky pathways. It felt like I was walking through ancient lands where druids and druidesses had once lived and legends created. Nature here seemed so *alive*.

It was early afternoon by the time I reached Foncebadón. The sky had turned grey and cloudy, the air cool and moist. By then I had walked almost 30km with only two small breaks. My legs were telling me it was time to stop. Foncebadón looked like an old ghost town from the wild west that had just recently returned to life. The main thoroughfare was nothing but a dusty dirt road lined by mainly derelict houses that looked like they were about to collapse. The roof of one house was even made of the left-overs from other old houses and it looked rather artistic in its incompleteness.

One of the first newer houses I came across was a recently built albergue that had a small food shop and a restaurant attached to it. A group of American college students were sitting outside, behaving as if Foncebadón was their runway. As I passed them, I hoped there would be an alternative albergue where I could avoid these 'newer types' of pilgrims. A little further on, I noticed wheel tracks disappearing between some old pine trees lining the side of the road. The scenery through the trees looked so attractive, I had no choice than to go and explore.

Up behind the trees a breathtaking view appeared and, to my surprise, down a small driveway stood a quiet albergue where I immediately checked in. The couple who owned the albergue received me kindly, and had in no time carried my backpack to my bed, showed me around and arranged to have my laundry done for me. After my shower I went straight to bed and slept for a few hours. When I later awoke, the dormitory was almost full. It was fairly quiet, since most of the pilgrims were either asleep or resting on their beds. I stayed in my bed a while longer, thinking and looking out the window.

I lazily stretched and reached for my pen and notebook. It seemed that no matter how hard I tried to keep track of my pen, it always managed to disappear. This time, it was hiding under some clothes, even though I thought I had zipped it up safely in the small pocket in my backpack. I wasn't sure how it had moved from there, but I had learnt to accept, that once I opened my backpack, its contents seemed to have a life of their own.

Taking my pen and notebook, I walked outside onto a large terrace to sit in the late afternoon sun and write up my day. I really liked it up here in the mountains. There was something very special about them; they spoke to me of forgotten dreams and times long gone.

What I could gather from the conversations I overheard around the albergue, was that most of these pilgrims had just started their Camino. I also found a few of the younger male pilgrims rather aggressive and uncomfortable to be around. At one point, I sat outside talking with a ballet dancer from Slovenia. In the middle of our discussion, a British man interrupted, saying some extremely rude and condescending things about women in general and about the subject of our conversation. I immediately stopped talking and looked firstly at him, and then at the ballet dancer. It was obvious to me that he had found a place where he could dump his own problems. I was, however, quite surprised to see the ballet dancer accept this kind of behaviour as being normal and invited him into our space. Not wanting to be a receptacle for all his rubbish and waste my good energy on him, I closed the conversation, got up and left.

Were these really the new kind of pilgrims I would meet from now on? The British man was the third person I had met that day who had been aggressive and condescending towards me and other female pilgrims. This had really shocked me. If they hated women so much, why didn't they just leave us alone? As I was walking away from the table, I received an unexpected phone call from Richard. I quickly rushed up the hill to get the best possible signal. We ended up talking for quite some time, with me standing in the middle of a dirt road that led away from the albergue. He told me he was getting ready to leave for the airport having spent the day finding presents for his five children.

He said with feeling: 'I hope they'll like the presents I have bought for them.' I could hear that meant a lot to him.

'I'm sure they will!' I answered.

Richard went on to describe his feelings about going back to Australia, and I told him about my experiences with the aggressive British man. I could hear, on the other end of the phone, Richard was really annoyed about the situation.

'I'm glad you walked away!' he said. 'Don't put up with people like that. They are not healthy to be around.'

I found it so comforting talking with Richard again. He enjoyed hearing about my walk and how much his hiking pole helped me through the rough terrain. I also told him about all the things I had seen in Astorga and the many new groups of pilgrims. I said laughingly: 'They walk with the same speed as Japanese tourists.'

I heard Richard's sympathetic laugh at the other end of the line. Prior to hanging up, Richard promised to call me when he arrived back in Australia. It hurt even more knowing that he would be travelling even further away from me now. Somehow Richard, the Camino, and myself belonged together.

Regarding my comment about the speed with which pilgrims on this section of the Camino travelled, I had begun to feel stressed about these groups, and at times I had ended up walking in the ditches to avoid being trampled by them. I soon realised that I had two choices: I could either run ahead or I could slow down and let them pass. I decided to do the latter. When I did this, and all the groups had passed, there was only myself and the other 'slow' pilgrims left. From then on, the walk had been great and not a bicycle anywhere.

Many of the newer pilgrims talked fearfully about the lack of albergues on the last part of the Camino. Now one had to rush ahead to get a bed. It was a first in-first served mentality, and it was obvious how this fear created a negative kind of competitive behaviour, especially as the cyclists usually arrived before the walking pilgrins and therefore took up many of the beds. Pilgrims even pushed other pilgrims out of the way, so they could overtake and be first to the next albergue. I chose to ignore them. In the worst-case scenario, I would have to sleep in a hotel or even a farm shed. I really couldn't see a problem with that. In the end, it would only give me new and different experiences.

Very early the next morning, while it was still dark, all the lights in the dormitory were abruptly switched on. The many groups of pilgrims immediately got up, talking loudly to each other across the room and letting their backpacks scratch noisily over the floor and bump into beds. There was absolutely no point in trying to go back to sleep. However, not wanting to start walking before it became light, I stayed in bed.

By 6.30, all the groups had left. Now it was the host who stood in the doorway, urging the rest of us to leave.

As I stood outside the albergue, moments later, I noticed I still had my comb in one hand and my toothbrush and toothpaste in the other. I hadn't had time to use either of them. When the host had said out, it meant out!

THE GIFT OF SILENCE

Over the next few days I continued my silent walk through the mountains. The closeness that had existed between the pilgrims had disappeared and been replaced with a negative and stressful energy that was felt everywhere. I only felt relaxed when walking by myself or together with the other 'slow' pilgrims.

The rudeness and insensitivity expressed by the newer groups was just incredible. There was nothing in their behaviour that recognised the presence of other pilgrims or the sacredness of this walk. Why did these people even bother coming on a pilgrimage?

I kept looking for my friend, Peter. It would have been so great to camp out with him. For if I had had a tent, I would have stayed as far away as possible from the albergues and, just like the druids, lived in the silence of the mountain forests. I had really come to cherish the silent tranquillity I experienced in the nature around me. Up here, I could really feel the flow of life that ran through the earth and beneath my feet. I had always thought that silence was emptiness and loneliness, but the pilgrimage had taught me that it was, in truth, full of life; this was the magic of the Camino.

TOMAS, A MODERN-DAY TEMPLAR

The path from Foncebadón up through Cruz de Ferro to Manjarin was really beautiful. Reaching Cruz de Ferro, at the height of 1500 metres, I was above the early-morning mist and the most incredible sunrise unfolded before my eyes. It filled the entire sky with soft shades of red, orange and purple. From where I stood, on the top of the mountain, the earth below seemed so small and the sky above so infinite.

All the groups were already ahead of me, so I was left to walk in peace. When I saw the signpost, indicating I had reached Manjarin, I started to feel excited, because this was where Tómas lived. When passing a little wooden tower to my right a bell rang. I had read earlier that this was one of Tómas's traditions. He would ring the bell every time a pilgrim passed by. I thought this was rather sweet, but figured he would spend a lot of time in that tower during the high season of the Camino.

Opposite the tower, to my left, stood a old-fashioned 'homemade' toilet. However, I found Tomás himself, in his Knights Templar outfit, standing talking to some pilgrims. He was standing inside a large canvas-covered structure that contained all his paraphernalia. The place worked as both a reception area and as a shop.

Tomás was a very short man, with dark brown eyes, horn-rimmed glasses and a bushy grey beard. There was a very warm presence about him. I felt like giving him a big hug, but greeted him instead in the normal way and shook his hand. In his broken English, he asked curiously where I was from.

'Denmark,' I replied, and wondered if he knew where that was.

'Oh, Denmark!' he said, pointing to a Danish flag that hung from an overhead roof beam. He then said something about the cross on the Danish flag and the Knights Templar's cross that I didn't completely understand.

I asked if it was okay if I had a photo taken of the two of us together.

'*Si, claro*!' he said with a laugh and posed for me. He seemed pretty accustomed to this request.

The first picture left us laughing out loud, with Tomás poking fun at the way he posed. The second photo turned out slightly better. We were still laughing in the picture and I looked rather huge standing next to this little man. He then stamped my pilgrim's pass even though, in principle, I wanted stamps only from the places I slept. But it was different with this modern Templar. I wanted a special memento of our meeting. I also bought some different things from his shop to support him.

When I left, Tómas walked me out to the road whilst constantly talking to me in Spanish. He was obviously trying to tell me something important that I couldn't understand, probably about the Templars. Tómas stood and waved as I walked away but, as soon as another pilgrim appeared, he rushed over to the tower again and rang the bell. I thought to myself, as I left Manjarin behind, that Richard would have loved to have met Tomás.

Ditte and Søren later told me they had slept there. They said it had been very cold, but they had also enjoyed meeting him. Tomás had lived a rather interesting life. Prior to becoming a Templar at Manjarin, which in itself was an interesting story, Tomás could also tell many other fascinating, funny and mystical accounts of his life. He had been very open about his spiritual beliefs and shared them with anyone who showed interest. I was definitely going to stay there the next time I walked the Camino.

FACING ANOTHER REALITY

After my short stay in Manjarin, I walked through the tiny township, Acebo, and spent the night in Molinaseca. There I experienced something rather shocking.

The village itself was newly renovated and particularly picturesque with a medieval stone bridge that crossed a large lake where the locals swam. There I met Pierre, who looked both stressed and annoyed. He invited me for a cup of tea and a chat. While sitting there, we were suddenly interrupted by a loudly spoken woman, who said something in French to Pierre that I didn't understand.

He answered her in a rather tired and irritated way. Then the woman walked off with a small group of other people, who again had been standing at a polite and respectful distance, waiting for their 'leader'. After we had finished our tea and coffee, Pierre left and I walked around to see the village's churches. On my way, I passed several groups of American college students sitting in the town's bars. They were getting drunk and behaving badly, and yet it was only three in the afternoon.

Changes were starting to occur with the churches after Astorga. First, there were far fewer of them, and they were a lot smaller. In the churches, as well, the signs and connections to the Knights Templars had basically disappeared. The major themes now were powerful madonnas in scarlet-red dresses depicted with crescent moons; women with towers and books; the Freemasonary ladder and the skull and cross-bone symbol; and, most surprisingly, Jesus together with his mother and father, as a real family. Joseph was even depicted with a halo around his head and just as important as Mary. It made me so happy to see Joseph back in the picture; the absent father had finally been allowed to return home.

As I strolled through the cobbled streets back towards my albergue, I met a handful of pilgrims I had known from the beginning of my Camino. They looked tired and were just as happy as me to see a familiar face. Knee and shoulder pains were a common issue for many, and the social changes of the Camino affected many of us in a negative way. The pilgrims I spoke to, even Pierre, felt stressed by the hordes of marching groups and their insensitive behaviour. I had to admit it was quite a relief to hear that I wasn't the only one suffering from these changes.

Back at my albergue I joined other pilgrims out on the terrace. Everyone was sitting there peacefully, either reading their books or writing in their journals whilst enjoying a cup of coffee or a beer. There was a closeness and presence that existed between us; a cosiness that reminded me of what the Camino had been like before Astorga. As I looked around, most of us sat with contented smiles on our faces. About this time, three American Catholic priests entered the terrace. They sat themselves down at the only available table, which happened to be next to mine. They were apparently the leaders of a group of teenagers, and I guessed they were all in their 40s.

Completely ignoring the social energy, tranquillity and closeness that existed between those of us who were already sitting there, the three priests began discussing and defending the Catholic church in loud voices. Many of my fellow pilgrims gave them annoyed looks and started clearing their throats. Others started to move around restlessly in their seats and sigh loudly. It was obvious to everyone that the priests hadn't noticed anything.

The way they sat and talked over us felt like they were doing this deliberately. They talked a lot louder than they needed to, and they behaved as if they were putting on an act for us, doing a 'hard sell' for their church. I was about to walk over and ask them to quieten down, when they began to, even more determinedly, defend the actions of the Catholic church, in complete disregard of the consequences. I was so shocked that I just stared at them, thinking I must have misunderstood them. But I hadn't. These three priests, who apparently held a lot of power in their community, sat, and not only questioned the veracity of thousands and thousands of children who had been sexually, physically and emotionally abused by Catholic institutions all over the world, they also said that we should forget about what had happened and *think forward*. Did they not know *anything* about the real history of their church?

I felt nauseated hearing all of this and could have thrown up. I was lost for words. All I could do was to collect my things and remove myself, as quickly as possible, from their presence. As I passed the other pilgrims, I saw disgust and anger written all over their faces. They, too, were starting to gather up their things and leave. Shorty after, the terrace that had just been full of happy people was empty, except for the three priests.

As I walked up to my dormitory, I felt violated both spiritually and emotionally. The shameless way that human beings could just sit there and defend these actions, and only talk about 'looking forward', deeply concerned me. Shivers of discomfort spread through my body, thinking that these men were a part of the church's next generation. No wonder people were leaving the church in droves. The priests had been so full of themselves, living in a world far removed from the rest of humanity, where compassion and responsibility were non-existent. The lack of empathy, and their shamelessness and coldness scared me.

As I lay there on my bed under my sleeping bag, I still felt cold and uneasy after the experience downstairs. The other pilgrims in my room, who had also been sitting down on the terrace, were all on their beds completely withdrawn into their own worlds. The community and closeness was gone and we felt it was unsafe to open up again. I wanted to reach out to them but couldn't. I felt shame, whereas the priests had felt none. We had all just walked away, and now we sat there, feeling terrible and alone.

Anger started to rise within me. I should have walked over and told them how unacceptable their behaviour was. Defending such actions was sick and destructive. I should have pointed out the violation they created with their attitudes. And last of all, I should have asked them to leave.

I felt so sorry that I hadn't said any of this; that none of us had said anything, but it clearly showed how easy it was for a powerful institution like the church to get away with almost anything. As Confucius once said:

To know what the right thing is, and not doing it, is lack of courage.

I felt this incident had confronted me with my own lack of courage. And I didn't like it. Later, when most of us went into town to eat, to escape from the poisonous atmosphere at our albergue, people started talking about the incident.

'I just can't wait to get away from these people!' many exclaimed with anger and disgust.

When we arrived back at the albergue, the feeling of community was starting to return. Thankfully, the priests and their group kept very much to themselves, away in their own room. For a long time after the lights had been turned off, I stayed awake thinking; how often did we humans let authorities treat us badly and suppress us, simply because they were in a position of power? How often had we stood up against them and demanded our rights? And how many times had we blindly accepted their lies and manipulation and thus lost another part of our self-respect?

Feelings of anger and sorrow swept through my very being, as I realised that by closing our eyes and doing nothing, we allowed this violence and human destruction to happen. In the end, it all came back to what we did, and to what we didn't do. Passivity always supported the perpetrator.

As I started meditating, the warm light of the sun slowly filled me up and brought me back into balance. The poison from the priests evaporated and I began to feel grounded with a new state of clarity. I realised these priests had taught me an important lesson about the world I lived in. I saw with my inner eye how history had a tendency to repeat itself because we refused to learn and grow as humans.

Exhausted from all the emotions and the hard walk that day, I finally feel asleep. That night I had this dream:

It is daytime, and I am standing outside in nature looking up into the sky. The atmosphere is dark and dirty. Far out in the universe, a red glowing meteor is heading for earth at an incredible speed. As it enters our atmosphere, it creates massive pressure waves that are forced down into the earth. The meteor lands, close to me, with an explosion. Lots of steam, smoke and dust emanate from it. Out of the dust and smoke appear three radiant and beautiful androgynous beings, walking towards me. They inform me they are here to cleanse the atmosphere.

They have a large number of emergency aeroplanes, helpers and other important survival gear with them. From where I stand, I can see how extremely efficient the three shining beings and all their helpers are. They clean the entire atmosphere with their love, and slowly, more and more light is allowed onto the earth. One of the radiant beings, who now looks more like a woman, points lovingly towards the still-smoking meteor, and says to me: 'You called, we heard you and we came.'

I woke up the next morning, feeling literally like a meteor had hit my atmosphere, and in the midst of all the smoke, dirt and confusion, I felt a growing kind of iron strength. I stood up and followed my usual routine before going downstairs to have breakfast. As I walked throught the reception area I saw the three priests standing in the doorway getting ready to leave. Without even thinking I walked over to them.

'Good morning!' I said and looked them in the eye.

They looked at me, a little surprised. 'Good morning,' they replied.

'I was wondering, do you remember yesterday afternoon, when you came and sat on the terrace with the other pilgrims?'

'Yes,' they replied, happily remembering the occasion.

'Good!' I said. 'Then do you also remember how everybody left the terrace, quite suddenly, soon after your arrival?'

Silence.

'Well, let me tell you then, we all left because we were sickened and felt violated listening to your overly obnoxious discussions, but none of us had the courage to tell you. The thing is, I believe people with attitudes and values likes yours, with a total lack of empathy, compassion and a total denial of responsibility, should not be permitted to be even near children or the teenagers you have in your group. Do you really know the history of your church? I mean, do you really understand the concepts you are defending? Think about it! Goodbye, and have a good day!'

The three priests looked at me, speechless and absolutely stunned. I didn't wait for them to say anything either. I just turned around and walked back into the dining room, shaking with anger. I had had enough of these sorts of people, seeing them getting away with inflicting so much pain, hate and destruction on to our world. This had nothing to do with God, Jesus, paganism or whatever they called it; it had to do with them being psychologically disturbed persons with distorted thinking. They needed psychiatric treatment, and all the Hail Mary's on earth couldn't help them there.

It took me all of breakfast time and the caring attention of my host before I calmed down. The experiences I had with the priests made me see, clearer than ever, what kind of confusion the loss of our innate spirituality had caused. I thought back to St Jean and the weeks walking all the way to Leon. I remembered fondly the incredible harmony, space and freedom within our pilgrim community. Even a love for just being alive. The Camino was a place where we had a chance to get off the 'hamster wheel', and actually start to listen to ourselves and *connect* with our real spirituality. The challenge now, was to bring these insights and experiences back with us and, after the Camino, have the courage to manifest them in our relationships and actions.

As I left Molinaseca, I wondered about the snake in paradise. Would we know it was paradise if the snake hadn't been there?

SOMETHING MYSTERIOUS

It was funny how much more dependent I had become on Brierley's guidebook now Richard had left. His book was filled with relevant information on many important issues, such as the distance between albergues, the local terrain and the places where I could buy food and drink. Brierley's guidebook mentioned there was a renovated Knights Templar castle in Ponferrada, which I was really keen to see. I wanted to take some pictures of it for Richard.

Whilst waiting for the castle to open, I sat down outside a nearby bar and watched the pilgrims pass by. Pierre's little group then appeared with a new girl in tow. He looked even more tired than he had the day before. When he saw me, he left his group, bought a Cortado, and then came over and joined me at my table. Standing close to us, a discussion arose between the new girl and the French women I had met the day before. Pierre said nothing, but looked at me as if he were saying, 'Give me strength'!

The girl, with a heavy Texan accent, was arguing with the French woman, saying: 'But I'm telling you, this is not a town! It doesn't have any highways, there aren't any skyscrapers and there are not even enough people to make a town!'

Silence descended on Pierre's group and the tables around us. Everybody turned around and stared at the girl, wondering how anyone could say something so dumb. Pierre rolled his eyes, shook his head and took another sip of his coffee.

'I'm serious!!' the girl cried out, 'a town does not look like this where I come from!'

Pierre smiled apologetically to me, and I smiled back, fully understanding the situation. I could see it wasn't easy for anyone.

'Pierre!' the French women called out, fed up with the girl.

He quickly finished his Cortado, ran his fingers through his thin hair and rose from the chair with a sigh.

'I have to go, Louise,' he said, looking at me. 'See you next time, then we will have time to talk.'

'Yeah, that will be great, Pierre. Take care, okay?'

As Pierre's little group moved off, I could hear the French women giving the girl a lecture about the world outside America, and how America wasn't the centre of the world.

Yes, the Camino had indeed changed. Pilgrims were now becoming cantankerous, and middle-aged Catholic priests flirted with the teenage girls in their groups. Many who had walked since the Pyrenees were now really tired and suffered a lot of pain. The newer pilgrims' constant noise and insestitivity was suffocating; young college students behaved as if the Camino was their own personal runway with spotlights, and I was starting to feel full. To make matters worse, the three priests from my albergue, suddenly turned up with their group of teenagers, but wisely stayed far away from me.

It was now my turn to run the fingers through my hair and sigh. The meteor had indeed hit the ground. I was only happy when the castle finally opened, and quickly rushed over to line up and buy my ticket. To my surprise – or disappointment – it was only the outer walls of the castle that had been renovated. The inside was one large grassy area with some tiny stonewall ruins dotted here and there. It wasn't until I entered its museum that I found anything interesting.

The exhibition displayed many beautiful books and pictures on alchemy – all locked up behind large glass display cases. There were also illustrations of medical treatments and examinations from the Middle Ages (I took a couple of photos of these for Richard as they were a bit funny), and, quite surprisingly, a book that once had belonged to Lorenzo de Medici. How did a book from the Italian Renaissance make it into a Templars collection dating from the Middle Ages? Unfortunately, all of the text was in Spanish, so I couldn't understand the information. However, the more I saw of the exhibition, the more I wondered about the spiritual and alchemical material it contained.

The central library of the Templars had, at one time, been located on Cyprus and had been burnt to the ground in the war against them. (Burning libraries was, sadly, a common occurrence in wars throughout history). Many historians said that the only documents we have left, relating to this order, were the testimonials given under torture before the Knights Templar were killed.

I vaguely recalled something the two Germans, Rolf and Carl, had mentioned in Viana. They had mentioned there were Knights Templar, who had been known as the warrior monks, and then there had been another order of knights called the Knights Hospitallers. The Hospitallers were more the carers, looking after sick and wounded travellers. According to Rolf and Carl, many confused these two groups believing them to be one and the same, which they weren't.

The way I saw it, all the medical material in the museum could be explained by the influence of the Knights Hospitallers, so I wondered if this museum was more about the Knights Hospitallers, and not the Templars? But it still didn't explain all the spiritual, astrological and alchemical materials I saw there. By this point in time, I had visited and studied every possible church, and their museums, along the Camino. I had met a living history, which I doubted was to be found in the mainstream history books written by so-called experts. With the enormous amount of historical documents that had been destroyed throughout history, together with the books and documents hidden in the Vatican library; and all the private collections and the research that had been held back because it challenged the 'truth' of the church, how could we say we knew the 'truth' about our history?

All of this made me wonder what our history would look like, if the libraries from those past eras, and the knowledge they contained, still existed? What if the library at the Vatican was open for everyone to see (before they had a chance to remove or burn anything)?

How would history look, if it was written, analysed, described and explained through the eyes of women? How would men be seen then? And what would our historical 'truth' look like then?

Walking the Camino had become the greatest eye-opening experience of my life. My understanding of psychology, sociology and so many other areas of life had been turned upside down. How could it be, that all these mighty women, who constantly filled the walls of the churches and ruins along the Camino, weren't mentioned anywhere? And how could it be, that the only person we seemed to hear about on the Camino was Saint James? One had to look very hard to find him, if at all, amongst the older sculptures and artwork. But the women and the traces of our ancient legacy, were everywhere!

I was, by now, starting to see increasing similarities between the legend of Saint James and the Emperor's New Clothes fairytale. There was little evidence to support the story of Saint James, and when one looked away from this empty tale, there was so much evidence of a world filled with important women and the sacred knowledge about deep spiritual transformation.

Back out on the small street I took a left turn and walked up into the centre of Ponferrada looking for a bar. I was thirsty and needed to get off my feet for a while. The street was quiet now; the groups had passed a long time ago, as had the cyclists. The only shops open here were a few boutiques that sold Camino souvenirs and T-shirts. I wondered if I should buy a Templar memento for Richard, but decided not to as I had already bought him a Camino T-shirt. While I was sitting and enjoying a cold drink, Ingrid and her husband, Kurt, stopped to have a chat. The Camino seemed to be one long honeymoon for them. Alice, the fast talking Canadian, passed by a short time later, and updated me on her latest plans. It had been a few days since I had last met her, but we used to run into each other frequently. Alice sounded as if she were in a rush to make it to Santiago, and only stopped a short while before walking on.

I wanted to move on, too, as I felt I had wasted precious walking hours visiting the castle. I felt restless about getting back out onto the pathway, but something kept holding me back. I duly paid for my drink, got up and walked off, not realising I had missed seeing a scallop shell. I continued up a narrow side street, which led me into a large empty plaza. There was something familiar about this square and, even though I wanted to move on, I felt I needed to stay.

I stood and looked around, thinking there might be a church or other old building that would be interesting for me to visit, but the square didn't seem to have anything to offer. Suddenly I heard the most beautiful organ music echoing across the square. Curious to see where it came from, the sounds led me to a massive stone wall. The wall had no visible windows or other indications of its use. However, this was where the music came from.

On closer inspection I saw a very small open doorway in the wall, leading into an otherwise hidden church. In front of the doorway, I noticed an unusual white light. Because everything else was in the shade, I kept staring at it, wondering what it could be. I cleaned my sunglasses; that didn't help. I rubbed my eyes; that didn't help, either.

'That's weird,' I said to myself. The white light was still there, so I walked a little closer, curious to see what caused it. As I walked nearer, I felt the light having an unusual effect on me. It surrounded me and I felt as if I were being wrapped in soft angora fur of unconditional love. It took me quite a while before I understood what I was experiencing. But the moment I did, I realised this wasn't just any kind of church. This was a very special place. So I walked through the doorway into the church, hoping I would find my answers there. Unfortunately, a service had just begun and visitors weren't allowed in until it was finished.

'When will it be over?' I asked the man standing in the doorway.

'In about an hour,' he said. 'The service has only just started.'

Darn it! I turned around, thinking about what I should do. I was still able to see and feel the white light. I began to focus on it more intensely when it suddenly struck me that it was actually the light that had drawn me to Ponferrada. It really was a mystical, strange, and very, very beautiful experience.

Walking away, I passed a tiny sign informing me that there once had been a vision of the Virgin Mary right here. It also said that the vision of the Virgin Mary had been seen in an oak tree. I later learnt this whole region had been covered with oak trees. Following the original vision, the oak tree in which the vision appeared had been chopped down and a church built on that very site. I questioned whether the apparition had actually been that of the Virgin Mary, since the oak tree had been the sacred dwelling place of the goddess Diana. She had been worshipped over large parts of pre-Christian Europe, also here in Spain.

The importance of the oak tree, made me think about studies that had been done on the Black Madonna sculptures. These studies showed that the Black Madonna had been made of wood. However, it was the treatment of the wood that had created the famous black colour. I now wondered if the Goddess Diana had been recreated in the form of the Black Madonna, in a shape acceptable to the Catholic church. It definitely seemed to fit with one of the theories about the origins of the Black Madonna.

A vision had indeed occured here in Ponferrada. Of that, I had no doubt. Maybe the light I experienced was a legacy from those ancient times. Or perhaps, the vision is still alive, but for what reason?

CACABELOS

The day I walked out of Ponferrada was my 27th day on the Camino. Looking back, I hardly recognised the person I had been four weeks earlier. It felt like a whole lifetime had passed.

Entering the world of the Camino had been like entering a world of timeless space with no walls and no roofs. My mysterious experience in Ponferrada had left me in a calm state of mind. As the many details about the Virgin Mary, Mary Magdalene and the 'other' women figures I had come to know came together, I felt a huge transformation taking place within myself. The more they stepped out of the shadows and came alive, so did I. In their light, I started to understand how society and my culture had shaped me and limited me, and the more I learnt, the more I freed myself. The thing was, that apart from the Virgin Mary and Mary Magdalene, all the other many women depicted along the way of the Camino, remained completely anonymous, whereas all the men, of course, were identified and easily recognisable.

In many ways, I felt that mirrored how my historical roots of identity and strength had been taken away from me. In the beginning, with all my dreams, I had thought it had been about me as a woman. But now, I realised it was about me as a human being. I was more than just a woman; I was a human being who had been discriminated against purely based on my gender. And, in my eyes, this treatment hadn't been beneficial to anyone.

After Ponferrada, the walking was easy and relaxing. The pathway led me along quiet country roads beside grassy fields, through small villages and later on, as I approached Cacabelos, large vineyards which spread out before me. It was midday and the weather was perfect. The sky was a brilliant blue and the sun shone warmly. As I was rather 'late', due to my long stopover at Ponferrada, there were only the 'slow' pilgrims like myself out on the Camino. I really enjoyed feeling these moments of community and tranquillity once again.

Upon entering the vineyards, the sealed road became dirt. As I walked along, a man in a four-wheel drive jeep drove up. Judging from the writing on the side of the car, he was the owner of a local adventure tourist business. And on this particular day he had apparently seen the need to go adventuring in his four-wheel drive, trying to pick up female pilgrims who were walking by themselves. As he drove past he slowed down, stared at me intensely and gave me a flirtatious look before speeding off. I thought he was an idiot and quickly forgot about him as he disappeared in a cloud of dust. But when he came back the second and then a third time, staring and 'making eyes at me' while driving slowly next to me for some minutes, I felt it was time to take some precautions. Shortly after this incident, I came to a paved road and stopped to wait for other pilgrims I could walk with. Thankfully a mature aged couple and a young woman soon appeared. I explained about the man in the jeep and asked if we could walk together.

'Of course!' they said.

They turned out to be really warmhearted people, but it wasn't long before the jeep reappeared, and this actually made me very angry. What was 'cool' about stalking women who were walking by themselves? It was neither 'adventurous', sexy nor macho-like; it was just plain loser behaviour. When he saw I was walking with other pilgrims he sped off and didn't return. However, when I reached the main pedestrian street that passed through Cacabelos I saw him waiting for me outside a bodega. He gazed at me as I walked past him before turning and walking into the bodega. I stared back at him coldly and, when close enough for him to hear me, I loudly and clearly called him 'a fucking asshole!'

My 'walk-in closet' albergue was located on the other side of Cacabelos. It had been described as a nicely rebuilt church. What the description really should have said was that the albergue was actually a separate building placed in a half-moon shape around the church. This ugly modern building consisted of numerous closet-style rooms containing two beds and a small table. The doors into these 'closets' were painted in a bright orange colour, dating from the 1970s. From the outside, they looked rather claustophobic but, once inside, they turned out to be surprisingly spacious, cool and comfortable.

Cacabelos was a good place to stop. It was filled with many different kinds of restaurants, which actually meant a lot because the pilgrims' diet had turned into a rather monotonous affair! It was a cosy little town where I spent my afternoon in the company of some wonderful people from New Mexico, France and Denmark. Aalt came passing through, but was heading towards the next town. Sitting outside a local bar, the topic of blisters arose again. After seeing some of them, I offered to treat the blisters when we got back to the albergue.

While sitting there with my new pilgrim friends, I discovered that some of them had also experienced the mysterious soft light in Ponferrada. They, too, had missed a scallop shell and ended up outside the church by chance. We all agreed that there was something mystifying going on there. None of them knew about the apparition of the Virgin Mary and were amazed when I told them about it.

As I visited the churches in Cacabelos in the late afternoon, something struck me. The areas the Camino had passed through after Astorga had been much poorer than the other municipalities I had walked through earlier on in my pilgrimage. Now the churches were not only much smaller and had less adornments on the outside, they also had very little on the inside. It was interesting, though, that the few remaining figures inside the churches were those of women! Especially the Madonna who was depicted holding a book, either reading from it or writing in it. I also noticed a couple a black Madonna's. As far as I knew, out of more than 80 gospels, the only significant text written by a woman, was the Gospel of Mary Magdalene, which, of course, wasn't canonical (not recognised by the Catholic church).

As I thought about it, it really struck me that so many other women had been depicted as teachers, writers and scholars, and they were ever-present along the Camino. They were often 'hidden' in the art of tapestries, glass-stained windows and paintings – even on carved wood panels. Why would I constantly see women holding books, writing in them and even teaching from them, when women officially hadn't written any church texts at all? They weren't even allowed to teach, let alone research or write! Yet, a massive amount of evidence present within these churches was telling me otherwise.

What on earth is going on? I asked myself.

I was certain that a woman holding a book, and maybe even reading from a book, would be explained away by the church as referring to the Virgin Mary holding the Bible, as she was the only woman with authority to do so. But it certainly didn't explain other women writing in books or reading from them, let alone acting as teachers on various academic subjects. Women weren't permitted to read or write and were basically kept illiterate for more than a thousand years, as were most men. So why would the church depict these women *reading and writing*? To encourage other women to learn how to read and write? Of course not! So who were all these women writing and teaching? What were they writing about, and what were they teaching? What was the book they were holding? Did it just signify knowledge or was it their own written works? If so, where are these works and why aren't they mentioned or recognised anywhere?

I wondered if all these unnamed female figures could have been actual women and teachers, of flesh and blood. Or were they merely symbolic, illustrating a 'hidden reality' and another way of approaching knowledge and spirituality? Like with Mary Magdalene, I figured it was both.

I sat down on the steps of an old small church outside, in the last of the day's sun. Here I began to write down all my thoughts. By the time I had finished, the sun had disappeared and I was now sitting in the cool shade of the evening. Pilgrims and locals were now eating in the many local restaurants and the wonderful smell of food wafted over me. My stomach grumbled. I was hungry, too. Really hungry, actually, so I walked over to find a place to eat. I ended up in a restaurant that advertised homemade hamburgers and large beef steaks.

Rather absentmindedly, I placed my order, sat down in one corner of the restaurant and watched the local news on a large television screen. Although I was really mentally tired, I couldn't stop thinking about all those women. I knew men and women had been considered equals in many cultures: the Cathars, the various pre-Christian cultures, and even within the Celts up until Christianity came on the scene. But could there really have been times, or places, where this equality had existed within the framework of the Catholic church? Even the church at large?

It was time for me to start organising my notes.

BUEN CAMINO!

After an early-morning phone call from Richard, who had by now arrived back in Australia, I started my day's walk. I had decided to take the longer and much-harder mountain route, one of the 'less travelled pathways' in Brierley's guidebook. This walk would be a difficult full day's walk, so I had to stay over at Villafranca Del Bierzo which was only a short distance from Cacabelos. This short walk passed through even more beautiful vineyards and surprisingly picturesque scenery.

Walking slowly along the dirt road, I found great amusement in kicking a stone ahead of me with my right foot. I had plenty of time, and figured I might as well spend it on the trail rather than hanging out at some albergue. Shortly after passing through Valtuille de Arriba, I noticed a young women ahead of me wearing a green-hooded jacket. She, too, was walking really slowly, stopping to look at the flowers and taking lots of photographs. I recognised her from Molinaseca and called out. Her name was Donna and she was from San Francisco where she worked as a nurse. She had only recently started on her pilgrimage and was in the midst of figuring out what it was all about.

After catching up, we walked together for a while. Donna then mentioned a route through the mountains she wanted to take.

'Have you heard about it?' she asked. 'I think it starts just outside Villafranca.'

I found my guidebook and opened it up at the page that showed the alternative route, marked in green, that crossed over three mountains.

'Is it this one?' I pointed to the map, and handed her the book. 'I had been thinking about going that way tomorrow myself. It's no fun walking beside the highways.'

Donna studied the map for a while and felt certain that this was the path she had heard about.

'Would you like to walk it together?' she asked.

'Yeah, that would be great!' I said. 'The description in the book will guide us through the mountains, since there are only one or two signs along this route.'

'Okay,' Donna answered slowly, studying the map one more time before handing it back to me. 'Cool!' she said. 'Let's have a closer look at the description in the guidebook when we come to Villafranca Del Bierzo. I need something to eat first.'

Early the next morning, with a full moon lighting our way, Donna and I left our albergue. It was only by looking towards the east one would know that the sun was about to rise. After we had rechecked our water supplies and food we set off, Donna leading the way with the open map in her hand. I figured there would be less chance of getting lost if a native English speaker read the English written instructions. I hoped so, anyway. Our instructions consisted of a list of directions containing phrases like 'opposite a grove of trees' and 'careful not to confuse the various local walking paths in this area' (Brierley, J.: 2011:232).

Steadily, and without talking much, Donna and I walked up the steep road that would eventually lead us into the wilderness of the mountains. As the sun rose, a grey mist descended, forcing us to take more care on the now wet, slippery and steep ascent. The smell of pine trees filled the air, and the only sounds we could hear were our boots hitting the asphalt and our heavy breathing. After following the road for about an hour, we finally saw a sign that indicated we needed to turn onto a small earthern pathway. And thus began our venture into the wilderness.

I very quickly understood that to do this walk by myself would have been too dangerous. I most likely would have got myself lost and then panicked. Just before we reached the peak of the first mountain, Donna and I entered the rural village of Dragonte where we were confronted by some vicious guard dogs barking savagely at us. We tried to ignore them, remain calm and keep walking. They didn't bite us but as we walked through the village we could feel the spit from their teeth and their hot breath on our legs. Once we reached the end of the village, they stopped and left us alone.

Donna and I looked at each other quite relieved. We had made it safely out of Dragonte, and hoped it wouldn't be like this every time we had to pass through a small village in these mountains. We continued on our great adventure, along the uphill path, until we reached the first mountain peak. I had no idea of how long we had walked, or what time it was, but we were rewarded with a most extraordinary view.

Grey rainclouds were now gathering in the sky and the air felt damp on our skin. The smell of earth and grass filled the air and made me think that it might start to rain soon. There was no doubt that the view would have looked even more stunning in sunshine, but I actually liked the roughness and wild look the grey sky lent to the scenery. In the distance, mountain peaks stretched out as far as our eyes could see. Below us, in the valley, old farm houses were dotted here and there, half-hidden behind trees. Small mountain roads snaked their way up and around the mountain sides. I took a deep breath and threw my arms out wide. What a place! I felt like an eagle who had spread its wings, soaring on the winds of freedom. Walking this less-travelled path was the best thing I could have done.

Donna and I decided to stop here and take a break so we could enjoy the view more. We had something to drink, ate some of my nuts and shared an apple. It was important that we were careful with our supplies, as there were no places along the way where we could re-stock. We then sat and took another look at the guidebook and carefully re-read the descriptions of the path we were to take. The descriptions in the guidebook, so far, had been reliable – as long as we paid close attention to them. However, this was the first place where we had to search the surroundings before we were sure which way to go. We had a long discussion and referred to the book many times before we reached an agreement. It was time for the steep descent into the first valley. The sky had cleared a little, letting in some sun, but not enough to dry the wet slippery stones.

There were many times Donna and I wondered if we were actually lost. Often we had to force our way through large dense bushes that were growing on a pathway that didn't really seem to exist. The track changed constantly, as did the scenery around us. Sometimes our pathway would take a sudden change of direction. Then there were the large slippery stones we had to constantly look out for, or a small creek we had to follow. At other times the pathway transformed into a narrow trail where we had to be careful not to fall. And then again, the trail transformed into wet two-wheeled earth tracks that took us through forests and small fields filled with many wild flowers. We were never quite sure we were on the right track until we found the next clue mentioned in Brierley's book.

At one point, Donna and I passed through a so-called village, which consisted of only a few farm houses and the usual pack of unfriendly dogs. We found the situation quite uncomfortable, but felt a kind of security with my stick and a large stone Donna had picked up before entering the village. As long as we ignored them and kept walking, the dogs left us alone.

Somewhere on the second mountain, Donna and I came upon a most enchanting and romantic remains of an old stone church. On one side of the ruins stood a small, beautifully crafted stone archway. It was the kind of place that made me think of Avalon, the priestesses and the Druids. It seemed to invite us to remember lost dreams and the stars we felt had been out of reach. Even Donna talked about the inspiration she felt in this place.

As I had come to expect, the church was closed and locked, so we had a bit of fun trying to balance on rocks to look through the windows. We didn't have much luck, though, and explored the rest of the grounds before we sat down to rest and eat our lunch. When I finished my sandwich, I lay down, hands resting under my head, looking up into the sky. After a short snooze, we explored the grounds of the stone church one more time before preparing to move on. We still had a long way to go that day. When walking in the mountains, it was important to keep an eye on the weather. The grey clouds had lifted a little, but here the weather could change without any notice, so I constantly found myself keeping an eye on the sky.

Mostly we walked together, but at other times, apart, each doing what we needed to do to make the most of this incredible walk. Being in better shape than Donna, I sometimes found myself some distance ahead of her. But I would always stop and wait so we never lost sight of each other.

It was about this time I had an epiphany. Maybe it was the amazing feeling of freedom and the intense experience of being alive, or the wild untouched nature, the endless sky and the emancipation that came with the insights given on the Camino, but whatever it was, I felt the energy from within these mountains filling me up and pulling me down, deeper and deeper into my body and into the dark earth. The strength in my legs carried me along the trails and my heart merged with my surroundings. I tilted my head back, stretched out my arms and yelled 'BUEN CAMINO!'

My call echoed throughout the mountains.

'BUEN CAMINO!!!!!' I yelled again, letting it all out.

I shouted out to the world *that I was truly alive*! That I was standing right here, in the middle of life and it was just fantastic. I shouted out to the visible and invisible, to whom I had been and to whom I was becoming. I shouted out to the Camino, feeling it! I heard it, I understood it and I was free! It was indeed my birthright to be free!

The Camino I had known was beginning to disappear amidst crazy priests and loud groups, but the golden energy of this sacred place would be ever present. No matter where on earth I was or what I was doing, it would always be a part of who I was. And if I lost my way, I would know how to find my way back. I had always found my way back, no matter how lost I had been. And the more 'lost' I became in the wilderness of these mountains, the more I found myself and my place amidst all the confusion in the world. The life of the Camino would always run through my veins; sometimes high and wild, at other times gentle like a summer breeze.

With my call still echoing in my ears, I looked up into the sky feeling like a warrior from ages past. The Camino was the way; the way into ourselves, the way into the future and the way back to our roots. It was the way we had walked for thousand of years, the way we had run away from and to which we had returned. I fell to my knees and just looked at the nature around me, feeling nothing but a silenced love for the Energy of Creation. What did we need churches for when we had the masterpiece of them all – our earth.

Donna came up and knelt down next to me. She held out her hand towards me in silence. It was full of red, sweet berries she had just picked. I smiled and took a few from her.

'Thank you, my friend.'

'You're welcome.'

After finishing the berries Donna had picked, we continued on together, discussing whether or not we also should attempt to walk over the third and last mountain. However, the answer became obvious to us as we reached the valley at the base of the second mountain. Neither of us had any food or water left, and I was running out of energy. It took us an hour or so to reach the road that would take us down to the highway where the other pilgrims walked. There we would find what we needed and a place to stay.

Since Villafranca del Bierzo, the other pilgrims' pathways followed alongside a busy highway. It was terrible. Trucks and cars passed extremely close to us at high speeds, spewing out large quantaties of exhaust fumes. And to make things worse, it also had started to rain – and the cyclists were back! In front of us, in the middle of the narrow pathway that ran alongside the highway, a Danish women was, for some unknown reason, having an acute anxiety attack. Donna and I had to walk her to a nearby hotel and help calm her down. Once back on the road, we passed two male pilgrims who were having a fight, and then looking further ahead, we saw a group of college students who were jumping up and down on the protective fence that ran alongside the highway. It was a great danger to the traffic and themselves.

'You wouldn't think they had brains enough to attend a university when acting like that,' Donna sighed.

When we finally reached a bar, we walked in to have something to eat and drink. We needed to recharge our batteries. I thought back to what Pierre had told me, and now realised what he had meant when he had said that the Camino would change. It wasn't a pilgrimage any more. It was just a crowded walk heading towards Santiago.

Feeling better after our break we continued on our way and passed through a number of tiny villages. Donna refused to stay at any of their albergues as many of them looked cold and damp. Then Donna remembered hearing something about an albergue called Do Brasil, so I looked it up in my book. I should have known, shouldn't I? The logo for the Brasilian albergue was the Black Madonna – a figure that had come to represent not only my deep connection to the earth, but also the source of knowedge, strength, spirituality and insight. Seeing her brought me to another realisation I found difficult to accept. *Tomorrow*, I said to myself, *tomorrow*. That would give me time to get used to the thought, but not today. Not here, and not so soon after the mountains. I wasn't ready yet.

Predictably, the albergue was owned by a Brazilian couple. The beds were very comfortable and made up with freshly ironed white sheets. I didn't know it at that time, but all prices went up upon reaching Galicia. A bed for the night, including dinner and breakfast would now cost me a whole day's budget. Even the laundry prices had gone up so much that I had to do it myself by hand. Ironically, it started to rain heavily the moment I hung my laundry out to dry. Feeling rather frustrated, I looked tiredly out through the window and watched the rain. It looked like it would go on forever, so Donna and I, and one newly arrived cyclist, ended up sharing the cost of using a clothes drier.

The rest of that afternoon was spent resting in our sleeping bags, trying to stay warm and comfortable. I wished there had been a cosy warm albergue for us up in the mountains. It would have been an incredible place to stay. I could picture it in my mind's eye: stone walls, wooden floors and an open fireplace. It would be a small albergue, a stone cottage maybe, and the kitchen would have one of those old-fashioned stoves. And, as the icing on the cake, there would be a hot spring close by, where the pilgrims could sit at night and watch the stars.

However, coming back to reality, I found my journal and began my usual scribbling. Later, after a hot shower, I just lay in my bed, staring out at the rain through the little window above Donna's bed. It was now raining 'cats and dogs'. Dinner was incredibly cosy. Much to our delight, our hosts served us a delicious Brazilian meal of protein-rich foods. There were candles on the table, a fire in the fireplace and the room echoed with laughter and good stories. Our hosts possessed an incredible giving energy and did so much to make us feel welcome. They told us about their lives in Brazil, although I never fully came to understand how they ended up owning an albergue on the Camino.

At nine o'clock the couple said goodnight and the rest of us prepared for bed. Just like on my high school camping trips, we lay there and talked for a while after the light had been turned off. I could live like this forever, I really could. As sleep found its way, silence fell over our room. The cyclist, who had chosen a bed at the other end of the room, started to snore gently. I just curled up in my sleeping bag and looked out into the darkness, remembering my walk through the mountains.

'Buen Camino!' I whispered to myself.

'Sorry, I didn't hear you,' Donna said quietly.

'Oh, nothing,' I whispered. 'It was nothing. Goodnight.'

'Goodnight.'

We all slept so deeply that our host actually had to come in and wake us in the morning.

'Time to get up! It's seven o'clock!' he said, as he turned on the lights. 'Breakfast will be ready in 20 minutes.' Because we were slow to get out of our beds, the host returned a few minutes later to hurry us along.

Upon waking, I felt really great about myself, but then I *remembered*. I quickly got up, ate a hurried breakfast and walked off without any explanation – not even to Donna. I walked like a madman through the ever-changing weather of rain, wind and moments of sunshine. I continued up and down mountains, along the wet slippery, stone pathways, ignoring all the new crazy pilgrims. The college students with their immature behaviour were not only a danger to themselves, but also to other pilgrims. They always seemed to be yelling at each other as they jostled and pushed past other pilgrims who were carefully walking along the narrow slippery pathways. Whereas my fellow pilgrims' facial expressions used to be open, bright and happy, they were now closed and hard. That community I had come to know on the Camino, was no longer there. It had completely disappeared.

I kept on walking, all through the morning and into the early afternoon, only stopping once for a cup of tea. I didn't even slow down to enjoy the Celtic atmosphere of Galicia or the charming village of O'Cebreiro. I just kept walking until I reached Hospital de la Condesa. Here I stopped only because I felt really uncomfortable from not having eaten anything since breakfast. It was a 1.45pm, 15 minutes before the albergue closed for pilgrims' registrations. I was lucky to get the last bed.

The small, 20-bed albergue was mostly full of Italians and Koreans. There was no hot water and it wasn't even worth trying to get in line to use the washing machine. This turned out to be one of the rare days where I actually didn't get to wash my clothes, and I didn't even care. Worried that my sleeping bag wouldn't be warm enough, in the now much-colder climate, I asked the albergue if they had a spare blanket I could borrow. They didn't.

'Okay,' I thought. Welcome to Galicia. By now my blood sugar was so low, that my hands were starting to shake, I felt nauseated and weak, and I had started to break out in a cold sweat. The food machine was out of order, so the only other option was to walk to a restaurant located five minutes down the road. Realising I was too exhausted to go, I went upstairs to sleep.

Resting there, slowly warming up in my sleeping bag, I thought about it again.

Why couldn't I just admit it? My Camino was over! It was finished and it was time for me to leave. The mountain walk had been its last gift to me, and it was now time to go home. But I didn't want to go home. I wanted to go back to St Jean and do it all over again. I wanted to walk in the sunshine again together with Richard. I wanted to laugh, be with my Camino friends and again feel the wonders of the hidden world of the Camino as it presented them to me. I wasn't ready to leave. I hadn't been given enough warning! But when the time was up, it was up. Every part of my body and intuition said it was time to go home, now.

Accepting the situation with a breaking heart, I fell into a deep sleep.

I am standing on the top of the Meseta. It is still dark and I can see the stars moving across the sky. Slowly, the large glowing sun rises in the east. I stand and watch how the rays of the sun light up the earth. The scenery constantly changes before my eyes and I experience how the diversity of life is the very expression of our own divinity.

I stand and watch the sun slowly rise, its warmth filling me up. Suddenly, I notice a bright full moon in the sky. It moves closer and closer to the sun until I can't see the difference between them any longer. I am a bird, a large bird soaring across the infinite sky. The world below me and the sky above me are my home and I can go wherever I want.

Upon waking, I felt much better. The stress and uneasiness I had previously experienced had now gone, and I felt reassured that I was doing the right thing. But I still missed Richard so much and wondered when I would stop missing him.

Hearing a voice in the bunk beneath me, I realised I recognised it, so I leant over and looked down.

'Hi!' I said with my head turned upside down.

The Hungarian women looked up from the book she was reading, and started to laugh.

'Who were you talking to?' I asked curiously.

'My boyfriend,' she said, showing me her cell phone. I last met the Hungarian women in Astorga, where we had shared dinner with a young German man. I was grateful to meet someone I knew.

After buying some sandwiches at the local restaurant, my Hungarian friend and I went back to our albergue and sat outside on the grass enjoying the last sunshine of the day. The biggest chickens I had ever seen in my life walked around us. They were as big as dogs! So I watched them closely, ready to run if they should start attacking me. They couldn't have cared less about me, however; they were too busy scratching in the moist soil in search of food.

While sitting there, I told my friend about my painful decision to leave the Camino one week before schedule. She understood. She was suffering terribly with blisters, and wondered how long she would be able to continue her journey. On hearing this, I immediately told her to wash her feet, while I went upstairs to fetch the Fixomull and cream so I could help treat her blisters.

'You will feel much better tomorrow,' I promised.

Early the next morning, while a thick fog was hanging over the countryside, my Hungarian friend walked me down to the bus stop on the corner. She gave me a big hug, said goodbye and then waved to me as the little shuttle bus drove away with me tucked safely into a seat. I cried inside because I didn't want to leave the Camino, but quickly found myself focusing on the road ahead. The bus driver drove like a maniac through the small, constantly winding roads. It was like sitting in a roller coaster where everybody clung to whatever they could so as not to be tossed around. It was crazy; the bus driver was crazy; and the roads were crazy. It was all crazy and I couldn't help but laugh out loud. Not that anybody noticed, though. Everybody had their eyes locked on the road ahead, terrified. Their faces were pale and someone in the back started to throw up.

'Fucking Cami-Crazy,' I mumbled to myself.

Three buses later, and without throwing up, I reached Santiago only to discover that it was impossible for me to change my ticket to an earlier flight back to Denmark. Fortunately, Santiago offered many other travel options so I managed to get a seat on a Eurobus to Paris the following day, and then a cheap flight with Scandinavian Airlines from Paris to Copenhagen that same night. It was perfect.

THE HIDDEN CAMINO

It was a weird feeling as the Eurobus drove out of Santiago. The bus pretty much followed the Camino all the way back to Burgos where it turned north towards the Pyrenees. I could see the mountains where I had walked falling away behind me. More than anything I remembered all the love, the everlasting sunshine and immense happiness I had experienced throughout my pilgrimage.

I looked at the mountains and hills as the sun bathed them in its light and warmth, smiling that special smile only a pilgrim who had experienced the magic of the Camino could smile. I sat peacefully watching, for many hours, the scenery pass before my eyes, and giving thanks. Then I took out my journal and opened it to the pages where I described the women I had seen along the Camino. After having read through my last notes, I looked out the window and thought. I wondered if these women's teachings could be found in the closed library of the Vatican. What could they possibly be saying that could be so dangerous for the church and its clergy? What knowledge could be so threatening that it required more than a thousand years of supression, persecution and disempowerment?

As the passengers around me began to fall asleep, I turned on my overhead light and carefully started to summarise the many symbols and women I had seen along the Camino. When finished, my list looked like this:

Mary Magdalene: a skull (seat of knowledge), the chalice (spring and the mystery of rebirth), a book (knowledge/teaching), an egg (the mystery of rebirth), the name Magdalene (meaning High Tower and referring to a leader and The Mother of Gods, Cybele). Magdalene is also the *Apostola Apostolorum*.

The Virgin Mary: together with a child (Isis, goddess Diana, even Cybele), crescent moons (goddess Diana, middle eastern ancient cultures), crown of stars/stars (goddess Diana as she belonged to the group of celestial gods and Cybele/ Asherah; the Queen of Heaven), the Virgin birth (myths from Egypt, Rome and the ancient Greece), serpent-dragons (innate spirituality from the earliest of times)

The 'third' Madonna: I had seen this figure often. She was depicted with at least one of the following: a serpent-dragon, a tower, a book/or writing one, and the oak tree. The oak tree was symbolic of the tree of life which also refered to the goddess Diana. However, the tree of life had actually been seen all over the world: in the Icelandic sagas, ancient Egypt, China, North America and in many other cultures.

The 'fourth' Madonna: she was always dressed in gold, had golden hair and often holding the grail cup. I had seen this Madonna frequently during the first part of my pilgrimage and I wasn't quite sure who she was or what she referred to, but she was definitely someone of great importance.

The tower: Its origins related back to Cybele, but it was also seen in the title Magdalene, which signified a position as a spiritual leader. However, did the many other women depicted with towers indicate that there were many more spiritual leaders like Mary Magdalene? Was Magdalene a title only a 'high priestess' could bear? And was the presence of all these women with towers evidence that the teachings of Mary Magdalene had been a part of a wider belief system spread through the known Roman world? I very much thought so.

The Grail: this had been seen as several different objects before taking the shape of a chalice in the Middle Ages. Common to them all was that the 'grail' was seen as a magical object representing spirit. A detail that explained why, in the Grail stories, the Grail was always carried by a woman.

Pregnant women: This had its roots all the way back to Cybele and even to paleolithic times. Pregnancy came to symbolise the coming of new life to the world. Springtime! I had seen Mary Magdalene and many unnamed women depicted as pregnant, also on the Camino, but never the Virgin Mary.

The rose: is one of the many forms of the flower of life. It is as ancient as time itself. During the Middle Ages it became a symbol of the Virgin Mary, as well as the feminine principle (spirit.)

Sitting in the silence and darkness of the bus, a clear picture began to emerge. At the beginning of my journey, I had been sure that Mary Magdalene and the Virgin Mary had been the only remaining women linking us to an incredible spiritual heritage. But now, at the end of my journey, I realised it was much larger than that and it was all there right in front of us if we just dared to look. All in front of us if we just dared to look… My memory went back to Astorga and the large tower on the altarpiece. A tower, as the centerpiece of attention in a catholic cathedral? A great light of clarity descended upon me and suddenly all the pieces of the puzzle, about Mary Magdalene and the women along the Camino, came together and made sense. There was Magda, an old Hebrew girls' name meaning High Tower, referring to one who is elevated above all others; Cybele, The Mother of Gods, with her crown of towers and the Apostolic letter from 1988, which officially had stated Mary Magdalene as The Apostle of the Apostles and a teacher. It was impossible that Mary Magdalene was 'just' one of the women who followed Christ! With titles and references like these, she would be a great leader and authority within the ancient spiritual and mystical traditions connected to the Mother of Gods! Magdalene was a title! And all those women along the Camino, seen holding a tower, were showing us their true titles and position of authority. They were the Magdalenes, women holding positions similar to Priestesses and the female Cathar Perfects. Could the Magdalenes have been the link between the ancient goddess Cultures and the Cathars?

In every possible way, this would explain why the Roman Catholic Church appeared so scared and threatened by Mary Magdalene and other women like her. As a person, and as a symbol, the real Mary Magdalene is evidence of times and places, where men and women could live together in equality and friendship; a way of life, we today have forgotten all about.

I was now convinced, that the ancient spiritual teachings of Cybele and Asherah had been present along the Camino, and probably even more widespread across Europe. Even during the early formative years of the Catholic church, there must have been times where women had actually existed in their own right, equal to men. Much knowledge and ancient inheritance had become dangerous, even burnt and destroyed, as the Roman Catholic religion had spread its tentacles across Europe. So maybe the secret societies weren't so secret after all. They had just believed in the freedom of knowledge and understood the rich legacy of their past. I now knew, that all these females, so present along the Camino Francés, carried with them, physically and symbolically, the sacred knowledge and meaning of this broad and powerful legacy.

We know the Camino Francés had originally been a Celtic path of initiation, and we know the Celtic's had inhabited large areas of Europe. Therefore, it was only natural that a Celtic relic, the skull, had been found associated with Mary Magdalene. Since the dawn of time, ancient teachings and belief systems have spread from culture to culture, always being adjusted as part of the integration process. Mary Magdalene and The Virgin Mary were the very proof of that. Today, the historical person, and the spiritual tradition they followed, has merged into one. But one thing the Camino had taught me was that these women had indeed once been great teachers and spiritual authorities – not as a wife and as a mother, but as independent beings in their own right! Anybody who thought them unimportant was wrong – very wrong!

If we wanted to understand the knowledge and wealth of resources held within each of us, it was our own responsibility to do the work. Experiences and self-insight would always create a maturity that would change our emotions, that again would change how we thought and acted. From a deep emotional and existential core, our ancient cultures had understood this, and they had understood how important it was to live in harmony with the earth and flow of life; inside and outside of ourselves.

I remembered Camille who had said: 'All I know for sure is, if you follow the scallop shell, you will always walk in the light of the Goddess.' Now I didn't think of the Goddess as a woman any more, I thought of her as an ancient symbol of Spirit and Divine energy. It wasn't about gender, race or Goddesses vs Gods. It was about moving beyond and above to Oneness, Connectedness and higher emotional consciousness. It was about opening our eyes and hearts so we could find the courage to explore the incredible beauty of Who we really are. And walking in the light of the scallop shell, had led me exactly there!

Magic always begins when we start listening to ourselves.

I RECEIVED AN INVITATION

On the Camino I was as free as a bird. I soared higher and higher up into the sky, embraced by the warmth of the sun and filled with nothing but an endless freedom of existence. In the most gentle and loving ways, my eyes and my heart were opened, and I heard.

I heard the pulse of life that ran through my veins and through the earth, and I heard the song of my own soul. I saw a river of stars across the infinite sky, embracing me with their magic and tales of forgotten times. It made me feel so content to know that I was embraced by, and loved by, this amazing universe of which I am undoubtedly a part of.

I saw the sun rise and bring light to so many areas of my life. It healed me, educated me and made me grow deep roots into the earth and strong branches reaching to the sun. It taught me to stop being afraid of who and what I was, and it pushed me to change where I needed to change.

The pilgrimage freed me from the supression of others and their fears. It made me believe in my dreams and the possibilites of life, and it taught me to trust the flow of energy that ran through me, the earth and the universe. It showed me things could be different in our world.

Many people wouldn't be able to understand me now, because they hadn't soared like me, seen what I had seen and met the Camino as I had. So the least I could do was to share my story and my Camino, knowing that there were others out there who also wanted to see and hear. Others, who longed to soar freely above the earth and beneath the stars, sharing their own unique beautiful songs of life. My story is for you.

I am no longer afraid of walking in the dark, because I have learnt to read the stars. I am no longer afraid to soar freely in the sky, because I know it is my birthright to do so. And I am no longer afraid to listen to my heart, because its songs are the songs of my innermost being.

The road that led me out, was also the road that led me home, and so the journey continues…

Buen Camino!

EPILOGUE

Well, Richard did come to Denmark for my birthday. We are today married and live in Australia. Becoming a spiritual person in my own right was, indeed, the result of my pilgrimage. I stepped out of the shadows with a strong feeling of who I was and what I had to give to this world. My journey of transformation continued after I had left the dusty pathways of northern Spain behind. There are still times when I suddenly experience another drop of wisdom and insight from my time on the Camino. It is still an incredible heart-warming sensation for me to realise that these insights and the knowledge they hold have not existed only since the beginning of time; they also exist deep inside me and – I believe – in every human being.

Now I know that many of my dreams referred to the original purpose of the Camino, and to the Celtic legend of Tir-na-Nóg. A legend, that in so many ways carries the essence of one of the most sacred initiations practiced by the Celts. In the legend of Tir-na-Nóg, white horses with golden manes were the only creatures who could transport you to the island in the west (Tir-Na-Nóg.) In Rubens' painting El Triunfo de la Iglesia (1626–1628), white horses with golden manes are pulling the chariot, which made me think the artist had known about the legend and the deeper meaning of women as spiritual guides. That might just be a coincidence, but who knows?

As I witnessed the numerous images of women along the Camino, I came to understand the importance of our historical inheritance. And so my journey of discovery continues as I delve deeper and deeper into the history of women and the mystery of our past.

It is incredible how much society still judges women based on those old, conservative, religious perspectives. When discussing this issue during a dinner party in Australia, a well-educated man said: 'It is better to keep women under control and let them know their place, otherwise we will lose our power. And if we lose our power, I lose my identity – and that freaks me out!' It says a lot, doesn't it? A healthy and strong sense of self is not based on a need to control others; it is based on a mature sense of identity and self-worth – a grounded presence within our own tree of life. This issue of control is not only sad; it also leaves us emotionally fragile and with little resilience to the realities of life. This is why I emphasise that men are also losing out in the war between the genders.

Two years after my pilgrimage, I watched a Danish TV series about the Camino. The program was about a journalist who walked the last part of the Camino. In one of the final episodes, the journalist had arrived in Santiago de Compostela and was attending the Pilgrims mass at the cathedral. As the priest began his service, he said in a clear and loud voice: 'Dear Brothers!' (but no 'Dear Sisters!') He didn't even officially recognise the many women in the congregation, not even the nuns. I was not only deeply offended when I saw this, I also felt extremely hurt! The Catholic Church seems to be doing all it can to avoid any change on how they view women and, thanks to the revelations along the Camino, we now know why. The following piece of text was edited out from the original manuscript, but I think it is relevant here:

It seemed to me we had learnt not to see; that we had eyes, but were blind. We could hear, but were deaf. We could feel, but had become numb. It was as if we humans didn't live in this world any longer. Instead we lived in a world of superficial mainstream 'truths' and 'fears' which we had made the pillars of self-understanding. We had been indoctrinated with these 'truths' and 'fears' for so long that we had stopped questioning them.

As I started to write about the Light I had experienced in Ponferrada, I felt inspired to look into other accounts of visions along the Camino Francés; how and where they happened and in connection with whom. Here I found it rather interesting how the visions, even after a Christian make-over, contained many details that belonged to our ancient goddess cultures. So the question was: had people really seen what the church-approved account told us, or was it merely an account of a spiritual experience that had been 'dressed up' to sell the Catholic faith? Maybe these spiritual experiences aren't so rare and special as we make them today, and maybe they are a natural part of being in contact with the energy of creation.

Today I see a connection between the original purpose of the Camino, and what the Native American Indians call spirit quests and the Australian Aborigines call walkabouts. All of these terms refer to walks out into the solitude of nature, with the purpose of creating a closer bond and connection to one's spirituality. It was a search for answers, visions, for clarity about issues and an opening up for an actual meeting with the divine. Aspects, such as solitude, tranquillity, looking inside and facing oneself are all a part of these special walks.

I have no doubt that walkabouts, spirit quests and pilgrimages are extremely important ways of connecting with our inner selves and gaining a feeling of balance, stillness, meaning and direction in our life. The irony of the Camino is that the more people who walk it, the more crowded it becomes, the harder it will be to actually hear, see and feel. But to look at it from a positive point of view, this might just encourage other countries to create their own pilgrimages: build albergues, create a safe place for women and those who walk alone, keep cyclists away from the walking pilgrims – those sorts of thing. Our planet is so amazing, and every country and every continent has something special and unique to offer. Every place in nature is suited to us meeting ourselves and feeling our connection to that special energy of creation. Given time, we will hopefully learn that it is not so dangerous to face ourselves.

As one final comment, I have to be honest and say that I did have more experiences than those mentioned in the book. I had, for example, several past life experiences, where I learnt background stories about people whose paths had interwoven with mine in this life. However, none of them were relevant to the topic of this book and were left out.

If you would like to learn more about all the topics and research I present in *The Hidden Camino*, please visit my blog at www.louisesommer.com

APPENDIX A
HELP DOCUMENT THIS INHERITANCE

My main concern about publishing my experiences is that the church might remove or cover up all the artifacts, symbols, the precious frescoes and significant women depicted in churches along the Camino. Unfortunately, this has happened in other places. I took many photos along the way, but I didn't get anywhere near enough to be able to document and save just a quarter of the amount of this inheritance. I would thus encourage everyone who feels the truth of this book to help me document and preserve it.

My aim is to create a website devoted solely to documenting everything I have written about: every small wooden panel, windblown stone figures, dusty hidden altars, frescoes, obvious decorations above doors and on altar pieces. Close-ups of fine details and even a few photos received will make a major difference. As a Danish saying goes: many small streams make one big river, which means every contribution counts.

With everyone's help, I should in time have a large detailed collection of good photos from every single village, town, museum and church from the Camino Francés. My hope is that this collection will keep growing and growing! Should you have relevant photos from other parts of the Camino, let me know. They could be significant and need to be documented, too.

Please send your photos and information to: authorlouisesommer@gmail.com with 'Camino inheritance' in the topic field. It is essential you provide the following information together with your photo(s):

1. The name of the church/place where the photo is taken
2. The name of the town, where the church/place is located
3. The date of the photo (month and year) if possible, so I can document any changes or removal of artifacts.

APPENDIX B
ADVICE ON PREPARATIONS

Many people neglect careful preparation before walking the Camino. This includes the 'wearing in' of new boots, getting physically fit and selecting the correct backpack. As I found out, walking the Camino was demanding enough in itself.

First, it is important to understand that proper preparation for the Camino is both a physical and mental task. As Benjamin Franklin once said: 'By failing to prepare, you are preparing to fail.'

On the following pages I write about my preparations and give some advice in areas that seem to be of common concern to pilgrims. Hopefully, this will help you avoid some of the mistakes that have ruined the experience for so many.

What to bring

Refer to the end of this appendix for details of what I took with me.

When packing, be clear that you are going on a pilgrimage, not a shopping trip to Paris. All you really need are two changes of clothing: one outfit for walking, and one for all other occasions.

Everything I ended up taking with me, including the backpack, was weighed on my kitchen scales. Here I took note of every single gram of weight. If something was too heavy, I would first ask myself, do I really need this? If the answer was yes, I would try to obtain it in a lighter material. By doing this, I was able to keep the total weight of the backpack and its contents down to 5.5kg.

The weight of a backback

Choose your backpack with great care. If buying a new one, ensure it is the correct size and is properly fitted in the store. When walking the Camino, go for the lightest and most durable possible. The right backpack should feel like an intergral part of your body, even when it is full. Fine tuning should be done during your training walks.

Wise heads say a woman should carry a backpack of no more than 8kg when full, or 10 percent of her own body weight. The 10 percent rule also applies to men. Remember, the further you walk, the heavier your backpack will feel. Yes, pilgrims can send their things ahead to the post office in Santiago, but why have the hassle and extra expense when you can avoid it.

Food and drink

It is important to remember that you will be carrying water, and often food, with you. One litre of water equals 1kg of weight. Keep in mind, that you are advised always to carry at least 500ml of water in reserve. This is for emergency situations that will arise at one time or the other. If it's not for you, it's for someone else. It is important to be aware, that there can be long distances where water and food are inaccessible.

Also, when you approach Burgos you will need to start buying water. The water in the fountains here, and later on, is often not safe to drink (no potable). This means you will have to carry even more water on this leg of the trip.

The boots

Remember that your boots are the things that will carry you through the 880km of the Camino. Your feet will be tired and sore just from the walking itself. So make sure there is room enough in your boots for your feet to swell. Some say that a pilgrim's foot swells at least one size during the day. I believe two or three. So try your new boots at the end of the day, when your feet are the biggest, together with the socks you plan to wear.

It is also recommended that you wear two pair of special hiking socks on each foot; an inner thinner sock and an out thicker sock. You may even need to add supportive innersoles in your footwear. All of this must be tested when you wear your boots and carry your gear on your preparatory walks.

Some pilgrims walk in jogging shoes and even sandals. Personally, I'm not too keen on these, because of their lack of support for your ankles and feet. However, it's your call, so spend enough time to find out what works for you.

If you are using new boots, note that it will take at least two months to wear them in so they can soften, and your feet will become accustomed to them. It's best to wear them all the time – even around the house,

The pilgrims pass

I purchased my pilgrims pass from the Danish Pilgrim Society. You can also buy it at the pilgrims office in St Jean. Many countries now have their own pilgrim associations, so hit Google and search for the office in your country. They will only be too glad to help.

St Jean-Pied-de-Port

St Jean is the only place on the Camino where it is possible for you to pre-book your bed at an albergue. The only other beds you can book in advance are in the hotels. To find an albergue in St Jean, hit Google and see what feels right for you.

I highly recommend that the booking includes dinner, breakfast and a packed lunch for the following day. Except for one albergue, halfway between St Jean and Roncesvalles, there are no places where you can buy food or drink. And if you get lost, as I did, it's a really bad idea having to depend on the few water taps along the way. I suggest that you carry two to three litres of water when you start off from St Jean.

Guidebook or not

I had only brought photocopies provided by the Danish Pilgrim Society that listed the names of towns I would pass through and what services these towns provided. As I discovered, this was not sufficient. Richard however, had purchased John Brierley's small guidebook, Camino de Santiago. I came to love and rely on this book more and more as I travelled the Camino.

Of all the guidebooks available, Brierley's book seems the best in every respect. It gives important detailed information on albergues and which ones are opened during the different seasons; where on the walk you can, and cannot, find water; the terrain; important landmarks, churches; and helpful maps. The great thing is that his books are also updated on a regular basis.

All in all, I recommend that you bring some kind of guidebook with you. But, again, be wise and consider its weight.

Bedbugs and fleas

You will most likely hear rumours about bedbugs being present in certain albergues. Take this with a grain of salt. I actually never met anyone, nor encountered any albergue, that had that problem. However, that could be because of the many precautions the albergues took to avoid infestations: no boots in the dormitories, no backpacks on the beds and plastic covers over the mattresses. In this respect, it is also important to bring your own pillowcase and sheet.

But fleas? That's a different story. I met some pilgrims suffering from flea bites because they had been patting a cat or a dog. So keep your hands away from animals or wash carefully afterwards.

My exercise plan

I started my preparations about five months before I left for the Camino. I was already a regular member of a gym and cycled every day. However, with the Camino coming up, I changed my exercise program (except for the cycling), which ended up looking like this:

February
I walked 18km p/w + 3 hours of gym p/w.

March
I walked 30km p/w + 3 hours of gym p/w

April
I walked 39km p/w + 3 hours of gym p/w

May
I walked 45km p/w + 2 hours in gym p/w. Now I started walking with my backpack on, with a total   weight of 9kg. I also tested out my planned outfit for walking and I had to make several adjustments to my gear.

June

In the last weeks before the Camino, I walked 45-50km in total per week, stopped going to the gym and started doing lots of extra stretching. During the last two weeks, I concentrated on getting my backpack down to the desired weight, which I then carried during my walks.

My final packing list

- A notebook and a pen
- 1 pair of good hiking boots
- 1 pair of lightweight flip-flops (to wear after walking, when it's good to air one's feet)
- 2 pairs of thin inner socks
- 2 pairs of thick outer socks
- 2 pairs of sports underwear
- 2 sports bras
- 1 thin long sleeved woollen blouse
- 1 pair of pants where I could unzip and remove the lower leggings (to walk in)
- 1 pair of comfortable shorts (for after the walk)
- 1 T-shirt (for after the walk)
- 1 blouse made of sweat-absorbent material (to walk in)
- 1 lightweight fleece jacket
- 1 lightweight, long blue cotton scarf (useful for many different purposes)
- 1 lightweight multipurpose bag
- Rain gear (Cheap gear is useless! Buy proper rain gear)
- 1 lightweight sleeping bag
- 1 very small chamois
- 1 small bottle of shampoo
- 1 small bottle of hair conditioner
- 1 small tube of face cream
- 1 comb
- 1 small bottle of body lotion
- Sunscreen factor 30
- A small packet of panadol

- 1 hat (very important!)
- Safety pins
- 1 small bar of soap (to wash my clothes with)
- 1 pair of nail scissors
- 1 nail file

Prepare your feet

Richard's advice, with respect to footcare, is that you remove all dead skin and callouses from your feet a couple of months before leaving. After that, use a pumice stone every time you have a shower, to keep the dead skin away. After that, massage lanolin cream into your feet, and keep your toenails carefully trimmed.

Personal security

The Camino is a safe place to walk, especially for women and those who walk by themselves. However, walkers should always follow the same precautions as anywhere else in the world when travelling. That is, don't accept lifts from strangers; women can be friendly, but not personal with men; and remember the cultural differences in Spain with respect to women.

Regretfully, it is known that money, passports, backpacks and even hiking boots have been stolen on the Camino. So be aware and keep your valuables and personal items especially secure at all times.

It must be noted that this is my advice, based on my own experience and reading. However, each pilgrim is entirely responsible for making their own decisions and is responsible for the outcomes of these.

REFERENCES

Today, there are thousands of websites, apps, books, homemade documentaries and other materials related to the Camino. In the following lists, you can find the information I have referred to or found relevant to mention. You can also visit my blog and learn more about the topics and research I present here in *The Hidden Camino*.

Books

Boer, E.D. (2006) *The Mary Magdalene cover-up – The sources behind the myth*. T&T Clark, New York.

Boer, E.D. (2006) *The Gospel of Mary – Listening to the Beloved Disciple*. Continuum, London

Brierley, J. (2011) *Camino de Santiago*. Findhorn Press, Scotland.

Clemens, M. & Forbord, I. (2008) *Gudinnens fortellinger*. Emilia Press AS, Oslo. (The book is about the ancient goddess cultures in Pre-Christian Europe, written from both an academic and a mythological point of view.)

Ellis, P. B. (1995) *Celtic Women: Women in Celtic Society and Literature*. Constable and Company Ltd, London.

Gimbutas, M. (I highly recommend all her books. Gimbutas was an outstanding researcher, and her works are continuing to make a real difference in this world. She was one of the best researchers of pre-Christian goddess cultures in (old) Europe.)

Green, M.J. (1995) *Celtic Goddesses: Warriors, Virgins and Mothers*. British Museum Press, UK.

Green, M.J & Green, M.A. (1993) *Celtic Myths: The Legendary Past*. University of Texas Press.

Leloup, J.Y. (2002) *The Gospel of Mary Magdalene.* Inner Traditions, Vermont

Narby, J. (1998) *The Cosmic Serpent: DNA and the Origins of Knowledge.* Phoenix, London.

Spike, M.K. (2004) Tuscan Countess: The *life and extraordinary times of Mathilde of Canossa.* The Vendome Press, New York.

Warner, M. (2013) *Alone Of All Her Sex – The myth & the cult of the Virgin Mary.* Oxford University Press, Oxford, United Kingdom

Apps
Beebe Bahrami 'The Esoteric Camino France & Spain'.

TV/DVD/Film
Bertelsen på Caminoen (meaning Berthelsen on the Camino). In 2010, Danish Television (Channel DR) aired a 24-episode program about the Camino. The 24 episodes follow a journalist who walks the last part of the Camino. The episodes used to be free online, but seem to have been removed. You can ask your local TV station to broadcast them. Richard and I really enjoyed the program.

Signs Out of Time (2008) (This is a great, but short documentary about Marija Gimbutas and her research. It is narrated by Olympia Dukakis.)

The Highlander (1986) (starring Christopher Lambert)

ACKNOWLEDGEMENTS

Richard, your never-failing support of me and this book, and all the hard work you have put into it, has been incredible. Your belief in me means everything, and always will.

I would also like to thank Ida, Karen, Susie, Dr. Brown, Dr. Gannon and family, Rick S, and my editor, Carol Campell. Also, a Thank You to Christina Larmer, for her empowering support and friendship. And last, thank you to all those wonderful pilgrims who became my friends along the way. It was an honour to meet you all.

ABOUT THE AUTHOR

For more than two decades Louise Sommer's passion has been investigating the role of women in European history. In an effort to understand where our modern-day thought patterns originate regarding gender (men, women, masculinity and femininity), she has educated herself through all manner of reference materials – from research papers, books and articles, as well as her extensive travels.

Through her research Louise realised the role Christianity has played in forming our current western gender roles. These studies led her to look even further back, examining pre-historical cultures in Europe (the goddess cultures from 12,000BC through until Christianity), as well as immersing herself into studies of various indigenous cultures.

Louise (b.1972) holds a Masters degree in Educational Psychology, a BA degree in Social Education and is specialised in trauma, complicated grief and crisis. She frequently writes articles for magazines and online societies worldwide: about travels, women in religion and history, psychology, the issues approached in her book *The Hidden Camino* as well as book and movie reviews. Louise is also a keen blogger. As well as having lived in Denmark, she has resided in the USA and Thailand, and now calls Australia home. Louise is often invited to do talks around Australia and Europe.

CONNECT WITH ME!

Thank you for reading my book. If you enjoyed it, won't you please take a moment to leave me a review at your favorite retailer? It'll mean a lot.

I would also love to hear from you! You can email me at authorlouisesommer@gmail.com or connect with me via Social Media:

- Louise Sommer Facebook

- The Hidden Camino Facebook

- Author Lou Sommer Pintrest

- and don't forget to visit my blog!

Much Love,
Louise Sommer

Printed in Great Britain
by Amazon

40865187R00158